"It is really exciting to see this book. At a time when environmental psychology is moving more towards addressing important and challenging issues of sustainability some of the fields critical contributions to architectural psychology can sometimes be left behind. This book brings some of the key concepts, models and theories within the field of Architectural Psychology into the 21st century and shows that these are still key concepts with significant importance in today's world – both from a scientific and practical perspective. This book is an important read for psychologists, architects, designers and environmentalists alike. I will certainly recommend it as essential reading to our Environmental Psychology masters and PhD students".

—Professor Birgitta Gatersleben,
Professor of Environmental Psychology,
Director of Environmental Psychology Research Group,
Programme Leader for MSc Environmental
Psychology, University of Surrey, UK

"This book provides the ingredients for understanding human behaviour in its broadest social and spatial dimensions. The author draws on his years of accumulated scientific experience, presenting environmental psychology's interpretation of human behaviour in many settings. Each topic opens a conversation in which the meanings of spatial behaviour in different contexts are discussed. In doing this, the reader is given a harmonious, pertinent and challenging analysis of current environmental and urban issues. This is an expertly constructed reference book for both present and future generations of environmental psychologists".

—Professor Ricardo García Mira,
Professor of Social Psychology,
Leader of the People-Environment Research Group,
Universidade da Coruña, Spain

SILVIO CARTA
EX LIBRIS

ENVIRONMENTAL AND ARCHITECTURAL PSYCHOLOGY

Environmental and Architectural Psychology: The Basics is a jargon-free and accessible introduction to the relationship between people and their natural and built environment.

Exploring everything from the effectiveness of open plan offices to how people respond to life-threatening disasters, the book addresses issues around sustainability, climate change, and behaviour, and is grounded in theory and ideas drawn from psychology, geography, and architecture. Author Ian Donald introduces both the theoretical underpinnings and the applications of environment-behaviour research to solving real world problems, encouraging readers to reflect on the role of design and policy in shaping the environments in which they live and work. With chapters considering the impact of environment on identity, wellbeing, crime, and spatial behaviour, Donald shows us not only how people shape and affect the environment, but also in turn how the environment shapes and affects people's thoughts, feelings, and behaviours.

Addressing some of the most important questions of our time, including how behaviour drives climate change, and what we can do about it, this is the ideal book for anyone interested in the interactions between architecture, the environment, and psychology.

Ian Donald is Emeritus Professor of Psychology at the University of Liverpool, UK, where he was previously Head of the School of Psychology. He was International Co-editor of the *Journal of Environmental Psychology* for ten years and on the Editorial Advisory Board for 25 years. Ian is an active researcher and has taught Environmental Psychology at undergraduate and postgraduate level in the UK and abroad.

The Basics Series

The Basics is a highly successful series of accessible guidebooks which provide an overview of the fundamental principles of a subject area in a jargon-free and undaunting format.

Intended for students approaching a subject for the first time, the books both introduce the essentials of a subject and provide an ideal springboard for further study. With over 50 titles spanning subjects from artificial intelligence (AI) to women's studies, *The Basics* are an ideal starting point for students seeking to understand a subject area.

Each text comes with recommendations for further study and gradually introduces the complexities and nuances within a subject.

COGNITIVE PSYCHOLOGY: THE BASICS
SANDIE TAYLOR AND LANCE WORKMAN

SOCIOLOGY (THIRD EDITION)
KEN PLUMMER

MUSIC COGNITION: THE BASICS
HENKJAN HONING

PERFORMANCE STUDIES
ANDREEA S. MICU

AMERICAN STUDIES
ANDREW DIX

PHYSICAL GEOGRAPHY (SECOND EDITION)
JOSEPH HOLDEN

WORLD PREHISTORY
BRIAN M. FAGAN AND NADIA DURRANI

FRENCH REVOLUTION
DARIUS VON GÜTTNER

RESEARCH METHODS (THIRD EDITION)
NICHOLAS WALLIMAN

ARCHAEOLOGY (FOURTH EDITION)
BRIAN M. FAGAN AND NADIA DURRANI

REAL ESTATE
JAN WILCOX AND JANE FORSYTH

MANAGEMENT (SECOND EDITION)
MORGEN WITZEL

SEMIOTICS (FOURTH EDITION)
DANIEL CHANDLER

CHOREOGRAPHY
JENNY ROCHE AND STEPHANIE BURRIDGE

LANGUAGE ACQUISITION
PAUL IBBOTSON

AIR POLLUTION AND CLIMATE CHANGE
JOHN PEARSON AND RICHARD DERWENT

INFANCY
MARC H. BORNSTEIN AND MARTHA E. ARTERBERRY

Other titles in the series can be found at: www.routledge.com/The-Basics/book-series/B

ENVIRONMENTAL AND ARCHITECTURAL PSYCHOLOGY

THE BASICS

Ian Donald

LONDON AND NEW YORK

Cover image: Getty

First published 2022
by Routledge
4 Park Square, Milton Park, Abingdon, Oxon OX14 4RN

and by Routledge
605 Third Avenue, New York, NY 10158

Routledge is an imprint of the Taylor & Francis Group, an informa business

British Library Cataloguing-in-Publication Data
A catalogue record for this book is available from the British Library

Library of Congress Cataloging-in-Publication Data
A catalog record has been requested for this book

ISBN: 978-0-367-22367-0 (hbk)
ISBN: 978-0-367-22368-7 (pbk)
ISBN: 978-0-429-27454-1 (ebk)

DOI: 10.4324/9780429274541

Typeset in Bembo
by codeMantra

For Oliver, of course.

CONTENTS

	List of figures	x
	Preface	xi
	Acknowledgements	xvi
1	**Introduction and Brief History of Environmental and Architectural Psychology**	1
2	**Place, Place Identity, and Place Attachment**	29
3	**Spatial Behaviour: Crowding, Privacy, Personal Space, and Territoriality**	57
4	**Behaviour During Disasters and Emergencies**	81
5	**Crime, Environment, and Geographical Profiling**	109
6	**Therapeutic, Supportive, and Restorative Environments**	134
7	**Office Environments**	167
8	**Environmental Sustainability and Pro-Environmental Behaviour**	197
	Index	241

FIGURES

4.1 General Model of Behaviour during Fires 97
8.1 Dimensions of curtailment and efficiency 206
8.2 Representation of Value-Belief-Norm theory 211
8.3 Representation of the theory of planned behaviour 218

PREFACE

Environmental psychology is why I became a psychologist. At the time I was an undergraduate, psychology was not the popular subject it is now, and many people had little idea what it entailed before they began to study it. So it was for me. I enrolled on a broad applied social science BA, with psychology as a minor subsidiary subject. I thought a little psychology might be useful, mainly because it would tell me about things like body language, which would come in handy at parties. Instead I was faced with lectures on perception, cognition, and the other mainstream experimental psychology subjects. This is not psychology I thought. But it was.

In my final year, I chose a module in environmental psychology, for timetabling reasons as much as an interest in the subject. It was immediately apparent that environmental psychology fitted with what I thought psychology should be about, and how I thought it should be done. Instead of putting subjects in laboratories and studying isolated variables, environmental psychologists were studying real people, in their real habitats, and trying to solve real problems. This was interesting, even exciting, and it was what I wanted to do. A year later I arrived at the University of Surrey to study for an MSc in Environmental Psychology, and exactly 40 years to the month after that, I am writing this preface. Naturally, a fair bit has happened to me and to environmental psychology during those intervening years.

In writing this book, one of the things that has struck me is how early in the development of environmental psychology it was at that time I was studying. It meant that I had the privilege to study with some of the first generation of environmental psychologists in the UK, including Terrance Lee and David Canter. Surrey also attracted international visitors who generously gave their time to us students. Off the top of my head, I can recall visits from David Stea, Henry Sanoff, and Claude Levy-Leboyer. At the same time, the first edition of the *Journal of Environmental Psychology* was being planned in the office next to our seminar room. Unfortunately it is only in retrospect that I can appreciate what a formative period this was.

Early on in writing this volume, I fixed a bright yellow sticky note to the edge of my computer screen. It is still there, and on it is scribbled 'THIS IS NOT A COMPREHENSIVE TEXTBOOK'. It was to remind me that I couldn't cover the entire body of research that has been published in the discipline. Instead, this volume is a specific, perhaps idiosyncratic, take on environmental psychology by someone who has worked in and out of the field for many years. It gives a flavour of what environmental psychology is and what environmental psychologists do. In writing the book, I have tried to provide the basics of environmental psychology, but also give a feel for some of the deeper questions.

Unusually, I have chosen to title this book *Environmental and Architectural Psychology*. In the early days of the discipline the terms architectural and environmental psychology were used pretty much interchangeably, reflecting the focus on the built (architectural) environment. Eventually environmental won out, probably because it was more all-encompassing and was the favoured term in North America. In recent years, there has been a significant shift in the emphasis of the discipline towards the natural environment and 'green' issues. That is completely appropriate and welcome. The focus on nature not buildings, and on changing behaviour not design, has led some to speculate that environmental psychology has fundamentally shifted and is now a discipline solely about conservation, sustainability, and pro-environmental behaviour. That, of course, is not the case. These subjects are the primary current focus of interest, as other areas of research have been in the past. Environmental psychology is doing what it has always done, which is researching and trying to help solve the pressing issues of the day. However, it does not hurt to remind people explicitly that buildings are still a part of the discipline, and so including architectural in the title of this book serves as that reminder.

In a field as broad as environmental psychology, the choice of areas for inclusion in a volume like this is always going to involve difficult decisions. The book could easily have been about schools, homes, and tourism, rather than about disasters, therapeutic environments, and offices. In making my choices I have tried to ensure that they cover many of the basic underlying processes that link people with their environment. I have attempted to write about quite a broad range of areas of research. I have also had an eye to what is available in existing texts in environmental psychology. I have left out several topics that are extensively covered elsewhere – the most obvious being environmental cognition and perception. I also do not include specific sections on research methods in environmental psychology. Those subjects are well considered in most environmental psychology texts. At the end of Chapter 1, I particularly recommend Bob Gifford's textbook for its coverage of those areas. I have also tried to include topics not available in other environmental psychology texts, such as behaviour during emergencies, and geographic profiling, along with more architecturally orientated subjects such as office design, which are not included in recent overviews. The inclusion of those subjects complements what is found in, for instance, Linda Steg and her colleague's recent edited textbook on environmental psychology, which I also recommend.

In Chapter 1 I begin with an overview of the field, what it is and how it works. In the section describing key developments I have limited the description primarily to the UK, with a focus on parts of the history and people that do not always appear in the major environmental texts. I also wanted the chapter to establish at the outset the different ways of thinking about person-environment relations, which, in my view, shapes the questions we ask and the way in which we think about them.

Chapter 2, on place, continues the discussion about how people and environments are related. Place is an important concept, but does not always get the coverage it deserves in introductory books. Although the concept of place can seem abstract, it has important applied implications that take us beyond the simple questions that most people tend to think of when they ask about the environment. For instance, it has something to say about resilience to environmental risk and threat, how we treat immigrants to our country, and the location of infrastructure.

Crowding, territoriality, and personal space are classic areas of study and were once central to environmental psychology. They are the focus of Chapter 3. Although they are less researched today as subjects in their own right, they are still important concepts in many applied areas of study, including crime prevention and office design.

Psychologists are often involved in studying the circumstances that precede various kinds of disasters, or in working with survivors after an event. Chapter 4 focuses on behaviour *during* life-threatening events, with a particular focus on fires. This is an area in which it is readily possible to claim that environmental psychology has led to changes that have saved lives. Despite this, it is often not covered in any detail in general environmental psychology books.

In Chapter 5, I consider crime and the environment from three different angles. The first two of these are found in earlier textbooks on environmental psychology. They are the idea that the weather causes crime, or at least facilitates it, and that the design of the environment can do the same. The third perspective looks at the way in which the environment can be used to help the investigation of crime and to identify potential offenders through geographical profiling.

Some of the earliest environmental psychology studies in the 1950s looked ways of improving ward and hospital design. The range of ways in which the environment can contribute to therapeutic settings and support their inhabitants has changed considerably since those early days. In Chapter 8 we look at the relationship between ideas of therapeutic support and the design of the settings in which people live or are treated. The second part of the chapter shifts to examine the idea of restorative environments and the theories that underlie them. In a sense, restoration is therapy for everyone.

Chapter 7 focuses on the built environment of offices – places in which millions of people spend large periods of their lives. In this chapter, I try to show again how the environment reflects prevailing theories from other disciplines, such as management theory. In this case, how theories about organisations and workers influence the design and management of the office, with particular emphasis on open plan designs.

The final chapter, Chapter 8, is about sustainability and pro-environmental behaviour. This represents the current largest and most active area of research endeavour in environmental psychology. In this chapter, I have covered the basic theoretical foundations of behaviour change, along with the practical interventions that are based on those theories. Although the research findings are varied, and sometimes contradictory, on the whole they present a reasonably coherent picture of the factors that underlie behaviour and how we could go about changing those behaviours.

As I write this preface, COP26 is about to take place in Glasgow, during which climate change and the fate of the world will be influenced by decisions made by world leaders. Fifty or more years of environmental psychology research on sustainability means that the tools to bring about change are available to politicians and policy makers, if they choose to make that change.

In writing this book, my aim has been to give people an insight into the nature of environmental psychology and perhaps even into their own relationship with the environment. I want to show that there is a lot more to environmental psychology than what colour we should paint the walls (a question that I do not answer in the text). Our relationship with the environment is much more subtle than that, as I hope I have conveyed. As I have been writing this book, I have been reminded of many of the things that I found so interesting back when I was an undergraduate. If, in these pages, I can communicate just a fraction of the excitement and enthusiasm I felt for environmental psychology when I first encountered it, I will be happy with what I have achieved here.

ACKNOWLEDGEMENTS

I would like to thank Oliver Donald for putting up with me writing this book. He is, as I type this, watching a film we are supposed to be watching together. I'm grateful to him for taking the time every day, including today, to ask how it is going. At last I can tell him, it's gone.

It is completely unreasonable to ask a friend and colleague to read and comment on a complete draft manuscript within two weeks of it needing to be submitted. As that is exactly what I have done, I am especially grateful to Dr Margaret Wilson for responding to such an unreasonable request and for still managing to laugh about it. Margaret is that rare person, a friend who can be an honest, sometimes ruthless critic. This book is significantly better because of her input.

I could not write acknowledgements for a book on environmental psychology without mentioning David Canter, whose influence on my thinking in psychology is clearly evident in this volume.

Eleanor Taylor at Routledge initially suggested the book and has been patient and supportive well beyond the call of duty. I am very grateful.

I would like to acknowledge and thank the University of Liverpool for its continued support. Without access to their library and other facilities this book would have been very much more difficult to write.

1

INTRODUCTION AND BRIEF HISTORY OF ENVIRONMENTAL AND ARCHITECTURAL PSYCHOLOGY

THE BEGINNING

Let's begin our exploration of environmental and architectural psychology with two observations. The first is that:

> A person's behaviour can be more accurately predicted from knowing where they are than knowing who they are.

To psychologists who have spent a lot of time developing measures of individual differences and personality tests from which to predict behaviour that might come as a worrying surprise. Nonetheless, it is the case that a person will behave very differently in a religious building, a sports stadium, or an office. The same group of students will act differently in a lecture theatre, an exam room, or when they are out for an evening together. There will, of course, be individual differences on display within each of those settings, but overall the framework for behaviour is provided by the place someone is in more than it is by their scores on the dimensions of a personality test. This obvious and basic observation has many implications, but for now we will stick with what it means for psychology.

Frequently, experimental psychologists see the environment as a hindrance. They spend a lot of time, thought, and energy designing experiments that remove as much of the environment as possible. The environment is controlled for and cancelled out, rather than

DOI: 10.4324/9780429274541-1

studied and understood as something intrinsic to behaviour. There is a very nice comment from Helen Ross (1974) in which she makes the point that "We know a great deal about the perception of a one-eyed man with his head in a clamp watching glowing lights in a dark room but surprisingly little about his perceptual ability in a real-life situation" (quoted in Canter, 1975, p. 5). Another way of saying this is that we know a lot about what people do in psychology laboratories, but much less about what they do in real environments.

If experimental psychology removes the environmental from research, environmental psychology puts it back. To understand behaviour, we need to situate it in its environment. That means, amongst other things, we need to know where the behaviour is, what the rules of that place are, how they are understood, what people are trying to achieve in that place, and who else is there. This takes us beyond the physical environment to a more complex understanding of a world that brings together many other elements, including social, physical, cultural, and cognitive phenomena. Complex as it may be, we understand how these components work together. We construct the environment in our minds and share a comprehension of it with others who use that place. If that were not the case, the places and settings we inhabit would not function. Interestingly, it is when one of the components does not work, or when we do not share an understanding with those around us, that we notice our environment. One instance of this is when we travel to different cultures. We soon discover that many places do not operate in the same ways as we are used to. Rarely in the West, for instance, are you asked to remove your shoes when you enter a restaurant. Western visitors can also, for example, find the proximity at which people stand in the Middle East uncomfortable. Therefore, if you remove all the elements that comprise our environment, and then try to understand how someone behaves, it is likely that you will have a very poor understanding of what people do when they leave the laboratory.

The second observation is that:

> The environment is not random. Everything you see around you is the product of human thought and decision-making.

What that means is that someone somewhere has made a decision that has produced the environment that surrounds us, all the time.

Each bit of our surroundings is the result of a conscious thought. The decisions may have resulted from social processes and movements, habits, fashions, or a host of other factors, but at the root will be found people making decisions. Very often those making the decisions will have a theory, implicit or explicit, about how people will perceive that environment and how they will behave in it. This might be small scale, such as when someone decorates their house, and assume their friends will like it, or a teacher rearranging a classroom to achieve a particular learning environment and change the way pupils interact. It can also be large scale, planning a city, or a country's transport infrastructure. One of the challenges that we face in making these decisions is whether our theories about how others will relate to those setting are correct or not. Through testing theories and rigorous empirical research, environmental psychology aims to provide a sound and valid basis for making those decisions and understanding the implications of those that have already been made.

It is worth pointing out that, although less obvious, the same is true for the natural environment, which is rarely the outcome of natural processes. The typical English landscape, for instance, of fields and dry stonewalls, or heather covered moors are the product of human decision-making. The choices people have made for agriculture, ownership, and commercial purposes have shaped our landscape. Forests have disappeared because tress have been felled, but less obviously more trees never get beyond a few inches because we graze animals that eat small shoots that will never grow and together form forests.

It is quite possible that in some parts of the world there are large areas of wilderness or unspoiled forest that are devoid of human influence. These might be found in the large regions of rainforest, or North American wilderness. But now even areas devoid of local human influence are being changed as human activity has a significant and detrimental impact on the planet's climate. The polar region's shrinking ice caps, and the fires and the droughts being seen around the world are the result of our choices.

Understanding that the environment is the product of our decision-making can lead to a great number of questions about why environments are the way they are and how they impact on the people who use them. Psychology, of course, is not alone in examining the environment and our relationship with it. One of the central claims of environmental psychology has always been that it is an interdisciplinary endeavour. In the next section, we will very briefly mention some of the other disciples and professions that have an interest in our surroundings.

DISCIPLINES WITH A STRONG INTEREST IN THE ENVIRONMENT

There are several disciplines that consider the environment and its relationship to behaviour. Some of these disciplines are directly related to psychology while others are not. As a multidisciplinary field environmental and architectural psychology is happy to draw on all of them.

Psychophysics is a discipline that is closely tied to mainstream perceptual psychology and could be argued to be the root of experimental psychology. Psychophysics tends to be concerned with the relationship between very specific, discrete environmental stimuli, such as a sound or light, and the resulting sensation or perception of that stimuli. The discipline therefore works at a reductionist level. In contrast, environmental and architectural psychology usually examines the environment at a molar level as well as including more subjective elements. That is not to say, however, that psychophysics is irrelevant to environmental psychology. It would perhaps be more accurate to say that it occupies a relatively small, specialised corner of the discipline.

Ergonomics or human factors is the design of products, systems, and processes to fit the physical capabilities of people. Its aim is to ensure that the environment fits the person, physically and psychologically, rather than the person having to adapt to the environment. The Chartered Institute of Ergonomics and Human Factors characterises the practice as bringing together knowledge from several disciplines including physiology, anatomy, engineering, and psychology. Traditionally focused on work environments and products, the field has expanded to incorporate cognitive ergonomics. It has also moved out of the workplace and is now applied in broader settings including in the design of household objects, cars, and an array of machines and appliances that we encounter every day.

Environmental sociology is focused on the interaction between societal issues and broader social movements (Lockie, 2015). It is less concerned with individual responses than psychophysics and ergonomics. Knight (2018) identifies four broad areas of interest to environmental sociologists: the social causes of environmental problems, the societal impacts and influences of the natural environment, how environmental threats and challenges are reacted to, and understanding social processes that can lead to environmental change and sustainability. While environmental sociology operates at a societal level, many of the areas of interest are shared with environmental psychology, which is more than happy to draw on and use the work and methods of sociologists.

Behavioural geography is perhaps, of all the other disciplines outside of psychology, the one that has most contributed to environmental psychology. There would even be an argument for the idea that it has contributed more to the development of the discipline than mainstream psychology. Behavioural geography texts often resemble the content of psychology books on environmental cognition. A geographer might put that the other way around. The history of behavioural geography in many ways parallels that of environmental psychology. Its development in earnest began in the 1960s, as a reaction against what has been characterised as descriptive geography and was an attempt to move towards a more theory-driven part of the discipline. It has made a significant contribution to our thinking and understanding of place, especially from a phenomenological perspective, as we will see in Chapter 2. Another major focus of geographers is environmental cognition. In this they borrow from psychology but also make a considerable contribution to it. As well as environmental cognition, behavioural geographers look at such things as the cognitive basis of spatial decision-making. While sociology tends to operate at a molar level, and psychophysics at a micro-level, like environmental psychology, behavioural geography works across the whole spectrum.

Some years ago, geographer John Gold (1980) characterised behavioural geography. Described by Gold, behavioural geography distinguishes between and examines both the 'objective' world and 'the world of the mind'. It recognises that people shape the world as well as respond to it. It focuses on the individual rather than on social groups or societies. Finally, behavioural geography has a multidisciplinary approach. Comparing Gold's description with Gifford's (2002) description of environmental psychology that we discuss below shows them to be at least siblings, if not twins. Many geographers have made contributions to environmental psychology and are an integral part of it (Kitchen, Blades & Golledge, 1997).

Planning is one of the main disciplines that create our environments. It is generally concerned with the large-scale locations or facilities and the routes between them. These include the layout of cities, neighbourhoods, and university campuses, for instance. Planning is often based on assumptions and data about how people move around, use information, navigate, make decisions, and interact socially. Planners are therefore interested in how people understand their environments and how they cognitively structure them. Planners have made some significant contributions to our understanding of person-environment relations and environmental psychology. The US planner Kevin Lynch was one of the pioneers of ideas behind mental mapping studies in relation to large-scale urban environments. His book *Image of the City* is one of the most influential writings on the topic of cognitive maps ever published (Lynch, 1960). It is worth noting that psychologists have made contributions to planning. Notable amongst those is pioneering environmental psychologist Terrence Lee in the UK, who influenced thinking on neighbourhood forms and school locations.

Architecture has provided a lot of material and raised many questions for psychologists to address. The impact of architects on environmental psychology and our understanding of person-environment relations have been relatively limited in recent times. That is not to say they have made no contribution. Especially in the UK architects such as Manning and Markus were highly influential, as were architecture schools at Liverpool, Strathclyde, Kingston, and Portsmouth, where several leading environmental psychologists began their research careers. Alan Lipman in academia and, in private practice, Frank Duffy also spring to mind. However, today the influence is perhaps less than would be expected for the discipline that designs, plans, and constructs buildings. There has however been a significant indirect contribution to our discipline.

Because many of the buildings that environmental psychologists study are created by architects, their intentions and assumptions in the designs they have produced are of course the subject of much research. Architects also have a significant focus on the aesthetics, raising questions about how people understand the styles and design of buildings. Several researchers have examined perception and understanding of meaning in architecture (e.g., Groat, 1982; Nasar, Stamps & Hanyu, 2005; Wilson & Canter, 1990), as well as how architects' training comes to shape their design styles (e.g., Wilson, 1996; Wilson & Canter, 1990). Although architects consider people's use of and responses to their settings, the direct influence of architectural psychology on architecture has been less than may have been hoped in the early days of the discipline.

BECOMING AN ENVIRONMENTAL PSYCHOLOGIST

Unlike clinical, forensic, or occupational psychology, for example, there is no registration, licenced or chartered status for environmental psychologists. Although the American Psychological Association has a division of environmental psychology, it is not a protected title in the same way other areas of psychology practice are. In some ways an environmental psychologist is a person who does environmental psychology. Terrance Lee made a similar point in 1976 when he wrote, "To understand the specie 'environmental psychologist', the first point to make is that the label derives from what he (sic) actually does and not from his (sic) university degree" (p. 17). Of course, that applies to most of the pioneers of the subject, who were recognised as environmental psychologists, but whose original training was often in a very different area. As researchers from other areas of psychology, including social psychology, start to notice the environment and publish their research on what are essentially traditional environmental psychology topics, we ought to add to the definition of an environmental psychologist as someone who does environmental psychology and identifies as an environmental psychologist.

Some environmental psychologists gain experience working with consultancies, large organisations, architecture practices, or in academia. They might set out to work on environmental issues or it may just happen as part of their role. For instance, working within a large organisation as a human relations specialist, someone might be tasked with facilitating design participation and a move to a new office building. More formally, and more usefully, the route to environmental psychology would be via postgraduate training in the subject. At masters level there is only one course in the UK that has environmental psychology in its title, but there are courses in ergonomics or social psychology that can be relevant. In most European countries, including Spain, France, Germany, the Netherlands, Italy, Sweden, and elsewhere, there are programmes that have significant environmental psychology content, even if they are not called that. In the USA there are programmes in many universities including the University of California, Irvine, and City University New York. It is also possible to pursue an interest in environmental psychology via doctoral research. In that case there is an even wider choice of universities as there are potential supervisors who work in environmental psychology but are not part of a large enough group to provide taught postgraduate courses.

DEFINITIONS OF ENVIRONMENTAL PSYCHOLOGY

Definitions put boundaries around a disciple, identifying what it is concerned with and how it might go about its business. There are several definitions of environmental psychology, which have changed over the years, recognising advances in research and in the complexity with which the environment is conceptualised. Despite the dynamic nature of the discipline, the definitions identify a consistent set of characteristics, some of which we will consider in more detail later.

At the start of the 1980s, David Canter and Ken Craik, in their opening introduction to the first issue of the *Journal of Environmental Psychology*, described the discipline as,

> that area of psychology that brings into conjunction and analyzes the transactions and interrelationships of human experience and actions with pertinent aspects of the socio-physical surroundings.
>
> (Canter & Craik, 1981, p. 2)

Canadian environmental psychologist Bob Gifford, who has written one of the best comprehensive textbooks in environmental psychology, now in its fifth edition, defined environmental psychology simply as,

> the study of transactions between individuals and their physical settings.
> (Gifford, 1987. p. 2)

Finally, one of the most recent good texts in environmental psychology, edited by Linda Steg and her colleagues in the Netherlands, describes environmental psychology as,

> the discipline that studies the interplay between individuals and their built and natural environment.
> (Steg, Van Den Berg & De Groot, 2013, p. 2)

There are some features of these definitions that are worth drawing out. Canter and Craik's, and Gifford's definitions highlight that the discipline is concerned with transactions with the environment. In the early days of environmental psychology many researchers assumed that there was a clear one-way relationship between the environment and people. This has gradually evolved to the point where the relationship is conceptualised as a transaction in which the environment and people mutually act on one another in a continuous cycle of change and influence.

While Gifford talks of physical settings, Canter and Craik, by specifying socio-physical surroundings, draw attention to the social environment as well the physical. Other people are part of our environment and so need to be considered along with the physical surroundings. As French environmental psychologist Claude Levy-Leboyer describes, "*. . . in reality, the social dimension is always there, because it constitutes the web of relationships between man and environment. . . The physical environment simultaneously symbolizes, makes concrete, and conditions the social environment*" (Levy-Leboyer, 1982, p. 15). As soon as we start to discuss the social relationships in an environment, and the social systems that give rise to them, the importance of other disciplines, such as sociology and anthropology, becomes more obvious.

Finally, it is worth emphasising Linda Steg and her colleagues' definition that highlights the built environment and the natural environment. This distinction was evident very early on in the development of the discipline. In what is perhaps the first text on environmental psychology, Ittelson et al. (1974) devote considerable attention to the natural, as well as the built environment.

CHARACTERISTICS OF ENVIRONMENTAL PSYCHOLOGY

To understand environmental psychology further, it is helpful to elaborate the discipline beyond the confines of the definitions we have seen. Within environmental psychology, there is a remarkable constancy in the characterisation of the field across writers and over time. Comparing the first texts on environmental psychology (Ittleson et al., 1974; Proshansky, Ittelson & Rivlin, 1976) with more contemporary volumes (Gifford, 1987, 2002; Steg, Van den Berg & De Groot, 2019) shows a consensus unusual in academic social science.

Gifford's (2002) description of the discipline is perhaps the best characterisation available. He argues that what sets environmental psychology apart is its commitment to research that subscribes to the following principles:

> Environmental psychology "*is ultimately capable of improving the built environment and our stewardship of natural resources*".
>
> (p. 4)

General and mainstream psychology has many everyday applications, but application is not always the central aim of research, and the way in which it can be applied is not always evident from the original experiments. This is like many scientific disciplines. In physics, for example, research on the atom was not aimed at a specific application and was only later used to develop atomic bombs and atomic power. Environmental psychology is not unique amongst other sub-areas of psychology, such as occupational and industrial psychology, and clinical, forensic, and health psychology, in being applied. Like those fields, environmental psychology research is strongly oriented to address challenges and, more uniquely, improving the environment. This is consistent with Ittleson et al.'s (1974) description written almost 50 years ago, in which they identified environmental psychology's aim as being to solve social problems. Proshansky et al. echoed this point at a similar time, when they wrote that the discipline directly grew out of attempts to answer pressing social challenges (Proshansky et al., 1976). It is important to note, however, that the applied nature of environmental psychology does not mean that it is without theory. That was a criticism in its early days, but today it can be characterised as a theory-based discipline, though it aims to use that theory to change the world. As Gifford makes clear, environmental psychology includes theory, research, and practice:

> Environmental psychology "*is carried out in everyday settings (or close simulations of them)*"
>
> (p. 4)

Earlier the point was made that it is possible to predict a person's behaviour more accurately from knowing where they are than who they are. Therefore, to understand people's behaviour in a particular environment, you need to study them in that environment. After all, a psychology laboratory is an environment. Consequently, studying behaviour in a laboratory will tell you about how people behave in a laboratory. It will not necessarily tell you about their behaviour in other environments. As soon as a person goes into a laboratory, they already have expectations that will influence their behaviour. If it is not possible to study people in the target environment, then they should be studied in an environment that is, in all important respects, a very close approximation of it . In traditional experimental psychology, researchers attempt to remove most of the influences on behaviour, but when environmental psychologists have to use a laboratory, they try to preserve them. This poses some unique challenges for environmental psychologists who have developed an array of research techniques, which are typically described in comprehensive textbooks on the discipline, or in texts devoted to research methods in environmental psychology (Gifford, 2016).

The third of Gifford's principles is:

> Environmental psychology "*considers the person and the setting to be a holistic entity*".
>
> (p. 4)

When examining people's behaviour in the world outside the laboratory we are usually looking at the whole environment. The holistic approach to studying the environment goes back to the beginning of environmental psychology and is commented on in the early work of Ittleson et al. (1974) and Proshansky et al. (1976). As Proshansky (1976) noted many years ago, environmental psychologists study people as part of their milieu. Beyond their physical and social qualities, environments come with a set of rules, expectations, and scripts that guide what people will do. These form part of their field's subject matter.

The fourth principle suggested by Gifford is:

> Environmental psychology "recognizes that individuals actively cope with and shape settings, rather than passively absorb environmental forces". (p. 4)

Although most areas of psychology have been moving away from the notion that people are passive responders to stimuli, it has long been central in environmental psychology that people do not just respond to the environment, they actively engage with it, adjusting the way they interact and changing the environment itself. Ittleson et al. (1974) referred to this as the "dynamic interchange" (p. 5). Slightly more fundamentally, within environmental psychology people are seen as having agency. In contrast to determinism in which a person's behaviour is a response directly determined or caused by the environment, agency has people acting on their world rather than simply responding to it. Without an external stimulus people do not remain passive and inert. They have goals and intentions, they make decisions and choices, and they carry out actions related to those choices. From this perspective the environment might help shape behaviour, but it does not cause it.

Gifford's final principle is:

> Environmental psychology "*is often performed in conjunction with other disciplines and professions*".
>
> (p. 4)

Because environmental psychologists tend to be problem-solving and work with real environments they often work alongside practitioners from other disciplines. These may include some of those we have already briefly mentioned, such as planners and architects, but can also include, amongst others, facilities managers, safety experts, and the police. Further, as environmental psychologists are dealing with a wide variety of environments and environmental issues, they will be one of an array of environmental scientists. Consequently, they are likely to find theories and ideas from other environmental disciplines more useful than would be the case if they were working in isolation. On top of that, they are also likely to find theories from disciplines not concerned with the environment to be helpful.

For instance, organisational theory may assist environmental psychologists in their understanding of the way in which work settings contribute to workers' experience and organisational functioning.

While this sounds very collaborative and ideal, working with different disciplines is not without its challenges. These can be as basic as language, for instance, what a psychologist means by objective data might not be what an architect or computer scientist means by that term. Sometimes the difficulties are deeper. The basic ways in which various disciplines conceive of and think about the world may also be different. Scientists for example often struggle with arts disciplines, where the reliance on empirical data is less important. Environmental psychology therefore requires an understanding not only of different technical languages but also of multiple perspectives and ways of conceptualising. They require a willingness to work in worlds that do not immediately fit with their own training and thinking. Overall, this is probably a positive feature.

A SKETCH OF THE (UK) ORIGINS OF ENVIRONMENTAL PSYCHOLOGY

It is impossible to do more than scratch the surface of the history of environmental and architectural psychology here. This is true for its development in just one country, for the field as a whole it is impossible. Therefore, in this very brief account we will focus on the UK, and even then, only a handful of the many people who created the discipline can be mentioned. However, help is at hand for those who want a more representative and comprehensive account. Almost all environmental psychology textbooks include detailed information about the history and development of the discipline. As they are accounts of historic events what they describe has not changed in any significant ways over the years, though some people and studies get added and others seem to disappear. Each account usually includes developments in North America, which dominated the discipline for 60 or so years. If the writer is from outside the USA, further details usually reflect the author's own country . Stokols and Altman's *Handbook of Environmental Psychology* (1986) has extensive descriptions of the history of the discipline in ten countries or regions including Australia, Japan, France, Germany, the

Netherlands, Sweden, Soviet Union, Latin America, North America, and the UK. Spanish environmental psychologist Enric Pol provides a broader international view of the contributions that researchers have made to the discipline than is often found in accounts given from an Anglo-American perspective (Pol, 2006, 2007). Bonnes and Secchiaroli (1995) also provide a wider account that includes detail on developments in Europe and elsewhere. Further, reviews of other disciplines are worth considering, especially behavioural geography (Gold, 1980; Kitchen et al., 1997).

The work of several psychologists at the start of the twentieth century, or even earlier, can be seen as foreshadowing research that later became part of environmental psychology. The first time the term environmental psychology (pschologie der umwelt) was used in a publication was probably by German psychologist Hellpach in 1924 (Kruse & Graumann, 1987; Pol, 2006). There were others working at this time and later that could be seen as pioneers; however, as Steg et al. (2013) contend, at that point it is too early to speak of an independent field of systematic research in environmental psychology. It is also probably too early to speak of these researchers as environmental psychologists in any real sense. However, that is not to deny their groundbreaking work, which laid foundations, influenced later eminent environmental psychologists, and included topics we would recognise as part of the discipline today.

Fleury-Bahi, Pol, and Navarro (2017) draw attention to the "contributions of Terrence Lee, David Canter and Harold Proshansky and those who founded 'the golden age' of architectural psychology in the 1960s and 1970s" (p. 3). At this time, environmental psychology as a discipline can more clearly be seen to emerge out of a collection of unrelated studies carried out primarily in Europe and North America, though an interest in Japan was visible too. The research began to coalesce during the 1960s with the emergence of the infrastructure of an academic discipline, including conferences, professional associations, texts, and university courses. By the late 1960s and early 1970s, the discipline had consolidated and been named.

The applied and problem-solving orientation of environmental psychology was perhaps set at this time. In most countries where the field began to emerge, it was the result of research into some of the pressing social issues of the time. In some countries, including the Netherlands, it may have been a lack of interest in applied psychology in favour of more traditional experimental and theoretical approaches to psychology that delayed the emergence of the discipline in them (Stringer & Kremer, 1987). Incidentally, the Netherlands is now a country with a very strong presence in environmental psychology. Because of its applied nature, environmental psychology also often emerged from research collaboration between different disciplines or professions. In the USA that was often with clinical psychologists and designers. In the UK psychologists tended to be involved with planners, architects, engineers, and others involved in the design of buildings.

Like much of the rest of Europe, the UK in the 1960s was dealing with the aftermath of the Second World War, which, we sometimes forget, had ended only 15–20 years before. During the 1950s and into the 1960s 'slum' housing and bomb-damaged buildings were being cleared and new towns were being consciously planned. Terrance Lee, a founder and pioneer of British environmental psychology, had carried out influential PhD research on the concept of neighbourhood at Cambridge, under the supervision of Sir Fred Bartlett. Lee, in the 1950s, applied Bartlett's innovative work on cognitive schema to the environment in what can be considered one of the earliest studies of both modern environmental psychology and environmental cognition (Lee, 1968). Lee's work went on to influence town planning and the development of new towns in the UK. His work also fed into ideas that had started in the previous century with the Garden Cities movement, which were an attempt to get away from the crowded cities that had evolved from the industrial revolution and throughout the Victorian era. With the reorganisation of education in the country, Lee also worked on a variety of topics to do with schools, including the impact of journey time on pupil learning.

Lee eventually moved, via other universities, to the University of Surrey where he became its first professor of psychology and head of the newly formed psychology department. David Canter was invited by Terrence Lee to move to Surrey University, where they established the UK's first masters course in environmental psychology, which took its first students in 1973. The course continues to run today, and several of its graduates can be found cited in the pages of this volume. Had the course been established a few years earlier it would probably have been called architectural psychology. Lee and Canter were later joined by Peter Stringer, a psychologist working in the Bartlett School of Architecture (part of University College, the University of London), and Ian Griffiths, who was working for the consulting firm Atkins. Surrey University consequently became perhaps the leading centre for environmental psychology outside of the USA at that time. The department remains an important hub of environmental psychology today.

As an aside, the course at Surrey provides an interesting microcosm of the multidisciplinary and multinational nature of environmental psychology. Originally the course was directed by David Canter, a psychologist, who had moved from a school of architecture. Directorship then moved to David Uzzell, originally a geographer, and most recently to Birgitta Gatersleben, a Dutch psychologist with a PhD from the University of Groningen, another European hub of environmental psychology.

In the UK architectural psychology was the prevailing term used for the emergent discipline. This probably reflected a focus on the built environment because many of the early environmental psychologists, such as Canter, could be found in the architecture departments of UK universities. Changes in design and the requirements for gaining an understanding of user needs, and a push by the Royal Institute of British Architects (RIBA) to include evaluations and feedback as part of the management of design, led to architects and social scientists working together. For instance, Brian Wells was undertaking studies of offices based in the architecture department at Liverpool University. David Canter was Brian Wells' PhD student working within the Pilkington Research Unit at Liverpool. Canter later moved to the school of architecture at Strathclyde University, along with the Pilkington Research Unit, which became the Building Performance Research Unit (BPRU), led by architect Tom Markus. The unit conducted several multidisciplinary studies into building types including offices, hospitals, and schools.

The Pilkington Research Unit at Liverpool was sponsored by a glass manufacturer interested in the role of natural lighting in buildings. The group conducted important research and developed ideas about people-environment interactions. For instance, Manning, an architect, published one of the most important studies of its time into office buildings. Manning was part of a movement arguing for greater notice to be taken of users and for systematic research to be incorporated into architectural design stages, something taken for granted now. Writing in 1965, Manning made the point that "design decisions affecting the social environment of office buildings are made entirely on the basis of expectations or personal prejudice rather than knowledge" (Manning, 1965, p. 41). The BPRU (1972) book on building performance was significant in including discussion on the nature of agency, human action, and the goal-directed nature of behaviour. That was not something typical in publications on building performance at the time.

There were symposia on architectural psychology at British Psychological Society conferences in the 1960s, the first being in 1963 at Reading University (Lee, 1976). The first significant full conference on architectural psychology was organised by the RIBA and Strathclyde School of Architecture and took place at Dalandhui near Glasgow. The meeting resulted in a book, edited by David Canter, entitled *Architectural Psychology* (Canter, 1970), which appeared the same year as Proshansky et al.'s (1970) edited volume, *Environmental Psychology*. Conferences followed at Kingston Polytechnic and Sheffield University, eventually evolving into the bi-annual IAPS conferences.

For disciplines to become established they need to have an infrastructure that maintains them and disseminates ideas and research. We have already seen that university departments established research groups and postgraduate courses. There are also research associations in several regions of the world. In the USA, the Environmental Design Research Association (EDRA) was established in 1968 and has held an annual conference since 1969, usually in North America. Interestingly, the EDRA grew out of a multidisciplinary session at the 1965 conference of the Association of American Geographers. In Europe the International Association for People-Environment Studies (IAPS), which has its roots in the Architectural Psychology Conferences that began in the 1960s and continued to use the term Architectural Psychology until IAPS, was founded in 1981. In agreeing the name of the association, the 'AP' of the *Architectural Psychology Newsletter*, edited by Sue-Ann Lee, was consciously preserved. In Asia and Australia, there is the People and Physical Environment Research (PAPER) association (1980) and the Man-Environment Research Association (MERA) was created in 1982 at the Architecture Department in the University of Osaka, Japan. As well as associations there are journals publishing peer-reviewed research. Although there is a plethora of these, often covering specific research areas such as transport or sustainability, there are two primary environmental psychology focused journals. *Environment and Behavior* was established in the USA in 1969 as a multidisciplinary publication. The other is the *Journal of Environmental Psychology* established by David Canter and Ken Craik in 1981.

Of the regions that pioneered environmental psychology at its inception, arguably the USA, followed by the UK and Sweden, where architectural psychology conferences were being organised in the 1960s, were perhaps at the forefront. Researchers in North America however have dominated the field since its beginnings. That may well have changed in more recent years. Gifford (2017) has observed that there is now more environmental psychology research conducted in other countries than is carried out in the USA. Comparing a new handbook of environmental psychology (Fleury-Bahi, Pol & Navarro, 2017) to that by Altman and Stokols published in 1987, he notes that the recent volume includes 73 authors from 14 countries, with only two from the USA. The 1987 handbook included 66 authors from 11 countries with 43 of them being from the USA. Whether this represents a shift in the volume of work generated in different regions is open to question. Even if that is the case, we are still comparing the work of one country with the rest of the world. But all of that aside, there are now researchers working in environmental psychology in most European countries and throughout the world, and the discipline we have today is the product of all of them.

PERSON-ENVIRONMENT RELATIONS: FROM REACTING TO TRANSACTING

Having set the scene of what environmental psychology is and where it came from, in the next chapters we will examine some conceptual issues and start to see what it is that environmental psychologists do. First we need to lay some groundwork for understanding the relationship between people and their environments. The final part of this chapter will consider the fundamental way in which the environment impacts on people and vice versa. The nature of that relationship has been the subject of debate throughout the history and development of the discipline. It is important to engage with that discussion because the way we think about how the environment and people relate to one another will strongly influence how we design environments, the policy we make about environments, and the research we do on environments.

There are several different ways of thinking about how people and the environment relate, but generally they can be distilled into the three main categories of determinism, interactionism, and transactionism (Canter, 1984). There are other ways of conceptualising person-environment relationships; however, these provide a useful, good, and broad categorisation that is reasonably easy to grasp.

ENVIRONMENTAL DETERMINISM

The clue to the meaning of environmental determinism is very much in the name; the physical environment determines behaviour. Strong determinism is the simplest, most basic way of viewing the person-environment relationship. It is also, and probably for that very reason, the way most people initially think about the connection. Within this approach, the environment is a simple stimulus, with behaviour being the direct, usually predictable, specific response. The response might be a behaviour, thought or feeling, but the path from stimulus to response will be direct. The environment directly causes the behaviour, thought, or feeling.

Some of the most common questions asked about the environment and its impact on people are often framed within a strong deterministic framework. This is especially true when the press or other media are seeking a comment on some environmental question or other. It is a way of thinking that tends to be visible in most media portrayals of environmental issues, as well as many of the questions and statements from politicians. If we look at some of these questions closely, we can see that often the deterministic conceptualisation does not hold up as an adequate explanation. Take for example the apparently simple question of how loud must noise be to be annoying. Within a deterministic framework it should be quite straightforward to answer that question, it is just a matter of establishing the decibel level at which people report being annoyed. We will then know that as long as sound is kept below that level, everyone will be happy. We hear the equivalent of this when people are reassured that the noise from traffic or a new airport runway is acceptable because it will not be above a certain level. However, it is, of course, not that simple, because it is not just the level or volume of the sound that is important. Many other characteristics of the noise play a role in determining if it is annoying or not. For instance, who is making the noise, what the qualities of the noise are, how much control is there over the noise, what the noise means, and how frequent and intermittent the sound is, are all important in determining how annoying it is (Gifford, 2013). If the noise is meaningful, predictable, and can be controlled, it will be less annoying than if it does not have these characteristics, even if the decibel level is the same (Evans & Cohen, 1987).

Throughout this book we will see many instances where researchers and others have assumed a direct and simple relationship between person and environment, only to be disappointed or confused when the relationship turns out not to be that straightforward. The Hawthorne studies (Roethlisberger and Dickson, 1949), which many psychologists are aware of because of the Hawthorne Effect, began by conceptualising research in terms of a direct relationship between lighting levels and work performance. As we will see in Chapter 7, when we look at work environments, the results revealed that such simple ideas cannot account for behaviour and that many other factors were involved. Interestingly, rather than abandoning determinism, the researchers involved in that study initially abandoned the environment as irrelevant to worker performance. Other, more insightful researchers realised that it is important, but that its influences are subtler.

Less extreme versions of determinism give a slightly more active role to people in their relationship with the environment. From a weak determinist perspective, it is recognised that people will have a set of experiences that will mediate between the environment and a person's reaction to it. Behaviour is therefore not the pure, direct result of the stimulus. However, the reasons why or how things come to have meaning are often ignored. The approach typically assumes that meaning is static; so does not take change and development into account. That is important because as meanings change, the same physical environment will have different effects over time. For instance, the site of a disaster will have very significant meaning for some people. Their response to the physical qualities of the site will be different pre- and post-disaster, even though those qualities have not changed.

ENVIRONMENTAL INTERACTIONISM

Once we move along the continuum from strong determinism to a weaker version, we are beginning to recognise interactionist ideas. An interactionist approach is a little more complex and better able to account for the relationships observed between people and their physical setting. The same approach can be found in Kurt Lewin's famous equation: $B=f(P, E)$, where *B=behaviour*, *P=person*, and *E=environment* (Lewin, 1936). The equation simply states that any behaviour will be the result, or function, of an interaction between the person and their environment. In this, Lewin was emphasising that the environment plays an important role in behaviour but that there is an interaction between the characteristics of the environment and the characteristics of the person. As he wrote, ". . . one can hope to understand the forces that govern behavior only if one includes in the representation the whole psychological situation" (Lewin, 1936, p. 12).

This approach contrasts with the simple stimulus-response model, which ignores characteristics of the individual, such as personality traits, or personal experience and history. Research showing that the impact of the environment may vary dramatically from one person to the other, with the same environmental stimuli resulting in very different behaviours, supports this perspective.

ENVIRONMENTAL TRANSACTIONISM

It is not only the case that settings impact on people, but also people change their settings. There is an evolution of the relationship between the people and the environment. The idea that the environment shapes behaviour and that the environment is shaped by our decision-making reflects a famous quote from Winston Churchill, reproduced in almost all environmental psychology texts, in which he said, "We shape our buildings and afterwards our buildings shape us" (Hansard, 1943). He was talking about the rebuilding of the chamber of the House of Commons in the British parliament and pointing out that the nature of British politics and parliamentary debate is shaped by the characteristics of the House, including it being too small and spatially organised to facilitate confrontation rather than cooperation, though he did not necessarily express it in that way.

Churchill's statement leads us to the third of the approaches that we will consider. The transactionist perspective recognises that people can change the physical nature of their surroundings and the meanings they have. Equally the experience of the environment can change those people. There is a mutual transaction between people and the environment. In some versions of this approach, it would be argued that to make a distinction between a person and their environment is a false dichotomy.

Because people change their physical environments to meet their needs and goals, it can be difficult for designers, managers, or owners to dictate how people will behave within an environment. Whenever you see employees reorganising office furniture, or shoppers going in through the out door, what we are seeing are people who are not simply responding to their environment, they are transacting with it.

Strong transactionalism is the most complex of the Person-Environment models we will consider. Here, people are defined by the environments they are in and they and their actions, in return, define that environment. The strong transactionist approach argues that to distinguish between action and context, and to assume that past relationships people have with their settings are the same as they have with them in the present, is illogical because both the person and the environment are evolving together. To understand the relationship we need to look at the objectives and goals people have and the way in which they are structured by the social processes of which an individual is a part.

The transaction between the environment and people has physical form but can also be virtual or imaginary. As Canter (1977) argues, when dealing with the environment, people have 'mental models' of it and of the implications of their surroundings for them and what they are trying to do. The image people create can be the basis of how they act in relation to the environment. In that sense people really do create the environment that they are acting in, because they are acting on the basis of a cognitive or psychological model or concept of the environment, or place, they are in. At this point you might say that the environment has become 'place'. We will go on to discuss the concept of place in the next chapter, but for now place can be described as a function of the synthesis of people, activities, conceptualisation, and meanings, along with programmes of action (Canter, 1977).

IMPLICATIONS OF THE PERSON-ENVIRONMENT MODEL

It is often useful when dealing with slightly abstract concepts such as these to look at an example that provides an illustration of the implications of adopting one or other of these models. One example that we will come back to in detail in Chapter 4 is how people behave during life-threatening events such as fires. Getting this right can, literally, be a matter of life and death. Much regulation and planning has traditionally been based on a strong determinist model. It assumes that there will be an environmental stimulus, such as smoke or an alarm, to which people will immediately or rapidly respond. Most often it is assumed that the direct response will be panic.

What research has consistently shown is that when faced with indicators that there might be a threat, say a fire, people try to make sense of the environment, fitting it into existing conceptualisations (Canter, Breaux & Sime, 1990). They may ignore or reinterpret alarms, often based on previous experience. They will try to construct a narrative for the events they are caught up in, and, without significant guidance from others, will act upon that narrative and the world they have actively constructed. In establishing their image or conceptualisation of the event, they will include the environment, but also observe others, consider their own experience and how the current situation relates to it, think about their original goals or reasons for being in the environment, and then make a plan of action based on interpretations and scripts (Donald & Canter, 1990, 1992). This can be a rapid process, or can take time, delaying their response to the threat. Further, the evidence is that this process can continue to the very end of a life-threatening event (Donald & Canter, 1992).

This example shows us that rather than simply responding to environmental stimuli in the mechanical and automatic way predicted by determinist models, people will construct a reality of their own, and then act based on that reality. Of course, the physical environment will be part of that construction, but it will be shaped and altered by many other factors related to the individual. The model used to make decisions about the relationship between the environment and behaviour is, then, central to what we do, how we design, and how we manage environments.

FINALLY

Environmental psychology, as we know it, is a relatively young discipline. Over its 70-year history, it has made significant progress, becoming an international disciple and generating a major body of original research. As an applied and interdisciplinary field of study, environmental psychology has drawn on a wide range of theory and literature and contributed to understanding and solving many problems. In the rest of this book, a selection of that work will be examined. First, in the next chapter we will look at the idea of place. Although it is a quite abstract concept, we will see that it helps us to understand many issues and has important practical implications.

REFERENCES

Bonnes, M., & Secchiaroli, G. (1995). *Environmental Psychology: A Psycho-social Introduction*. London: Sage.

Building Performance Research Unit (1972). *Building Performance*. London: Applied Science.

Canter, D. (1970). *Architectural Psychology*. London: RIBA.

Canter, D. (1975). An introduction to environmental psychology. In D. Canter and P. Stringer (eds.), *Environmental Interaction: Psychological Approaches to our Physical Surroundings* (pp. 1–19). London: Surrey University Press.

Canter, D. (1977). *The Psychology of Place*. London: Architectural Press.

Canter, D. (1985). *Applying Psychology. Inaugural Lecture.* Guildford: University of Surrey.

Canter, D., Breaux J., & Sime J. (1980). Domestic, multiple occupancy and hospital fires. In D. Canter (ed.), *Fires and Human Behaviour* (pp. 117–136). Chichester: Wiley.

Canter, D., & Craik, K. (1981). Environmental psychology. *Journal of Environmental Psychology,* 1, 1–11.

Donald, I., & Canter, D. (1990). Behavioural aspects of the King's Cross Disaster. In D. Canter (ed.), *Fires and Human Behaviour, Second Edition* (pp. 15–30). London: David Fulton.

Donald, I., & Canter, D. (1992). Intentionality and fatality during the King's Cross Underground fire. *European Journal of Social Psychology*, 22, 203–218.

Evans, G. W., & Cohen, S. (1987). Environmental stress. In D. Stokols & I. Altman (eds.), *Handbook of Environmental Psychology, Volume 1* (pp. 571–610). Chichester: Wiley.

Fleury-Bahi, G., Pol, E., & Navarro, O. (2017). Introduction: Environmental psychology and quality of life. In G. Fleury-Bahi, E. Pol & O. Navarro (eds.), *Handbook of Environmental Psychology and Quality of Life Research* (pp. 1–9). New York: Springer.

Gifford, R. (1987). *Environmental Psychology: Principles and Practice.* London: Allyn & Bacon.

Gifford, R. (2002). *Environmental Psychology: Principles and Practice, Third Edition.* Colville, WA: Optimal Books.

Gifford, R. (Ed.) (2016). *Research Methods for Environmental Psychology.* Chichester: Wiley.

Gifford, R. (2017). Preface. In G. Fleury-Bahi, E. Pol & O. Navarro (eds.), *Handbook of Environmental Psychology and Quality of Life Research* (pp. v–vi). New York: Springer.

Gold, J. R. (1980). *An Introduction to Behavioural Geography*. Oxford: Oxford University Press.

Groat, L. (1982). Meaning in post modern architecture: An examination using the multiple sorting task. *Journal of Environmental Psychology*, 2, 2–22.

Hansard (1943). House of commons rebuilding. *Parliamentary Debates, House of Commons*, 393(114), 403–407. London: HMSO.

Ittelson, W. H., Proshansky, H. M., Rivilin, L. G., & Winkel, G. (1974). *An Introduction to Environmental Psychology*. New York: Holt Rinehart and Winston.

Kitchen, R. M., Blades, M., & Golledge, R. G. (1997). Relations between psychology and geography. *Environment and Behavior*, 29, 554–573.

Knight, K. W. (2018). *Environmental Sociology*. Oxford Bibliographies in Environmental Science. doi: 10.1093/obo/9780199363445-0100

Kruse, L., & Graumann, C. F. (1987). Environmental psychology in Germany. In D. Stokols & I. Altman (eds.), *Handbook of Environmental Psychology, Volume 2* (pp. 1195–1225). New York: John Wiley and Sons.

Küller, R. (1987). Environmental psychology from a Swedish perspective. In D. Stokols & I. Altman (eds.), *Handbook of Environmental Psychology, Volume 2* (pp. 1243–1279). New York: John Wiley and Sons.

Lee, T. (1968). Urban neighbourhood as a socio-spatial scheme. *Human Relations*, 21, 241–267.

Lee, T. (1976). *Psychology and the Environment*. London: Methuen.

Levy-Leboyer, C. (1982). *Psychology and Environment*. London: Sage.

Lewin, K. (1936). *Principles of Topological Psychology*. New York: McGraw Hill.

Lockie, S. (2015). What is environmental sociology? *Environmental Sociology*, 1(3), 139–142.

Lynch, K. (1960). *The Image of the City*. Cambridge, MA: MIT Press.

Manning, P. (Ed.) (1965). *Office Design: A Study of Environment*. Pilkington Research Unit, University of Liverpool. https://files.eric.ed.gov/fulltext/ED033529.pdf

Nasar, J., Stamps, A., & Hanyu, K. (2005). Form and function in public buildings. *Journal of Environmental Psychology*, 25, 159–165.

Pol, E. (2006). Blueprints for a history of environmental psychology (I): From first birth to American transition. *Medio Ambiente y Comportamiento Humano*, 7(2), 95–113.

Pol, E. (2007). Blueprints for a history of environmental psychology (II): From architectural psychology to the challenge of sustainability. *Medio Ambiente y Comportamiento Humano*, 8, 1–28.

Proshansky, H. M., Ittelson, W. H., & Rivlin, L. G. (Eds.) (1970). *Environmental Psychology: Man and His Physical Settings*. New York: Holt Rinehart and Winston.

Proshansky, H. M., Ittelson, W. H., & Rivlin, L. G. (Eds.) (1976). *Environmental Psychology: People and Their Physical Settings, Second Edition*. New York: Holt Rinehart and Winston.

Roethlisberger, F. J., & Dickson, W. J. (1949). *Management and the Worker*. Cambridge, MA: Harvard University Press.

Ross, H. (1974). *Behaviour and Perception in Strange Environments*. London: Allen and Unwin.

Steg, L., Van den Berg, A. E., & De Groot, J. I. M. (2013). Environmental psychology: History, scope and methods. In L. Steg, A. E. Van den Berg, & J. I. M. De Groot (eds.), *Environmental Psychology: An Introduction* (pp. 1–11). Oxford: BPS Blackwell.

Steg, L., Van den Berg, A. E., & De Groot, J. I. M. (Eds.) (2019). *Environmental Psychology: An Introduction, Second Edition*. Oxford: BPS Blackwell.

Stringer, P., & Kremer, A. (1987). Environmental psychology in the Netherlands. In D. Stokols & I. Altman (eds.), *Handbook of Environmental Psychology, Volume 2* (pp. 1227–1241). New York: John Wiley and Sons.

Wilson, M. A. (1996). The socialization of architectural preference. *Journal of Environmental Psychology*, 16, 33–44.

Wilson, M. A., & Canter, D. (1990). The development of central concepts during professional education: An example of a multivariate model of the concept of architectural style. *Applied Psychology: An International Review*, 39, 431–455.

SUGGESTED READING

Almost any introductory text in environmental psychology will provide a good overview of the history and nature of the discipline. Two can be particularly recommended.

Gifford, R. (2013). *Environmental Psychology: Principles and Practice, Fifth Edition.* Victoria, BC: Optimal Books.

Steg, L., Van den Berg, A. E., & De Groot, J. I. M. (Eds.) (2019). *Environmental Psychology: An Introduction, Second Edition.* Oxford: BPS Blackwell.

There have been several accounts of the discipline included in the *Annual Review of Psychology* series. Each summaries the research since the previous review, and are all worth looking at. However the most recent is

Gifford, R. (2014). Environmental psychology matters. *Annual Review of Psychology*, 65, 541–579.

For the history of environmental psychology any environmental text will provide details. Particular useful from a European perspective is Pol's account.

Pol, E. (2006). Blueprints for a history of environmental psychology (I): From first birth to American transition. *Medio Ambiente y Comportamiento Humano*, 7(2), 95–113.

Pol, E. (2007). Blueprints for a history of environmental psychology (II): From architectural psychology to the challenge of sustainability. *Medio Ambiente y Comportamiento Humano*, 8, 1–28.

2

PLACE, PLACE IDENTITY, AND PLACE ATTACHMENT

INTRODUCTION

In this chapter we explore the concepts of place, place identity, and place attachment. These may seem quite abstract and sometimes philosophical ideas, but they do relate directly to some of the fundamental elements of our own lives and identity. They also provide concepts to explain how we interact with the environment. These ideas help us answer questions such as why people resist changes to their neighbourhood, why they get homesick, why some choose to live on the side of an active volcano despite the risks, and why some people, but not others, object to power stations and wind farms being built near to them. Understanding the concepts in this chapter will, more generally, help our understanding of how people are part of place, and how place forms a part of them.

PLACE AND APPROACHES TO PLACE

Of all the disciplines that are concerned with the environment, the one that has had the greatest focus on place, and perhaps made the greatest contribution to it, is geography. Cresswell, in his excellent book *Place*, writes, "*Place is one of the two or three most important terms for my discipline – geography. If pushed, I would argue that it is the most important of them all*". He goes on to add, ". . .*But place is not the property of geography – it is a concept that travels quite freely between disciplines and the study of place benefits from an interdisciplinary approach*" (Cresswell, 2015. p. 1). He also quotes the Australian philosopher and writer on place Malpas (e.g., 2018), as saying, "*it is perhaps the*

DOI: 10.4324/9780429274541-2

key term for interdisciplinary research in the arts, humanities and social sciences in the twenty-first century" (Malpas, 2010, cited in Cresswell, 2015, p. 1).

It may be the disciplinary ubiquity of place as a concept, along with the philosophical orientations of the different disciplines that have led to some of the ambiguity in defining what it is. For instance, within geography two of the most influential writers on place, Yi Fu Tuan and Edward Relph, set much of the theoretical agenda, and both write from a *phenomenological* tradition (Relph, 1976; Tuan, 1974a,b). Psychologists, in contrast, have tended to take a positivist or empiricist perspective (Canter, 1997; Graumann, 2002), often focusing on hypothesis testing and the measurement of the psychological processes related to place. Stedman (2002) has discussed the difficulties these two positions create for place research.

> We are thus left with a paradox: On one hand are interesting statements that sound like testable hypotheses but are derived from the phenomenological tradition that avoids positivistic hypothesis testing; on the other hand are quantitative treatments of place that have often failed to engage these important theoretical tenets.
>
> (p. 562)

Some authors consider the diversity of approaches to place to be a benefit, arguing that "*rather than being a single body of literature, research on* place attachment *forms, and benefits from, a diverse multiplicity of inquiry*" (Williams & Miller, 2021, p. 13). Others consider attempts to try to unify the different perspectives as a 'false quest' (Patterson & Williams, 2005). Whether the differences are beneficial or not, there are, in fact, some strong similarities between the ideas of many writers on what place is.

Looking at the basic idea of place, Cresswell (2015) provides a very succinct summary, describing it as "*a meaningful location*" (p. 12). Though a simple statement, this brings together the two primary components of place, which are physical existence and attributed meaning. Several writers have elaborated on this dichotomy. Agnew, a political geographer, for instance argues that a place has a location (where it is), a locale (what its physical properties are), and a sense of place – usually how it is experienced (Agnew, 1987). Canter, an environmental psychologist, proposed a similar model, suggesting that place exists at the conjunction of three facets: the physical properties of the setting (location and locale, in Agnew's terms), the activities that happen in the setting or the goals that people have for being in that setting, and people's conceptualisations of that environment or place (similar to Agnew's sense of place) (Canter, 1977). Later Canter added other facets to his model, but essentially the core remains the same (Canter, 1997). As sociologist Richard Stedman (2003) summarises, common to definitions of place "is a three component view that weaves together the physical environment, human behaviours, and social and/or psychological processes" (p. 671).

Beyond this basic idea, there is a lot of complex and subtle discussion around the nature of place. Here we will limit that discussion and briefly examine two issues. The first is whether it is possible to have a 'placeless place', and the second, whether meaning is intrinsic to a place, or whether it is attributed to it. The answers to these questions do seem to evidence a difference between writers in geography and psychology.

Relph, who has written extensively on the subject over the last 50 years or so, describes placelessness as a place or environment that is devoid of meaning (Relph, 1976); it has no *sense of place*. In his writings, Relph seems to be, some extent, responding to the architecture and planning of the 1950s and 1960s onwards, in which homogenised shopping malls, out-of-town retail parks, and uniform high-rise developments proliferated, leading to some characterless and alienating environments. As should become clear as we progress, within the geography tradition it makes sense to talk of placelessness. However, for psychology it would be possible to take a different perspective. For instance, taking Canter's (1977) formulation of place, it could be argued that an environment cannot be placeless, in the sense of being devoid of characteristics or a quality of meaning. It is possible that the alienation, lack of quality, and feeling of anonymity that might lead to Relph describing somewhere as placeless are the characteristics that define and give meaning to that environment. Its placelessness, in a sense, is a characteristic that gives the place its meaning. These represent different perspectives, and there seems little point arguing which is correct and which is wrong. It is probably the roots these perspectives have in their different disciplines and traditions that lead to this contradiction, rather than any fundamental problem with either theory.

Answering the second question of whether meaning is intrinsic to a place, to some extent, also speaks to the first question of whether a place can be placeless. There has been debate about whether settings can have an intrinsic sense of place, which results from its qualities, regardless of whether people imbue it with feelings or meaning. Or, alternatively, whether a setting only has meaning if people give it meaning. Stedman (2003) points to Jackson's succinct summary of the two sides of the question:

> It is my own belief that a sense of place is something that we ourselves create in the course of time. It is the result of habit or custom. But others disagree. They believe that a sense of place comes from our response to features that are already there – either a beautiful natural setting or well-designed architecture. They believe that a sense of place comes from being in an unusual composition of spaces and forms – natural or man-made.
>
> (Jackson, 1994, p. 151)

Architects David Seamon in the USA and Norwegian Christian Norberg-Schulz, both phenomenologists, are particularly strong proponents of the idea of sense of place existing independently of meaning imposed on it by people. A helpful description of place provided by Seamon is that

> Place refers not only to the geographical location but also to the essential character of a site which makes it different from other locations. Place. . .is the way in which dimensions of landscape come together in a location to produce a distinct environment and particular sense of locality.
>
> (Seamon, 1982, p. 130)

The description fits with those given previously, but a clear point made here is that there are "*essential qualities of the site*" that give it its sense of place and differentiate it from other places. A place has essence. The suggestion is then that sense of place can exist without social construction. That sense comes from the nature of the place and its physical characteristics, not from the meaning imbued by those who interact with it, though of course they are likely to experience the sense of the place.

Norberg-Schulz also supports this perspective. A modernist architect who wrote extensively on architectural phenomenology, he drew on Roman beliefs and mythology using their idea of *genius loci*, or the spirit of place. The mythological roots of genius loci are found in the natural environment. Traditionally natural settings, it was believed, have a spirit that looks over them. Drawing on this idea Norberg-Schulz argues that every place has a *genius loci* or spirit (Norberg-Schultz, 1980). The characteristics that contribute to giving a setting a spirit are *Thing and Order* (spatial qualities), *Character and Light* (overall atmosphere), and *Time* (constancy and change). It is these physical characteristics that give an environment or location a sense of place. We can see that, from this perspective, it would be possible for a location to be placeless if its characteristics or form did not make it a 'distinct environment' or did not have a spirit.

In contrast to this view, other voices see a place's meaning as an individual or social *construction* (Canter, 1977; Fried, 2000; Greider & Garkovich, 1994; Hummon, 1992; Proshansky, Fabian & Kaminoff, 1983; Scannell & Gifford, 2010a). These and other authors argue that place only develops its meaning, its *placeness*, through people's interaction with it. In some senses it could be said that place is all in the mind. The experiences that people have with an environment, the things they do there, and the associations they have with it are what create meaning.

Throwing further light on this, some theories tie place to the assumption of *intentionality* or the *purposive* nature of place activity (Canter, 1977, 1997). This recognises that people have goals, things they are trying to achieve in an environment, or place. The purposes they have shape their interactions with the environment, and the way they behave and experience that environment, and therefore the nature of the place for them. The purposes people have in a setting will be related to their roles. For instance, in a hospital, the *roles* of patient, doctor, and porter all have different purposes, reasons for being in the building, which will affect their interactions with the setting. Some roles will be quite specific to one setting, while others will be more generic. Canter has tried to incorporate into his theory of place the idea of different roles and how they relate to the environment by introducing the concept of environmental role, which is "*that aspect of a person's role which is related to his (sic) dealing with his physical environment*" (Canter, 1977, p. 128). Because people have different roles and purposes in a place they will experience it differently. This has two implications. The first is that you would expect similarity in perceptions of place between people who occupy the same or similar roles. Second, if meaning is a defining characteristic of a place, and different people or groups attribute different meanings to a place, to speak of an environment being a single place is problematic. Further, if people experience a place differently, attributing different meaning, then does it make sense to say that place has intrinsic meaning, or a sense of place?

In terms of the discussion of different conceptualisations of person–environment relations, this position stands in opposition to environmental determinism in the sense that the meaning of place is constructed not (only) by the physical characteristics of the environment but by the meaning people give to it. However, if person-environment relations are a transaction, it follows that it is unlikely that the meaning that evolves, turning an environment into a place, is constructed without reference to the setting's physical characteristics. So, you can argue that the physical qualities contribute to the development of the meaning of a place, but the nature of that meaning is attributed by the people in that place. Research evidence supports this and suggests that both attribution and characteristics do play a role in sense of place, place attachment, and place satisfaction, but often in complex and indirect ways (Stedman, 2002). Overall, it can be suggested that the transformation of a physical setting into a place is a transactional process that evolves and changes over time between person and environment.

At first sight it might appear a purely academic discussion as to whether a place has *essential* qualities, an intrinsic *essence*, or whether, in contrast, it is cognitively and emotionally constructed and given its meaning by those who interact with it. However, there are important practical implications from the way in which people, including academics, see the nature of place. The difference between the two approaches is related to *essentialist* or *anti-essentialist* (or non-essentialist) ideas that can shape how we respond to events. Within the framework of essentialism, places have an intrinsic quality that is bounded with a historic continuity. To make any changes to the place will therefore be a threat to its very essence. To change a place is, in a sense, to destroy that place. A non-essentialist framework sees a place as socially constructed and open to evolution, ongoing change, and reinvention. Places are considered dynamic; therefore, change is part of them rather than a threat to their 'being'. As we will see, which of these perspectives someone takes has consequences for how change and environmental issues are dealt with.

PLACE IDENTITY AND PLACE ATTACHMENT

In the next sections we will consider place attachment and place identity, two of the most important concepts in place research, with significant implications across many topics of environmental and architectural psychology. Unfortunately, and unhelpfully, environmental psychologists as a group have not always been clear about what each of these concepts means or even whether they are distinct (Hidalgo and Hernández, 2001; Hernández et al., 2007). Hernández and his colleagues, for instance, have identified at least four different ways in which the terms have been used. These include being used as meaning the same thing, attachment being seen as a component of identity, identity as a component of attachment, or both as sub-components of some other overall concept. The debate, which at times can be very complex and subtle, does not seem completely resolved. So here a pragmatic position will be taken, acknowledging the debate, but getting on with presenting general definitions and identifying some distinguishing qualities of each concept.

PLACE IDENTITY

Place identity borrows from and contributes to the more general concepts of identity and self that are central within social psychology. Place identity can be considered to be the incorporation of place into a person's concept of self. This is an interesting idea, though something that people often are not consciously aware of, even though they may express place identity in everyday conversation. One relatively straightforward way of thinking about place identity is as *place identification*, in which a person identifies *with* a place (Twigger-Ross & Uzzell, 1996). For instance, a person might see himself or herself as a New Yorker, for another, being Liverpudlian might be an important part of their self. It is possible to identify with several places at one or more levels simultaneously, for instance, British and European. Place identification does not have to be with particular towns, cities, or countries, for instance one individual could identify as an urbanite, and someone else might see themselves as a country type person. There are of course many components of identity but it is likely that the physical environment will be part of it.

Place-related identification is one part of place identity. In expanding upon and theoretically developing the idea of place identity, Twigger-Ross and Uzzell (2010) draw on social psychologist Glynis Breakwell's identity process model (Breakwell, 1986, 1993), which has subsequently successfully been applied by others examining place identity (Bonaiuto et al., 2002; Knez, 2005). The model specifies four principles of identity: *distinctiveness*, *continuity*, *self-esteem*, and *self-efficacy*. To some extent these can also be thought of as the functions of place identity – what it contributes to the individual or what we get from it. The authors also argue that place identity is not a sub-part of social identity, as others contend (Proshansky et al., 1983, p. 59), but that, as all identity is physically situated, place must be an integrated, essential part of all identity. That is, you cannot have identity without place. This is in keeping with the transactional perspective in which people are conceptualised as always being embedded in rather than separate from their environment.

It is perhaps useful to look in a little more detail at Breakwell's four principles of identity as they apply to place. Distinctiveness is essentially the same as place identification. By identifying with a place people are distinguishing themselves from everyone who is not from there. So, for example, being from where you grew up makes you distinct from everyone who did not grow up there. It does not take a big jump to see how this could relate to ideas of nationalism and exclusion, a topic we will look at later. While here the example is given of identifying with the place you are from, other places can form part of your identity.

Continuity of identity is also facilitated by place providing links to the past and prospects in the future. Although Breakwell's processes model was developed independently of environmental psychology, the role of continuity is recognised by Proshansky et al. (1983) when they write

> At the core of such physical environment-related cognitions is the 'environmental past' of the person; a past consisting of places, spaces and their properties which have served instrumentally in the satisfaction of the person's biological, psychological, social, and cultural needs.
>
> (Proshansky et al., 1983, p. 59)

Continuity with a place, for instance your hometown, can help you refer to past selves, reinforcing your sense of who you are. Continuity though does not have to be at an individual level. Historic sites can have a role in reinforcing national identities. We can call this form of continuity *referent continuity* because it refers to a particular place or places.

Twigger-Ross and Uzzell (2010) distinguish referent from *congruent continuity*, which is the continuity of *type* of place. In this case the specific setting might change, but the *type* of setting is consistent. That might be a place that is physically similar, such as someone who always lives in a small cottage, or someone else who chooses to live in the centre of a busy city. It can also be congruent with the values that are associated with a place. For instance, many cities have liberal bohemian areas. When a person whose self-identity is as a liberal bohemian moves to a new city, they might seek out the bohemian or liberal areas as the place to live. The location would then reinforce their sense of who they are and communicate that to others as well.

The role of place identity in Breakwell's last two principles, *self-esteem* and *self-efficacy*, is relatively straightforward. The first of these is deriving self-esteem from the place you identify with. That can include the physical characteristics as well as the people who are associated with it, its history, or other features. Being associated with somewhere that you like is also an evaluation of yourself, because the place is part of you, and you are part of it (Twigger-Ross & Uzzell, 2010). It is also possible of course that a person's self-esteem could be undermined by the place that they identify with. This might happen, for instance, if a person loses their job and has to move to a neighbourhood that they have previously held negative views towards.

The final component of the identity process is *self-efficacy*, which is a person's belief that they can achieve what is needed to meet the demands of their life. Simply, the extent to which a setting can hinder or facilitate a person reaching their goals will impact on their feelings of self-efficacy. Before looking at the research and implications related to place identity we will first consider place attachment.

PLACE ATTACHMENT

Place attachment is a related concept to place identity, but it is distinct from it (Rollero & Piccoli, 2010a). The concept refers to a deep and meaningful bond that a person feels for a place. Hidalgo and Hernández (2001), drawing on general attachment theory, also include the desire to maintain closeness to the place as part of attachment. Taking those two parts together they define place attachment as "*a positive affective bond between an individual and a specific place, the main characteristic of which is the tendency of the individual to maintain closeness to such a place*" (p. 274).

While it tends to be the case that place attachment research focuses on the level of community or neighbourhood (Hidalgo & Hernández, 2001), attachment can be to any scale of the environment, from objects to the planet (Altman & Low, 1992). Given the high degree of research interest at neighbourhood level, it is interesting that the two studies that have compared attachment at different levels have both found less attachment to neighbourhood than to region/city and home or dwelling (Cuba & Hummon, 1993; Hidalgo & Hernández (2001). Finally, in the same way that someone can form attachments with several people, it is possible to be attached to more than one place.

In an attempt to integrate the components of place attachment, Scannell and Gifford provide a useful model that gives some structure to the research studies (Scannell & Gifford, 2010a). They see three principal dimensions or components of place attachment. The *person* experiencing the attachment, the *place* towards which a person feels attachment, and the *process* by which attachment is achieved. We will briefly look at each of these.

Under the *person* component of their model is included individual factors, such as experience of the place, along with cultural experience such as historical significance. This facet of the model emphasises that place attachment can be an individual experience, or can have a socio-cultural element, in which case there is a shared attachment. Under *place* is a distinction between the physical and social characteristics of a setting. People can become attached to a place because of their interactions with others. In a home for example that could be family members. In the neighbourhood it might be friends, or shopkeepers with whom there is regular interaction. Research suggests that both the social and physical environment are important to attachment. Finally, the psychological *processes* that can lead to attachment draw on the three components consistently identified in psychological research, which are cognitive (thought), affective (emotion), and instrumental (behaviour) action. For instance, people will have memories (cognitive) that are attached to a physical setting, along with meanings that have evolved for that place. Those meanings might be shared – social – and pertinent to specific cultural groups. Feelings of happiness, love, or other emotions can be associated with an environment, potentially converting it from a physical locale to a place to which a person is attached. And finally, behaviour, such as visiting an environment or engaging in important activities there, can be associated with place attachment (Scannell & Gifford, 2010a). In some ways this brings us back to the earlier models of place as comprising activities, people, and conceptualisations (Canter, 1977). As well as Scannell and Gifford's paper, there are several reviews of the place attachment literature that take the exploration of the concept further and are worth consulting (e.g., Giuliani, 2003; Lewicka, 2011).

APPLICATIONS AND IMPLICATIONS

A lot of this discussion of place has focused on theoretical and conceptual issues and debates. That is only right as they provide the foundation for research, problem solving, policy formulation, and place-based interventions. Understanding place, place identity, and place attachment helps to give insight into people's experience and behaviour in many areas of environmental psychology. The importance of place grows as we face what Manzo and Divine-Wright (2021) describe as a socio-spatially precarious time, with challenges of "*a global climate crisis, increased migration, displacement, rapid urbanization, and even pandemics*" (p. 1). Research on place and particularly place attachment has contributed to understanding each of these and other significant issues. We will consider some of these in the remaining paragraphs of this chapter.

It is not only the major existential challenges that can be better understood and addressed using place-related concepts. For instance, at a more personal, day-to-day level, there has been research examining the impact of place on restoration (Ratcliffe & Korpela, 2017), a subject we will come back to in Chapter 6. There have been studies throwing light on the role of place attachment in people rejecting infrastructure projects near their residence (Divine-Wright, 2013). That research taps into a rich seam of work on home, which is often seen as central to ideas of place, particularly amongst geographers (Relph, 1976; Tuan, 1974), though not neglected by psychologists (Moore, 2000). Another aspect of home is considered by several studies examining homesickness (e.g., Scopelliti & Tiberio, 2010), especially amongst students. The importance of place and homesickness will apply to any movement away from any attached place, so, for example, the research is of relevance to the experience of refugees, which we touch on below. As people around the world experience Covid-19-related lockdowns, there have been calls to reconsider issues around place and the home (Divine-Wright et al., 2020). Also relevant to lockdowns, place attachment research has given us insight into the use and underuse of urban parks (Moulay et al., 2018).

While most research focuses on the impact of place and place attachment on our feelings, experience, and behaviour, studies have also looked at how experience impacts on place attachment. For instance, being a victim of crime can reduce feelings of neighbourhood attachment (Zahnow & Tsai, 2021). Finally, demonstrating the variety of topics examined, research has also looked at attachment to where people were born and live and their choice of a 'final resting place' (Aimée, Aragonés & Moser, 2010). In the rest of the chapter we will focus on a sample of research that relates to some of the challenges identified by Manzo and Divine-Wright (2021) when warning of our precarious position: migration and displacement, responding to environmental threat, and response to the locating of energy infrastructure.

PLACE AND MIGRATION

Perhaps one of the strongest themes running through place attachment and identity research is change, or *place disruption* (Brown & Perkins, 1992). In some cases, that change represents a threat to place identity, and people's fundamental self-identity (Bonaiuto, Breakwell & Cano, 1996; Divine-Wright, 2009). Communities, countries, and our species are threatened by climate change, extreme weather events, and the large-scale migration that have been predicted and are now being seen. With the inevitably of increased migration understanding the processes that underlie whether people are welcomed or treated with hostility is important. Of course, the attitudes, policy, and rhetoric of governments are also critical in this, especially when they exploit place identity and attachment to create a 'hostile environment'.

Earlier we discussed the concepts of place *essentialism* and *non/ anti-essentialism*. We can use those ideas to help us understand people's response to the arrival of diverse groups into established communities. As we saw earlier, essentialism is a belief that places have an essential character, beyond that given to it by people, and that if there are significant changes to the qualities of that place, its essence, its specialness will be destroyed. Anti-essentialism argues that the meaning of places is imbued by the people who inhabit it, and that all places evolve and change over time, and there is little that is intrinsic to the place that makes it what it is. The way in which a person thinks about, or is led to think about, a place in either of these terms is likely to affect their response to change. For instance, if you think in essentialist terms, you are more likely to oppose diversity and less likely to welcome new groups into a place because they will change its essence. The reverse of this is true if you hold an anti-essentialist position (Wnuk et al., 2021). These feelings are likely to be amplified by place attachment because places are more likely to be perceived as essentialist amongst people with greater place attachment to them than people with less attachment (Wnuk et al., 2021).

With increased mobility and migration, understanding the role of perceptions of the nature of place and place attachment play in people's experience, in addition to social, political, and economic issues, is important. Often the environment is seen simply as a backdrop to integration or desegregation. But place identity and attachment can include deeper and more fundamental feelings that need to be addressed. This is illustrated in a study carried out in South Africa as it emerged from apartheid. The research examined areas of desegregation, revealing the loss white South Africans felt when beaches were opened to multiracial use (Dixon & Durrheim, 2004). White users experienced a loss of sense of attachment and familiarity and experienced the change as removing the setting's restorative qualities. The importance of this study, and other studies, is that it shows that far from being a backdrop, through place attachment the environment can generate resistance to change – in this case resistance to desegregation. Of course other ideological views have a strong or stronger affect too, but the role of place should not be forgotten during the implementation of policy and change.

Toruńczyk-Ruiz and Martinović (2000) found that length of residence was associated with feelings of entitlement towards an environment or place, a phenomenon referred to as *autochthony*. Other research carried out in 11 European countries found that autochthony was associated with intention to protest against refugees (Hasbún López et al., 2019). However, this was only found amongst people whose self-identity was national. Those with international (global) identification, as might be expected, had lower autochthony and lower intention to protest. A European identification was not related to intention protest or to autochthony. The study did not directly examine place attachment, but as there is a positive relationship between attachment and sense of entitlement, it is quite likely that those with a sense of autochthony also had a stronger sense of place attachment, and so intention to protest.

Despite these place-related difficulties of accepting diversity, other studies have demonstrated that objections to newcomers are not inevitable and that there is evidence that acceptance of 'outside' groups is sometimes affected positively by place attachment. In a study of Dutch and British residents, Toruńczyk-Ruiz and Martinović (2020) found that within a British sample place attachment was positively related to openness to both international newcomers and newcomers from other parts of the UK. Interestingly in the Dutch sample place attachment was not related one way or the other.

Understanding the psychological processes that underlie opposition to refugees is important to promoting acceptance and inclusiveness (Hasbún López et al., 2019), which in turn can help foster new place attachment for those that have been displaced. It is important that people do develop a sense of attachment and belonging, not least because of the positive benefits that have been identified as stemming from strong place attachment. Scannell and Gifford (2017) examined the places to which people felt attached. They identified 13 benefits: memories, belonging, relaxation, positive emotions, activity support, comfort-security, personal growth, freedom, entertainment, connection to nature, practical benefits, privacy, and aesthetics. Rollero and Piccoli (2010b), drawing on Fried (2000), also describe the benefits and outcomes of strong place attachment, "*(place attachment) encourages greater freedom of behaviour, exploration, confidence and affective responsiveness within the local community*"

(Rollero & Piccoli, 2010b, p. 234). It is enlightening to think of these in terms of the experience of newly arrived migrants and how they could benefit from being able to develop place attachment and the role host nations could play in facilitating that.

Research has shown the significance of 'enclaves' in helping immigrants deal with moving from one country and culture to another and in mitigating against the shock of the new. Enclaves can be areas such as parks (Main, 2013) or sections of cities that are home to communities of immigrants that have settled recently or over a protracted period (Mazumdar et al., 2000). Discussing the role of enclaves for Vietnamese-Americans, Mazumdar et al. (2000) explain their importance,

> (they) play a significant role in the immigrant's experience (Abrahamson, 1996; Gold, 1992; Zhou, 1992) by mitigating the psychological trauma of displacement, providing alternative economic structures, and facilitating the preservation of cultural traditions. The literature asserts that migration is often traumatic, involving physical and social displacement accompanied with feelings of loss, separation and helplessness. (Gold, 1992; Handlin, 1951; Kramer, 1970)
>
> (Mazumdar et al., 2000, p. 219)

Also writing about enclaves Kelly Main highlights identity processes that we discussed earlier. She writes, "*immigrants can achieve continuity of identity through continuity with past places of importance*" (Main, 2013, p. 292).

As research shows that place attachment for 'non-natives' develops before place identify (Hernandez et al., 2007), there needs to be stability in the location of newcomers so that they can develop attachment to place and then identity. Refugees are likely to have lost much that confirms their identity. Therefore, policy, however well meaning, which seeks to relocate and distribute them throughout a country so as not to have large groups in one place, will undermine the formation of their new identity related to their new country and exacerbate the losses they feel from their old life.

PLACE ATTACHMENT AND RISK

Perhaps the most direct manifestation of the threat of climate change to human populations has been the increased incidence and severity of wildfires, flooding, droughts, hurricanes, and other extreme weather-related events. Individuals and communities need to adapt to the effects of climate change in order to mitigate some of their consequences. How individuals and communities respond to these threats will be related to many factors, with place attachment being amongst them (e.g., Guillard et al., 2021). In the introduction to their meta-analysis of motivation and adaptive behaviour, van Valkengoed and Steg (2019) describe what is meant by adaptation and what it might involve for households,

> Adaptation to climate change, defined as the process of adjustment so that negative impacts of climate change can be reduced or avoided. . . Household-level adaptation behaviours include preparatory actions (for example, having an emergency kit or moving furniture), purchasing insurance, seeking information about climate-related hazards or how to adapt, evacuating from climate-related hazards, and supporting climate adaptation policies.
>
> (van Valkengoed & Steg, 2020, p. 158)

There are several examples in the research literature which show that place attachment can lead people to accept increased risk, or, in some cases, to perceive a reduced level of risk. Useful reviews of place attachment and natural hazards are provided by both van Valkengoed and Steg (2020) and Bonaiuto and colleagues (Bonaiuto et al., 2016). Here we will briefly look at a sample of this research. For instance, following hurricane Katrina in the USA, residents of New Orleans included place attachment as one of the reasons to return to the area after the disaster, despite the uncertain nature of the environment and it remaining hazardous (Chamlee-Wright & Storr, 2009). Of course, there are also economic and other reasons to return to a risky area, but place attachment exerts a significant influence. The role of place attachment is not straightforward however, and research reflects a mixed picture of its influence. For instance, although Chamlee-Wright and Storr show the increased risk taking associated with place attachment in relation to floods in New Orleans, research looking at flood risk response in India revealed that place attachment is related positively to preparedness (Mishra, Mazumdar & Suar, 2010). That research also found preparedness varied depending on the basis for the attachment. As we have seen elsewhere, place attachment comprises several areas of experience including the physical environment, but also social and cultural factors. In their study, Mishra and her colleagues found that place attachment based on genealogy (family association with a place) and economics predicts preparedness, but religious place attachment does not.

As well as floods, climate change is increasing the incidence, duration, and intensity of wildfires around the world, including the USA, Europe, and Australia. Examining response to wildfires in Australia, researchers found that residents with higher levels of place attachment displayed less intention to leave in the event of fires than those with low place attachment (Paton, Bürgelt & Prior, 2008). However, that does not necessarily signify that higher levels of place attachment mean people are blasé or are ignoring the risks. Anton and Lawrence (2016) also examined response to the threat of wildfires in Australia. In this case they found that inhabitants of rural areas take more mitigation actions the greater their place attachment. So while those with higher place attachment might stay in the event of a fire, they are likely to also do more planning for it. Interestingly, Anton and Lawrence did not find the same preparedness-attachment relationship for those in urban areas.

Risks from natural, non-climate related events have long been part of life. Even so, it often seems strange that people will knowingly chose to live in areas prone to threat, such as on the slopes of an active volcano. There are many reasons why people might do that, including economic and family ties. Although research results are mixed there does appear to be a general tendency for people with strong place attachment to underestimate risk, and further, people living close to potential hazards also tend to perceive lower risks (Bonaiuto et al., 2016). In their review of research on place attachment and natural hazard risk, Bonaiuto et al. (2016) found studies that demonstrated that place attachment played an important role in people remaining or returning to risky areas. Interestingly, the studies showed the development of a sub-culture that influenced behaviour. For example, in Iceland, rural residents with high place attachment developed their own evacuation plans rejecting the official ones as inappropriate. This and other studies demonstrate the advantage of engaging with communities (Garcia-Mira et al., 2012), especially those with high levels of attachment, when developing mitigation strategies.

The mixed picture suggested by the research is evident in the meta-analysis of motivations and preparedness by van Valkengoed and Steg (2019) who found that place attachment only played a marginal role in people's adaption to risk. These and other research findings suggest that place attachment can, in some circumstances, be associated with being prepared and taking mitigating action, but that it is a complex relationship that needs more detailed and subtle consideration to comprehend it. As threats from climate change increase and new risks emerge, understanding people's relationship to place and its implications will become more urgent. Interestingly, in light of the 2020–2021 experience of the Covid-19 pandemic, van Valkengoed and Steg (2019) could not find any studies that examine adaptive behaviour in relation to risk from vector-borne diseases. That will probably change.

It is of concern that, in their review of research on preparedness for threats, van Valkengoed and Steg (2019) could find no studies carried out in Central and South America and only 3% of the studies related to Africa. These are both regions that are currently at threat from the most extreme consequences of climate change. The authors found that most studies were conducted in the West, with some in Asia. By region, the percentage of research studies broke down as North America 39%, Europe 35%, Asia 12%, and Australia 11%. Unless we assume that there is a universal cultural validity to the research, there is urgent need for research in more areas of the world.

PLACE AND SUSTAINABILITY

The final area that we will consider briefly is the impact of place attachment on pro-environmental behaviour. As we cover sustainability in some detail in Chapter 8, we will limit discussion here to the locating of low carbon energy generators.

It might be expected that place attachment would be associated with behaviour that is consistent with attempts to reduce climate-damaging behaviours. However, studies tend to show that the picture is more complex than that with several factors, including quality of the environment and place identity playing a role (e.g., Uzzell & Badenas, 2002). Part of that complexity comes from the multidimensional quality of place attachment. Research has demonstrated that although we speak of place attachment as if it is a single entity, it is multidimensional and we need to be clear about which dimensions of place attachment the research is considering (Mishra et al., 2010). In their study, for example, Scannell and Gifford (2010b) distinguish between *civic* and *natural* place attachment. Civic place attachment is based on the idea of the community and the municipality of the environment. Natural place attachment, however, comes from nature within and around the place. So, for instance, civic attachment might be related to shops or monuments, and natural attachment to the trees, parks, and surrounding countryside, if it is a part of the place. The authors found that it is only place attachment to the nature within a place that predicts pro-environmental behaviour. This might help explain the study we looked at earlier in which urban residents did not engage in threat preparedness regardless of place attachment, but those with high levels of attachment in rural areas did (Anton & Lawrence, 2016).

The pursuit of a low-carbon economies and lifestyles will require major infrastructure changes. These are likely to impinge on many people's environments and so may well face objection, delay, and possibly abandonment. Dismissing objections as NIMBYism (Not In My BackYard) is not helpful. Instead, conceptualising objections to renewable energy generation sites in terms of place attachment is more productive and helps better understand opposition (Divine-Wright, 2013). Research to date in this area paints a complex picture. In two studies, Divine-Wright and colleague examined local village responses to tidal energy power generation (Divine-Wright, 2011) and a proposed coastal wind farm site on the North Wales coast (Divine-Wright & Howes, 2010). In the latter study Divine-Wright and Howes compared the responses of residents of two towns. In one of the locations high levels of place attachment were associated with negative views and with being in opposition to the wind farm. In the other town, with a similar view and proximity to the site, there was no significant correlation between place attachment and attitudes towards the site. The researchers found that the objection to the site was primarily based on disruption to place attachment, in the form of disruption of natural beauty and impact on tourists who visit the town. The lack or relationship found between place attachment and negative opinions of the wind farm evident in the other town was due to it being less concerned with tourism. The research then points to the importance of taking contextual factors into account.

Place attachment can lead to favourable perceptions of power generation sites. A study in Ireland comparing two villages' responses to an existing tidal energy generator revealed that there was a positive relationship between attachment and acceptance of the site in both villages. The research further showed that for one village the installation was experienced as positively *enhancing* place because of its symbolic meaning related to the vitality of the village (Divine-Wright & Howes, 2010). The authors note that the results point to the importance of governments and developers taking emotional bonds, place attachment, and symbolic meaning into account when planning and engaging with communities.

The potential positive view of existing generation sites has also been found in relation to nuclear power. Many early nuclear power stations have already or are about to come to the end of their life. Within the UK it is likely that replacement stations will be proposed and built in the same or proximate locations (Venables et al., 2012). The pattern of attitudes and objections to the site of nuclear power stations is interesting and sometimes, perhaps, counter-intuitive. For *new* hazardous or stigmatised technology, the closer people live to the proposed site the greater their objection (Vorkinn & Riese, 2001). However, when a facility is being situated where there is an existing one, the response is more positive (e.g., Freudenberg & Davidson, 2007). There are several reasons that might explain that outcome, including that the lack of previous accidents, familiarity, awareness of economic benefits, and less uncertainty for those used to living with the power stations. However, Venables et al. (2012) found that sense of place (conceptualised as incorporating both place identity and place attachment) was the main factor in determining attitudes to a new build. In effect, it would seem, the power stations have come to be part of the essence of the places where they are located. It is possible that those who could not integrate the facility into their sense of place have moved on to live in a different location.

These studies suggest that a more positive approach can be taken to development, and to understanding people's objections. As the authors note,

> The findings affirm the relevance of place attachment and place-related meanings to understand public responses to local development proposals, demonstrate how energy projects may enhance emotional attachments to place, suggest that a narrow focus upon public objections overlooks potentially ambivalent as well as supportive responses by local residents, and reveal how local responses vary by context.
>
> (Divine-Wright & Howes, 2010, p. 342)

The relationship between place attachment and objection or acceptance of renewable and other energy sites is, as would be expected, complex.

FINALLY

This chapter has demonstrated that the relationship between the environment and people is not a simple, direct one. To understand people's behaviour, it is important to understand the environment as place. As these brief examples show us, place can be associated with feelings of rootedness, belonging, safety, and comfort. However, it can also expose people to hazard and threat, and perhaps even generate hostility to others. Understanding place, place attachment, and place identity can help us to create better places in which to live.

REFERENCES

Abrahamson, M. (1996). *Urban Enclaves: Identity and Place in America.* New York: St Martin's Press.

Agnew, J. A. (1987). *Place and Politics: The Geographical Mediation of State and Society.* Boston, MA: Allen and Unwin.

Aimée, C., Aragonés, J. I., & Moser, G. (2010). Attachment forever: Environmental and social dimensions, temporal perspective and choice of one's last resting place. *Environment and Behavior,* 42, 765–778.

Altman, I. & Low, S. (1992). *Place Attachment.* New York: Plenum.

Anton, C. E. & Lawrence, C. (2016). Does place attachment predict wildfire mitigation and preparedness? A comparison of wildland–urban interface and rural communities. *Environmental Management*, 57, 148–162.

Bonaiuto, M., Alves, S., De Dominicis, S., & Pertruccelli, I. (2016). Place attachment and natural hazard risk: Research review and agenda. *Journal of Environmental Psychology*, 6, 33–53.

Bonaiuto, M., Breakwell, G. M., & Cano, I. (1996). Identity processes and environmental threat: The effects of nationalism and local identity upon perception of beach pollution. *Journal of Community and Applied Social Psychology*, 6, 157–175.

Bonaiuto, M., Carrus, G., Martorella, H., & Bonnes, M. (2002). Local identity processes and environmental attitudes in land use changes: The case of natural protected area. *Journal of Economic Psychology*, 23, 631–653.

Boon, H. J. (2014). Disaster resilience in a flood impacted rural Australian town. *Natural Hazards*, 71, 683–701.

Breakwell, G. M. (1986). *Coping with Threatened Identity.* London: Methuen.

Breakwell, G. M. (1993). Integrating paradigms: Methodological implications. In G. M. Breakwell & D.V. Canter (eds.), *Empirical Approaches to Social Representations* (pp. 189–201). Oxford: Clarendon Press.

Brown, B., & Perkins, D. D. (1992). Disruptions to place attachment. In I. Altman & S. Low (eds.), *Place Attachment* (pp. 279–304). New York: Plenum.

Canter, D. (1977). *The Psychology of Place*. London: Architectural Press.

Canter, D. (1997). The facets of place. In G. T. Moore & R. W. Marans (eds.), *Toward the Integration of Theory, Methods, Research, and Utilization. Advances in Environment, Behavior and Design, Volume 4* (pp. 109–147). Boston, MA: Springer.

Chamlee-Wright, E. & Storr, V. H. (2009). 'There's No place like New Orleans': Sense of place and community recovery in the ninth ward after Hurricane Katrina. *Journal of Urban Affairs*, 31, 615–634.d

Cresswell, T. (2015). *Place: An Introduction, Second Edition*. Chichester: Wiley.

Cuba, L., & Hummon, D. M. (1993). A place to call home: Identification with dwelling, community and region. *The Sociological Quarterly*, 34, 111–131.

Divine-Wright, P. (2011). Place attachment and public acceptance of renewable energy: A tidal energy case. *Journal of Environmental Psychology*, 31, 336–342.

Divine-Wright, P. (2013). Explaining "NIMBY" objections to a power line: The role of personal, place attachment and project related factors. *Environment and Behavior*, 54, 761–781.

Divine-Wright, P., de Carvalho, L. P., Di Masso, A., Lewicka, M., Manzo, L., & Williams, D. R. (2020) "Re-placed" – Reconsidering relationships with place and lessons from a pandemic. *Journal of Environmental Psychology*, 72. Available on-line 29 October 2020. https://doi.org/10.1016/j.jenvp.2020.101514.

Divine-Wright, P., & Howes, Y. (2010). Disruption to place attachment and the protection of restorative environments: A wind energy case study. *Journal of Environmental Psychology*, 30, 271–280.

Dixon, J. & Durrheim, K. (2004). Dislocating identity: Desegregation and the transformation of place. *Journal of Environmental Psychology*, 24, 455–473.

Freudenberg, W. & Davidson, D. (2007). Nuclear families and nuclear risk: The effects of gender, geography and progeny on attitudes towards a nuclear waste facility. *Rural Sociology*, 72, 215–243.

Fried, M. (2000). Continuities and discontinuities of place. *Journal of Environmental Psychology*, 20, 193–205.

Garcia-Mira, R., García-González, C., Dumitru, A., & Barreiro-Rivas, X. L. (2012), The social dimension of forest fires: Risk, responsibility, and participation. In S. Kabisch, A. Kunath, P. Schweizer-Ries, & A. Steinführer (Eds.), *Vulnerability, Risks, and Complexity. Impacts of Global Change on Human Habitats* (pp. 103–119). Cambridge, MA: Hogrefe.

Gifford, R. (2013). *Environmental Psychology: Principles and Practice, Fifth Edition.* Victoria, BC: Optimal Books.

Giuliani, M. V. (2003). Theory of attachment and place attachment. In M. Bonnes, T. Lee, & M. Bonaiuto (eds.), *Psychological Theories for Environmental Issues* (pp. 137–170). Aldershot: Ashgate.

Gold, S. J. (1992). *Refugee Communities: A Comparative Field Study*. Newbury Park, CA: Sage.

Graumann, C. F. (2002). The phenomenological approach to people-environment studies. In R. B. Bechtel and A. Chrchman, (Eds.), *Handbook of Environmental Psychology* (pp. 95–113). Chichester: Wiley.

Greider, T., & Garkovich, L. (1994). Landscapes: The social construction of nature and the environment. *Rural Sociology*, 59(1), 1–24.

Guillard, M., Navarro, O., Cortes, S., & Fleury-Bahi, G. (2021). How do we adapt when we are faced with the effects of climate change? *International Journal of Disaster Risk Reduction*, 65. https://doi.org/10.1016/j.ijdrr.2021.102586.

Handlin, O. (1951). *The Uprooted*. Boston: Little, Brown & Co.

Hasbún López, P., Martinović, B., Bobowik, M., Chryssochoou, X., Cichocka, A., Ernst-Vintila, A., Lamberty, P., Leone, G., Licata, L., & Žeželj, I. (2019). Support for collective action against refugees: The role of national, European, and global identifications, and autochthony beliefs. *European Journal of Social Psychology*, 49, 1439–1455.

Hernandez, B., Hidalgo, C., Salazar-Laplace, M. E., & Hess, S. (2007). Place attachment and place identity in natives and non-natives. *Journal of Environmental Psychology*, 27, 310–319.

Hidalgo, M. C., & Hernández, B. (2001). Place attachment: Conceptual and empirical questions. *Journal of Environmental Psychology*, 21, 273–281.

Hummon, D. M. 1992. Community attachment: Local sentiment and sense of place. In I. Altman & S. M. Low (eds.), *Place Attachment* (pp. 253–278). New York: Plenum.

Jackson, J. B. (1994). *A Sense of Place, a Sense of Time*. New Haven, CT: Yale University Press.

Knez, I. (2005). Attachment and identity as related to a place and its perceived climate. *Journal of Environmental Psychology*, 25, 207–218.

Kramer, J. R. (1970). *The American Minority Community*. New York: Thomas W. Growell Co.

Lewicka, M. (2011). Place attachment: How far have we come in the last 40 years? *Journal of Environmental Psychology*, 31, 207–230.

Main, K. (2013). Planting roots in foreign soil? – Immigrant place meanings in an urban park. *Journal of Environmental Psychology*, 36, 291–304.

Malpas, J. (2010). Place Research Network. *Progressive Geographies*. https://progressivegeographies.com/2010/11/04/place-research-network/

Malpas, J. E. (2018). *Place and Experience: A Philosophical Topography, Second Edition*. London: Routledge.

Manzo, L. C., & Divine-Wright, P. (2021). Introduction. In L. C. Manzo & P. Divine-Wright (eds.), *Place Attachment: Advances in Theory, Methods and Applications, Second Edition* (pp. 1–9). London: Routledge.

Mazumdar, S., Mazumdar, S., Docuyanan, F., & McLaughlin, C. M. (2000). Creating a sense of place: The Vietnamese-Americans and Little Saigon. *Journal of Environmental Psychology*, 20, 319–333.

Mishra, S., Mazumdar, S., & Suar, D. (2010) Place attachment and flood preparedness. *Journal of Environmental Psychology*, 30, 187–197.

Moore, J. (2000). Placing *home* in context. *Journal of Environmental Psychology*, 20, 207–217.

Moulay, A., Ujang, N., Maulan, S., & Ismail, S. (2018). Understanding the process of parks' attachment: Interrelation between place attachment, behavioural tendencies, and the use of public place. *City, Culture and Society, 14, 28–36.*

Norberg-Schultz, C. (1980). *Genius Loci: Towards a Phenomenology of Architecture*. New York: Rizzoli.

Paton, D., Bürgelt, P. T., & Prior, T. (2008). Living with bushfire risk: Social and environmental influences on preparedness. *Australian Journal of Emergency Management,* 23, 41–48.

Patterson, M. E., & Williams, D. R. (2005). Maintaining research traditions on place: Diversity of thought and scientific progress. *Journal of Environmental Psychology*, 25, 361–380.

Proshansky, H., Fabian, H. K., & Kaminoff, R. (1983). Place identity: Physical world socialisation of the self. *Journal of Environmental Psychology*, 3, 57–83.

Ratcliffe, E., & Korpela, K. M. (2017). Time-and self-related memories predict restorative perceptions of favourite places. *Environment and Behavior*, 50, 690–720.

Relph, E. (1976). *Place and Placelessness*. London: Pion.

Rollero, C., & De Piccoli, N. (2010a). Place attachment, identification and environment perception: An empirical study. *Journal of Environmental Psychology*, 20, 198–205.

Rollero, C., & De Piccoli, N. (2010b). Est-ce que l'attachement à l'environnement conditionne le bien-être social? *Revue européenne de psychologie appliquée*, 60, 233–238.

Scannell, L., & Gifford, R. (2010a). Defining place attachment: A tripartite organizing framework. *Journal of Environmental Psychology*, 30, 1–10.

Scannell, L., & Gifford, R. (2010b). The relations between natural and civic place attachment and pro-environmental behavior. *Journal of Environmental Psychology*, 30, 289–297.

Scannell, L., & Gifford, R. (2017). The experienced psychological benefits of place attachment. *Journal of Environmental Psychology*, 51, 256–269.

Scopelliti, M., & Tuberio, L. (2010). Homesickness in university students: The role of multiple place attachment. *Environment and Behavior*, 42, 335–350.

Stedman, R. C. (2002). Toward a social psychology of place: Predicting behavior from place-based cognitions, attitude, and identity. *Environment and Behavior*, 34(5), 405–425.

Stedman, R. C. (2003). Is it really just a social construction?: The contribution of the physical environment to sense of place. *Society and Natural Resources*, 16(8), 671–685.

Toruńczyk-Ruiz, S., & Martinović, B. (2020). The bright and dark sides of length of residence in the neighbourhood: Consequences for local participation and openness to newcomers. *Journal of Environmental Psychology*, 67, Available online 14 December 2019. https://doi.org/10.1016/j.jenvp.2019.101383

Tuan, Y.- F. (1974a). *Topophilia: A Study of Environmental Perceptions, Attitudes, and Values.* Englewood Cliffs, NJ: Prentice Hall.

Tuan, Y.-F. (1974b). *Space and Place: The Perspective of Experience*. Minneapolis: University of Minnesota Press.

Twigger-Ross, C. L., & Uzzell, D. L. (1996). Place and identity process. *Journal of Environmental Psychology*, 16, 205–220.

Uzzell, D., Pol, E., & Badenas, D. (2002). Place identification, social cohesion and environmental sustainability. *Environment and Behaviour*, 34, 26–53.

van Valkengoed, A. M., & Steg, L. (2019). Meta-analyses of factors motivating climate change adaptation behaviour. *Nature Climate Change*, 9, 158–163.

Venables, D., Pidgeon, N. F., Parkhill, K. A., Henwood, K. L., & Simmons, P. (2012). Living with nuclear power: Sense of place, proximity and risk perceptions in local host communities. *Journal of Environmental Psychology*, 32, 371–383.

Vorkinn, M., & Riese, H. (2001). Environmental concern in a local context: The significance of place attachment. *Environment and Behavior*, 33, 1249–1263.

Williams, D, R., & Miller, B. A. (2021). Methodological moments in place attachment research: Seeking clarity in diversity. In L. C. Manzo & P. Divine-Wright (eds.), *Place Attachment: Advances in Theory, Methods and Applications, Second Edition* (pp. 13–28). London: Routledge.

Wnuk, A., Oleksy, T., Toruńczyk-Ruiz, S., & Lewicka, M. (2021). The way we perceive a place implies who can live there: Essentialisation of place and attitudes towards diversity. *Journal of Environmental Psychology*, 75. https://doi.org/10.1016/j.jenvp.2021.101600.

Zahnow, R., & Tsai, A. (2021). Crime victimization, place attachment, and the moderating role of neighborhood social ties and neighborhood behaviour. *Environment and Behavior*, 53, 40–68.

Zhou, M. (1992). *Chinatown: The Socioeconomic Potential of an Urban Enclave.* Philadelphia, PA: Temple University Press.

SUGGESTED READING

One of the best books on place in general is by Cresswell. This gives an account of place from a geographer's perspective.

Cresswell, T. (2015). *Place: An Introduction, Second Edition*. Chichester: Wiley.

For a psychology view on place, there are several texts. But these are a useful place to start.

Altman, I., & Low, S. (1992). *Place Attachment*. New York: Plenum.

Manzo, L. C., & Divine-Wright, P. (eds.) (2021). *Place Attachment: Advances in Theory, Methods and Applications, Second Edition*. London: Routledge.

The review article by Scannell and Gifford is also worth consulting.

Scannell, L., & Gifford, R. (2010a). Defining place attachment: A tripartite organizing framework. *Journal of Environmental Psychology*, 30, 1–10.

3

SPATIAL BEHAVIOUR

CROWDING, PRIVACY, PERSONAL SPACE, AND TERRITORIALITY

INTRODUCTION

In this chapter we will look at the relationship between the spatial environment and people's behaviour. We will focus on how people use, structure, and experience space to regulate social interaction, achieve their goals, and reduce stress. The emphasis of the chapter will be on the main concepts of spatial behaviour: crowding, privacy, personal space, and territoriality. Although these are distinct concepts with their own research and literature, they can be linked into a system that regulates social interaction. In this chapter we will consider each of the four concepts and how they are linked.

EARLY RESEARCH

Much of the agenda for spatial research was set during the 1960s. During this period, there was a significant concern about rising populations and the increase in inner-city crime, which was often believed to be a result of the overcrowding. The concerns were further fuelled by influential books including Ehrlich's bestseller *The Population Bomb* (1968), in which the author, an entomologist at Stanford University, warned of the calamitous consequences of population growth and the need for population control. Attention was drawn to the speed with which world population was growing. It had been rising very modestly over thousands of years, eventually

DOI: 10.4324/9780429274541-3

achieving one billion in around 1800. Over the next 100 years the population doubled to two billion. By the end of the twentieth century and the beginning of the twenty-first, world population increased by a billion approximately every 10–15 years. Coincidently, the 1960s were also a time of considerable civil unrest, especially in the USA, with riots in major cities throughout the country. As we will discuss those more in Chapter 5 when we look at crime and the environment, for now we can just note that they added to the notion that something was seriously wrong in the Western world and that crowding might be at the root of it.

Coinciding with concerns over crime and population growth, two early studies provoked anxiety about overcrowding by seeming to support some of the worst predictions of social breakdown. Both studies were carried out on animals, and then generalised to more complex human populations. The first of these found that amongst deer, mortality rate significantly increased as density increases (Christian, 1961), a prediction Ehrlich would go on to make for human societies. More influential than Christian's research, however, was a series of studies of rats (Calhoun, 1962) that generated concern about social disintegration which fit with some perceptions of parts of US society. The studies developed other ideas that, as we shall see, are still echoed in policy debates today. In Calhoun's research' groups of rats were bred in purposefully designed enclosures until the spaces became densely populated. Under normal densities, the rats had a coherent, functional social structure. The males tended to accumulate a harem of females with whom they would mate, and they would not mate with female rats that were not part of their harem. The males defended their territory, but generally did not fight. The females built nests, had babies, and raised the young. They would resist males other than the one to whose harem they belonged. Like the males, the female rats tended not to fight. Social norms were adopted by both male and female rats, which allowed them to avoid violence and the damage that it would do to their social structures.

Under medium-high density rats seemed to attempt something resembling normal behaviour. In the highest density parts of the pens however the change away from normal behaviour was very significant for both males and females. These high-density pens were described as *behavioural sinks*. In the sink pens groups of males worked together to pursue female rats. There was a high level of disease and pregnancy, with a 50% female mortality rate. There was little caring for offspring by the females (or the males) with infant mortality of 80%–96%. In the slightly lower-density parts of the pens infant mortality was 50%. Overall, the highest density was associated with widespread breakdown of the normal social structure and functioning, and new dysfunctional structures emerging. The rats that lived in behavioural sinks were hyperactive, hypersexual, homosexual, and cannibalistic, with the females having no maternal functions. This was in sharp contrast to those in slightly less crowded environment that behaved similar to normal rats.

The results and conclusions from Calhoun's (1962) studies were generalised to human populations, painting a picture of a rather dystopian world, but one that again fit with many people's perceptions of a breakdown in society in 1960s USA. The research influenced thinking well beyond that decade. The idea of dysfunctional behavioural sinks, created by environmental conditions, caught on during the 1970s and 1980s. In the UK, for instance, British governments started to talk about *sink estates*, a concept that still enjoys some currency today. According to the *Guardian* newspaper, sink estates are characterised by high levels of economic and social deprivation. Such estates are not always high-crime areas, although there is a strong association between crime rates and sink estates in large urban areas. Different governments have attempted to 'clean up' these estates and in some cases demolish them. In her critique of housing in Britain, Coleman argued that the concept of sink estate – "populated by the dregs of humanity" – was used to blame the residents for the deprivation rather than architectural and socio-economic conditions (Coleman, 1985, p. 20).

There are of course significant problems with generalising from rats to human populations and then to housing estates, as there usually are when animal findings are applied to humans. At a general level, other countries, such as Japan, did not experience the same crime and social problems as the USA, despite significantly higher density living. Moreover, in many of the so-called sink estates, the population densities were not particularly high. What were important in these areas were the lack of investment in the buildings, the levels of social and economic deprivation, and the impact of unemployment and poor educational standards. However, the environment tended to be given the blame and provided a convenient scapegoat. Nevertheless, the research did spark interest in human studies of crowding and led to the realisation that density and crowding are complex issues.

HUMAN CROWDING

Although it is used regularly as an informal everyday term, it is not always clear what crowding means. Researchers examining the topic make an important distinction between crowding and density, and then between social density and spatial density (Stokols, 1972). What most people think of as crowding is in fact density, which is a physical concept. *Social density* is the number of people per unit of space. *Spatial density* is the area (e.g., square metre) of space each person has. As density is simply an objective physical measure, it can be neither good nor bad. Crowding, however, is a psychological phenomenon. It can be defined as the experience of discomfort that arises when a person feels that there are too many people within a space and/or that the amount of space they have is inadequate to meet their goals or needs. As, by definition, crowding is a negative experience, it makes little sense to ask whether crowding is good or bad. However, the idea that crowding is psychological rather than physical was not always evident in early crowding research, and even today researchers will speak of enjoyable versus stressful crowding (e.g., Novelli, Drury & Reicher, 2010). The negative feeling of crowding is often experienced as environmental stress, and results in the detrimental consequences of that pressure (Stokols, 1972). Thus, if someone feels negative about the number of people in a space, we can say that it is crowded. If, however, they experience positive feelings about the density, it is not crowded. In other words, high density is only crowded if it is unpleasant, which is why crowding is only mildly related to population density (Gifford, Steg & Reser, 2011). Another way of putting this is that crowding is an interaction or transaction between the density of a place and those experiencing that place.

As with other areas of environmental psychology, our experience of density rests with what we are trying to achieve; what our goals or purposes for being in a place are. Not all occasions when people experience high density will it lead to discomfort or crowding.

There are many places and occasions where high density is positive and low density would be undesirable. For instance, a party to which only a couple of people turn up, or a football match with only a handful of spectators would be uncomfortable. On these occasions higher density enhances the positive experience of the events. During national lockdowns because of the Covid-19 pandemic, supporters were not allowed into stadia to watch sports. A lot was said about how the games lacked atmosphere. Television coverage, at least in the UK, used soundtracks of crowds responding to the game to enhance the viewing experience. When small numbers were allowed in to watch, they sometimes reported that 'it just isn't the same'. Here high density is desired and integral to the positive experience. It is, of course, equally the case that there are many contexts in which high density is not at all desired. High density in a library or on a tube train, for instance, can be unpleasant and stressful.

We can see that where density is too high, crowding stress is experienced, and when density is too low, there can also be a negative impact and people can experience the unpleasant feeling of *isolation*. Like crowding, isolation is a psychological experience and when environmental psychologists talk about isolation it generally has negative connotations. Some consequences of isolation include feelings of loneliness, increased depression, and decreased happiness. There is even evidence that isolation results in a shorter life span (Holt-Lunstad, 2017; Holt-Lunstad et al., 2015). Isolation is not necessarily the consequence of being alone, sometimes that is desirable; rather, it relates to *feeling* isolated, which can also occur in the presence of others.

PRIVACY

Altman defines privacy as "selective control of access to self or to one's group" (Altman, 1975, p. 18). This short definition contains two essential qualities of privacy. First, in environmental psychology privacy is a way of controlling rather than preventing interactions. As Altman notes, "*Privacy is a* dialectic *process, which involves both a restriction of interaction and a seeking of interaction*" (Altman, 1975, p. 11). The level of privacy a person wants will change over time as well as between places, so the degree of interaction that is desired varies. The second part of Altman's definition points to the need for privacy for groups as well as individuals. For instance, family groups may require privacy from others, as may groups of work colleagues or adolescents.

Privacy fulfils several functions, which is why the ability to regulate it is important (Altman, 1975; Pedersen, 1979, 1999). One of the primary facets of privacy is the control and management of interpersonal interaction. This allows people to manage what Goffman (1959) referred to as 'front stage' and 'backstage' behaviour. Our front stage behaviour can be observed by an audience just like actors when they are on stage. But when backstage, like an actor, an individual can relax and rejuvenate because there is no one watching (Altman, 1975; Pedersen, 1999). Being able to control whether you are observed allows you to have control over what information you share about yourself. Another way of looking at this is that privacy allows you to maximise your freedom of choice (Proshansky, Ittleson & Rivlin, 1972). Further, privacy can help creative processes (Pedersen, 1979), as Virginia Woolf pointed to in *A Room of One's Own* almost a hundred years ago (Woolf, 1929).

Although control of information is important in its own right, the management of interaction is also important for self-definition and self-identity (Altman, 1975). The mechanisms for controlling interactions help define a person's own limits or boundaries. The time and space that the control of interaction gives allows people to reflect on, contemplate, and then integrate and assimilate their experiences (Altman, 1975; Pedersen, 1999). It allows the examination of future and possible relationships and social comparisons to be made. All of these processes would be more difficult if an individual were front stage and observed all the time. Using the stage metaphor, it would, for instance, be difficult for an actor to reflect on their performance, ensure they brought the right qualities to their role, and practise their lines if they remained onstage and in front of the audience all the time. *Self-identity* can also be facilitated through self-observation. Further, personal autonomy (Altman, 1975; Pedersen, 1979) can be developed as part of being alone to do what we want and how we want to do it. Also, individuality can be enhanced by time spent alone or with specific groups, which in the latter case will allow members the opportunity to confide in one another (Pedersen, 1999). It is probably no coincidence that as teenagers develop their sense of self and identity during adolescence they seem to demand more privacy.

There are different types of privacy, which vary by situation and the relationships involved. Using factor analysis, Pedersen (1997, 1999) identified six kinds: intimacy with family (being alone with family), intimacy with friends (being alone with friends), solitude (freedom from observation), isolation (being geographically removed and free from observation), anonymity (being seen but not identified or identifiable), and reserve (not revealing personal aspects of oneself). Each type of privacy meets different needs or objectives. Pedersen (1999) points to five needs that he empirically validated using factor analysis, which are, to confide, rejuvenation, contemplation, autonomy, and creativity. An objective can be achieved by more than one type of privacy. The need to *confide* is best achieved by creating intimacy with friends or family, but of course would not be met by isolation. Rejuvenation can be achieved by isolation or by intimacy with friends. Contemplation and creativity, for example, are most likely met by isolation and solitude. The final need from Pedersen's privacy functions is autonomy. His research showed that autonomy was facilitated reasonably well by most types of privacy.

Because of the central role privacy plays in many areas of our lives, the ability to regulate levels of privacy is important. Regulation is achieved by a combination of personal and situational factors. For instance, our personality will play a role in how we regulate access by others, as will our individual need for privacy. Other factors like our social skills may also be important to how we deal with social interaction in a way that allows us to achieve our desired level of privacy. In the remainder of this chapter, we will look at some of the primary mechanisms for regulating privacy. While these can include verbal regulation, such as telling people to 'go away', from our perspective those involving the use of the environment are the most interesting.

ENVIRONMENT AND SOCIAL REGULATION

In a moment we will move on to territoriality and personal space as ways of controlling privacy and social interaction. Before that we will look at how the design and layout of an environment can facilitate or inhibit the control of interaction. Some design features straightforwardly influence contact. A door on a bedroom or office performs the function of allowing or denying access. Designers can create different experiences and encourage behaviours by exploiting environmental characteristics in more subtle ways. One of the earliest studies in environmental psychology (Osmond, 1959) examined how design influenced patients on psychiatric wards. From the results of his research Osmond suggested two broad types of spatial arrangement, *sociopetal* and *sociofugal*. A sociopetal space is one that is arranged in a way that brings people together, facilitating interaction and encouraging conversations. Sociofugal space is the converse, having the effect of separating people and inhibiting interaction, for instance, an arrangement of chairs in a straight line or around the edge of a room. It is quite easy to remember which is which if you think of socio*fugal* as working in the same way as centri*fugal* force, which pushes bodies out and away from one another.

Sociopetal and sociofugal spaces are neither good nor bad. Which type of arrangement is best depends on your intentions, goals, feelings, and social motivations (Meagher & Marsh, 2017). If you want to limit interaction, a sociofugal arrangement will be helpful. However, if you want to engage in conversation and social activities, a sociopetal space will be most appropriate. Examples of sociopetal and sociofugal space can be readily found. The architect and psychologist Bryan Lawson in his interesting book *The Language of Space* (Lawson, 2001) draws our attention to the example of Antoni Gaudi's Parc Guell in Barcelona. A central feature of the park is a terrace with a balustrade, which also forms a tiled bench. The bench stretches the length of the terrace, forming undulating curves reminiscent of a snake or sea serpent. The concave, inward bends provide sociopetal spaces, in which people can sit and interact. The apex of the bends provides sociofugal spaces. Here people do not face each other when sitting, so interaction is not encouraged and people can remain alone in their thoughts. Whether the original intention was to create spaces that worked in this way is not known. But it is a good example of clever design that uses both types of space within one design element. It shows how a variety of space can be provided in one area that fulfils the different needs of people using the space.

An everyday example of a layout that does not work, and that most of us are be familiar with, is a room that is meant for socialising but is arranged in a sociopetal way. A typical example might be the resident's social room in a care home. The purpose of the room is for the users to interact and socialise during the day. To facilitate this, space should be arranged in a sociopetal form. However, to pick up an example we saw earlier, sometimes seating is arranged around the walls of a room, with few seats facing or at an angle to one another. This sociofugal inhibits the desired interaction leaving residents isolated in the same room. The arrangement is, however, convenient for cleaning or maintenance. During the 1950s and 1960s, sociofugal arrangement of social spaces was relatively common in psychiatric institutions as well as care homes. Some of these institutions were locations for the first studies to take place in environmental psychology and, happily, lessons have been learned with sociofugal spaces now being relatively rare.

It is easy to think of examples of space that is arranged appropriately to meet its design intent. If we consider a typical British pub, the tables and seating are clearly arranged to promote socialising and interaction. The waiting rooms at Doctor's surgeries, however, are usually configured in ways that do not facilitate conversation. Perhaps this recognises that the patient might not want to discuss their ailment or interact with someone who might be contagious. In some instances, there can be incompatible, competing goals in a space. For instance, departure lounges in airport tend to comprise linear rows of seats. The intention here is that users will not spend large amounts of time sitting around socialising but will wait for their flight, pay attention to announcements, and leave. The design also encourages people to move around the terminal and use shops and might help propel groups of passengers to the eating and drinking areas with their more sociable seating.

Usually, this arrangement works well for the airports. It perhaps works less well for groups of travellers and families, especially when there is a significant flight delay. For instance, the linear seating is not effective in allowing parents to supervise children unless their children entertain themselves and sit quietly. Groups travelling together will also wish to speak with one another which they will find difficult with the departure lounge arrangement. In response, it is quite common to see groups of travellers sitting on the floor in a small circle, disrupting the intention of the airport seating designer and creating for themselves sociopetal spaces. They are also showing that environmental determinism rarely works.

Before moving on to territoriality, let us briefly look at shopping. It might not be immediately apparent that our shopping experience is influenced by the types of spatial arrangements retailers adopt. In some shops the merchant wants customers to interact with both people (assistants and one another) and the products. In other environments the aim is the more rapid movement of shopper through the environment without them lingering too long. The archetype of this sociofugal space is the supermarket. The linear rows of goods on shelves facilitate movement or traffic as it is sometimes called. Customers can easily see what is available, take the product they want, and move on. That can be contrasted to a farmers' market or some clothes retailers, for example, where arrangement of the space invites shoppers to look at the goods, handle them, and discover new products. Sociofugal and sociopetal spaces are evident in a wide range of settings, from parks, to shops, to airports, yet the aim is the same. Designs are produced that either facilitate or inhibit interaction. Whether you experience that as good or bad will depend on the purposes that bring you to that place.

TERRITORIALITY

If we take the earlier example of a group of travellers sitting in a circle on the floor of an airport departures lounge, we can also see that they are marking out an area for themselves. Now, consider what would happen if a person, a stranger to the group, arrived and sat in the middle of the circle or anywhere within its 'boundary'. It would be seen as a very odd, and perhaps even a provocative thing to do. That is because the area they are occupying has become *their territory*. Most people will recognise and understand the demarcation without any need for explanation and know that the unspoken rule is that you do not 'invade' that space. The territory they have defined will allow within – group interaction and provide a barrier to outsiders. It allows the group to control access, and so can be seen as a privacy regulation mechanism.

We can define territoriality as one of the primary physical mechanisms for regulating social interaction, allowing control of interaction to achieve goals (Edney, 1976; Proshansky et al., 1972). It is a boundary regulation mechanism that involves marking an area or place and identifying it as belonging to an individual or group (Altman, 1975). Territories are areas that a person or group feels some sort of ownership of, and which are often defended physically or by verbal and non-verbal communication.

The idea of territoriality grew out of work on animal ecology and has been generalised to humans. An animal's territory is relatively simple and serves clear functions such as defending breeding opportunities or ensuring food supply. When applied to people, territoriality is more complex. Altman (1975) has argued that a wider variety of things can be included within the general idea of territory than just physical locations, including ideas and objects. In that sense, copyright is a type of territorial claim. The development of the internet and virtual space raises new issues around territory, which have yet to receive a significant research interest (Joinson & Paine, 2007). This inclusion of ideas and objects suggests an overlap between the concept of territory and the idea of ownership, which might be a better term to use in relation to human behaviour than the analogy of animal territory.

Although human territoriality comes from the concept of animal territory, there are several differences between the two (Altman, 1975). For instance, animal territory is often, though not always, small scale, owned by a single-group membership or single animal, and often relates to a single location. In contrast, human territory is both small and large scale, from tables to countries. Human territory has a greater diversity of membership than is the case for animals. People occupy and have territories in multiple locations. Further, as mentioned, humans territoriality can apply to a variety of domains, including ideas. In animals, territory is almost exclusively confined to environments. Finally, given the social intricacy of humans compared to other animals, the responses to the violation of territory can be complicated and various, while an animal's response will usually be simple and aggressive.

Ever since the early writings on territory, researchers have subdivided it into several types, usually coinciding with environmental scale. At the smallest and closest scale is individual *primary* (Altman, 1975) or *body territory* (Lyman & Scott, 1967). This level is thought to be important for a person's sense of self and identity. Primary territories include a person's body, their own room, or their whole home (Altman, 1975; Brower, 1965). Some writers, confusingly, classify home as a larger, more distant level of territory (Lyman & Scott, 1967), which suggests it might be an intermediary level between the boundaries of two territorial levels. Primary territories can also include mobile environments, such as cars. This is an interesting example as a car is a private territory but is in a public territory (road). As we will see later, this can lead to some confusion in social interaction. A key feature of primary territory is that it reflects something about the person who owns or is associated with it. Primary territories reflect the owner's choices and are the areas in which people tend to be most invested. The proximity and importance of primary territory is reflected in the degree and enthusiasm with which it is controlled and defended.

Secondary territory is more public, and is often a group space (Altman, 1975). This type of territory might be permanent, or temporary. For instance, a person or group might appropriate a table in a bar, which then becomes their territory for as long as they are there. Once they leave, the space will then be 'claimed' by another group for a period. Although these territorial locations might be temporary and not owned in the same way that a primary territory is, feelings related to their possession can still be quite powerful. Similar to the example of invading a circle of people sitting on the floor in an airport, imagine what the response might be if a stranger in a bar decided to sit, without invitation, at a table already occupied by a group of friends. There are circumstances in which some form of negotiation might take place, which allows a stranger to share your territory. For example, if an environment such as a bar is very crowded, it would be acceptable if a stranger asked to sit at an already occupied table, if there are spare seats. The same behaviour would not be considered appropriate if the bar was half empty. The context of a full bar allows the sharing of a table by a stranger, as does an overt verbal exchange – asking if they can sit there.

The final category is *public territory*, which is a non-owned space. As the name suggests this type of territory is open to the public. This could be, for instance, a beach, a piazza, or a park. However, while a space is public, markers can still be used to appropriate areas for individuals or groups, creating secondary territories. In the case of a beach, for instance, a towel or sunshade can be used to mark off a small area for personal use. As with other territories, once part of a public area is appropriated, it can feel threatening if that space is intruded upon.

It is not necessary for you to be present to occupy a territory. People leave markers to reserve territory while they are elsewhere. These too are generally understood and observed, and when they are not, it can be annoying. For instance, if you have left some possessions on a table in a library while you go to look for a book, and when you come back another person has moved the items and sat there him or herself, you would probably feel rather irritated. Even on crowded trains, people sometimes look quite disgruntled if you ask them to move their coat from the empty seat next to them so that you can sit down.

TWO APPLICATIONS OF TERRITORIALITY SPACE TO UNDERSTANDING EVERYDAY QUESTIONS

There has been a significant amount of research examining territoriality, its characteristics, and how it impacts behaviour. Most of the research on territoriality took place in the 1960s and 1970s, but some interesting work is still conducted. We will look at applications and influences of territory and territorial behaviour when we examine other areas of environmental psychology, including defensible space and crime. To demonstrate the far-reaching implications of territorial behaviour for understanding people's actions, in the remainder of this chapter we will consider two very different pieces of research. The first examines road rage from a territorial perspective, and the second applies the concept to understanding home advantage in competitive sport.

We have seen that most territory is fixed to one static location, with occasional exceptions including people's vehicles. Szlemko and his colleagues explored the implications of vehicles as territory as an explanation of driver aggression, often called road rage (Szlemko et al., 2008). Their central idea is that when you are in your vehicle, because you occupy both public and private territories simultaneously, confusion can arise. That confusion can then lead to aggression if a person experiences their personal territory being impinged even though the act is appropriate for and related to public space.

Vehicles fulfil criteria of primary territories: long-term ownership, control of access, recognisable ownership, and personalisation. As a result, people are likely to defend their primary vehicle territory aggressively, as they would other primary territory such as their home. Public roads are not individually owned. The occupation of roads is for a relatively short time, they are not usually personalised, and markers are not used, unless for instance it is space outside someone's home.

The authors found that people whose vehicles show more territorial markers, in the form of displays of ownership and personalisation, were more aggressive on the road and had more moving traffic violations. They also found attachment to vehicles – in a sense a place attachment – independently predicted aggressive behaviour as well being related to personalisation. Extrapolating from the study may also help shed light on why people continue to use their mobile phones while driving, fail to wear seatbelts or why they break the speed limits. Being in their own territory they may feel that they define the rules of behaviour and ignore those imposed by others. There are further safety implications, for instance, when people remain in their cars when making sea crossings by ferries or trains. Usually, smoking is forbidden while on the train; however, if the car is a primary territory, it may be more likely that the owner will ignore those instructions because they feel governed by their own rules. It is clear that there are practical implications from the concept of territory that need to be taken into account for day-to-day behaviour, especially when primary and public territory coincide. For instance, in some situations it might be wise to have people make crossing separated from their vehicles, as happens on most longer distance ferry crossings.

The second example of territory playing a role in everyday life is drawn from research that tries to explain why in sporting events home teams have an advantage over visitors. Neave and Wolfson (2003) directly addressed that question arguing that, in animals, there is an increase in testosterone when territory is threatened or encroached upon. If testosterone is linked to assertiveness, dominance, and fighting harder to defend territory, there might be alterations in testosterone of humans when playing home games, in which ritualised aggression is exhibited in defence of territory.

The results of research carried out on football players in the UK did in fact show that testosterone levels were significantly higher before home games than levels before either away games or home training sessions played against other members of their football club. Further, testosterone levels were higher when the opposing team were 'extreme' rivals. The authors did take into account other factors that might account for home advantage, including familiarity with the ground, travel fatigue of the opposition, crowd noise, and referee bias.

Neave and Wolfson (2003) note that the precise mechanisms that translate increased testosterone into more successful performance during a game are not known and need to be established. And, of course, a lot of caution needs to be exercised when generalising from animal studies and behaviour. However, this study provides an intriguing, if tentative, indication of some of the array of areas, often unexpected, that territoriality might have implications for and provide insight into.

PERSONAL SPACE

The other primary spatial mechanism for regulating privacy and controlling interaction is *personal space*. Like territoriality, many of the ideas behind personal space were derived from animal research, especially Hediger's studies of *individual distance* amongst captive zoo animals (Hediger, 1950). During the late 1950s and 1960s, several researchers were thinking and writing about ideas of individual space and interpersonal distance. Anthropologist Edward Hall's closely related idea of *proxemics* describes a similar regulating mechanism to personal space and has been very influential with other thinkers. Goffman (1971), a leading sociologist, also considered personal space, and although he did not use the term, he described the same phenomenon, "*the space surrounding an individual where within which an entering other causes the individual to feel encroached upon, leading him to show displeasure and sometimes withdraw*" (p. 30). However, it was environmental psychologist Bob Sommer who brought the concept of human personal space to wide attention in the 1960s (Sommer, 1959, 1969), ultimately resulting in it becoming part of everyday language (Sommer, 2002).

Altman (1975), describing the concept, writes, "*The idea of personal space. . . deals with the boundary around the self*" (p. 53). "(it is) *An area with an invisible boundary surrounding the person's body into which intruders may not come*" (Sommer, 1969, p. 26). Like privacy, personal space is a dialectic in which people can feel uncomfortable with too much distance, as well as the too little (Hall, 1966; Sommer, 2002).

The discomfort of too much distance as well as people being too close was experienced by some during the Coronavirus lockdowns of 2020 and 2021. The recommendation in the UK and some other countries was that people should maintain a distance of at least two metres, or yards, from one another. In several situations that is inappropriately far and initially was often experienced as awkward or even unpleasant. Moving to a greater distance from people when passing in the street was also a common response to the Covid-19 pandemic. Although anecdotal, in the early days people would often smile or in some way acknowledge each other as they gave a wide berth when passing. The inappropriately large distances communicated a non-verbal message that people countered by other cues, in a way almost explaining or at least acknowledging the inappropriate distance. As time progressed and further distances became more normal, the use of smiles and other indicators appeared to drop off. A new situational distance norm had been established.

While infringement of personal space is likely to lead to discomfort and environmental stress, like other experiences, it depends on who is doing the infringing and in what circumstances they are doing it. In other words, perception of space and appropriate personal space is dynamic. As Hall (1966) wrote in his book *The Hidden Dimension*, "*. . . we can think of man (sic) as surrounded by a series of expanding and contracting fields which provide information of many kinds. . .*" (p. 115). These fields or zones depend on people's activities and who else is there. In specifying distances Hall is emphasising that different relationships, behaviours, and experiences are related to different sizes of personal space. What is appropriate within one distance is not appropriate within another. Further, the shape of personal space is not uniform around the body; rather, it is like the shape of a traditional egg timer, with larger distances at the front and rear of a person, and smaller at the sides (Sommer, 2002).

In Hall's proxemics there are four zones of interpersonal distance, which are *intimate* (touching, 6–18 inches), *personal* (1.5–4 ft/45–120 cm), *social* (4–12 ft/45 cm–4 m), and *public* (greater than 4 m). The intimate zone is generally the distance of those with an intimate relationship. The zone can be split into near intimate distance, in which there is body contact, and far intimate distance, which would be appropriate for sharing a quiet conversation. It is possible to think of many instances in which physical contact is made but is not intimate in the usual sense. For example, a visit to a doctor or dentist will often involve contact at the near intimate distance. The same happens during contact sports. In those circumstances, the normal mutually understood rules of interaction are transgressed, but they are usually governed by professional or social rules that regulate them and make them acceptable. As we saw with territory, context and circumstances allow general rules of space and interaction to be temporarily suspended, such as when there is high density in a place.

The *personal zone* usually involves interactions with good friends or intimate partners in a social setting. This is a good example showing that the acceptable interaction with the same people varies by context. In a social setting even if people are intimate partners they are expected to behave appropriately and maintain personal distance. If they behave as they might when they are alone, they may well be told to 'get a room'. When spatial rules are being transgressed, other regulatory mechanisms, in this case verbal, come into play.

Beyond the personal zone, interactions can also include strangers. The first of these regions is the *social zone*, which is often the distance at which business takes place. Generally, the more formal the interaction the further the distance between the people involved. At the extreme is the *public zone*. An example of this is the distance between speaker and their audience. At these distances, the concept of proxemics extends beyond personal space and may move into territory. There are, however, some significant differences between personal space and territoriality.

A criticism of the concept of personal space is that it lacks a sound theoretical basis for explaining why people maintain distance from others (Evans & Howard, 1973; Sommer, 2002). In response there have been several attempts to provide a personal space theory or explanation, including stress reduction, overload, arousal, and attraction (Sommer, 2002). One approach that appears to have quite a strong explanatory power is evolutionary theory. Briefly, this suggests that personal space is likely to have served an important evolutionary function in humans, as it still does for other animals. In earlier more primitive societies keeping others, in particular rivals, at a distance has the advantage of avoiding fights, keeping a mate, and reducing food loss. Allowing kin to be closer and forming a coherent social unit also provides a strong evolutionary advantage. Research indicates that there is a difference in acceptable personal space or personal space distance choice related to groups with shared identity (Novelli et al., 2010). Members of groups with whom a person identifies are allowed closer and are more likely to be helped than other group members, even if both individuals are strangers (Glick, Demorest & Hotze, 1988).

There is some evidence that to a degree space regulation is most probably physiological and innate, which supports evolutionary explanations. It is known that the amygdala plays a role in social approach behaviour in primates. Kennedy and his colleagues (2009) conducted an intriguing study indicating that the same process may apply to humans. Using a case study of a 42-year-old woman with complete bilateral amygdala lesions, they found that, when asked to select an appropriate distance to stand, she consistently stood half the distance from the experimenter that control participants would stand. Sometimes she would be within touching distance. She described feeling perfectly comfortable at those distances. The experimenter felt quite uncomfortable. Interestingly, she was aware of personal space and, although she underestimated the distance, was able to predict at what point other people would feel uncomfortable. She therefore had a cognitive, learned awareness, but not an emotional one. The researchers found further evidence that the amygdala plays a crucial role in the emotional experience of personal space from fMRI studies, giving more support to a biological basis of the phenomenon.

It seems that although humans have sophisticated social conventions that allow interaction, older biological systems continue to influence behaviour. It would be expected that there would be overlay of complex socially evolved behaviour on top of biological processes, which would be reflected in universality along with culturally specific differences. In other words, evolutionary biological processes would result in the need for distance, but over time diverse culture would shape that need into culturally specific spatial conventions. Research supports this prediction. The size of personal space zones is relatively stable *within* cultures. But, as anyone who has travelled widely will have experienced, the size and management of personal space can vary significantly *across* cultures. Cultures with close (small) personal space include Asia, Middle East, and Latin countries (including Southern European and Mediterranean countries) (Hall, 1966). Those with *more* distant personal space are found in Northern Europe, Canada, the USA, Australia, and some parts of the Far East, including Japan (Beaulieu, 2004; Evans, Lepore & Allen, 2000). Naturally, these are generalisations and there is variation within them, but there is a clear cultural pattern to the use and need for personal space across these cultures.

Beyond culture, research has identified many of the factors that affect people's experience of personal space. Sommer first started using and developing the concept to improve conditions in hospitals (Sommer & Ross, 1958). The applied use of theories of personal space continues, although work on the topic is no longer central to environmental psychology. In the USA, for instance, the concept has been used in legal cases of sexual harassment and where distances are cited as evidence of improper behaviour. The concept has also been used in court cases aimed at protecting women entering abortion clinics from anti-abortion protesters, and has suggested that the concept is now used in legal contexts as much as in design (Sommer, 2002). Personal space has then become one of those relatively rare ideas that transfer from psychological sciences into the mainstream.

PERSONAL SPACE AND TERRITORIALITY

Before concluding it is worth differentiating personal space and territoriality. While there are some overlaps, for instance, markers may be used to define territories and to prevent the invasion of personal space, there are important differences between the two concepts. A fundamental quality differentiating them is that personal space is *person centred* and moves with the individual. In that sense, personal space is *portable*. Territory in contrast is *place centred*. Therefore, when a person leaves a territory, such as their home, that territory remains where it is. Personal space is an invisible boundary – when it is crossed, a person might choose an aggressive response, but they can also withdraw in which case their personal space is no longer being infringed. This contrasts with territory, which is usually delineated with visible boundaries, which might be permanent, like fences, or temporary, such as coats or a pile of books. Because permanent territory is environmentally anchored in one place, it is difficult for it to be withdrawn in the same way that a person can withdraw their personal space if it is invaded.

BRINGING IT ALL TOGETHER

The spatial concepts of privacy, crowding, isolation, personal space, and territoriality can be interlinked. When doing this *privacy* is considered the key concept. In describing the interrelationships between the spatial concepts we have discussed, Altman wrote:

> Privacy is central. . .it is a central regulatory process by which a person (or group) makes himself (sic) more or less accessible and open to others. . . the concepts of personal space and territoriality are mechanisms that are set in motion to achieve desired levels of privacy. Crowding. . . (is) a social condition in which privacy mechanisms have not functioned effectively, resulting in an excess of undesired social contact.
>
> (Altman, 1975, p. 3)

FINALLY

In the early days of environmental psychology, the issues of crowding, privacy, personal space, and territoriality were central to the discipline. Many of its early, pioneering studies were based around these concepts. Their heyday in terms of research interest has waned somewhat in environmental psychology, as Uzzell and Horne (2006) have noted in relation to personal space. However, a small but steady stream of studies still emerge each year, and the concepts continue to be used in discussions of many areas. As we will see later, the ideas can be found in other chapters, for instance in relation to crime, work environments, and therapeutic settings. Outside of environmental they are also being used to better understand privacy regulation including, for instance on the internet (Joinson & Paine, 2007).

REFERENCES

Altman, I. (1975). *The Environment and Social Behavior.* Monterey: Brooks/Cole.

Beaulieu, C. (2004). Intercultural study of personal space: A case study. *Journal of Applied Social Psychology*, 34, 794–805.

Brower (1965). The signs we learn to read. *Landscape*, 15, 9–12.

Calhoun, J. B. (1962). Population density and social pathology. *Scientific American*, 206(2), 139–149.

Christian, J. J. (1961). Phenomena associated with population density. *Proceedings of the National Academy of Sciences*, 47, 428–449.

Coleman, A. (1985). *Utopia on Trial: Vision and Reality in Planned Housing.* London: Hilary Shipman Ltd.

Edney, J. J. (1976). Human territoriality. In H. Proshansky, W. Ittleson, and L. Rivlin (eds.), *Environmental Psychology: 2nd Edition. People and Their Physical Settings* (pp. 189–205). New York: Holt, Rinehart and Winston.

Ehrlich, P. R. (1968). *The Population Bomb.* New York: Ballantine Books.

Evans, G. W. & Howard, R. B. (1973). Personal space. *Psychological Bulletin*, 80, 334–344.

Evans, G. W., Lepore, S. J., & Allen, K. M. (2000). Cross cultural differences in tolerance for crowding: Fact of fiction. *Journal of Personality and Social Psychology*, 79, 204–210.

Gifford, R., Steg, L., & Reser, J. P. (2011). Environmental psychology. In P. R. Martin, F. M. Cheung, M. C. Knowles, M. Kyrios, L. Littlefield, J. B. Overmier, & J. M. Prieto (eds.), *The IAAP Hand Book of Applied Psychology, First Edition* (pp. 440–470). Oxford: Blackwell Publishing Ltd.

Glick, P., Demorest, J. A., & Hotze, C. A. (1988). Keeping your distance: Group membership, personal space, and requests for small favors. *Journal of Applied Social Psychology*, 18(4), 315–330.

Goffman, E. (1959). *The Presentation of Self in Everyday Life.* New York: Doubleday.

Goffman, E. (1971). *Relations in Public: Microstudies of Public Order.* New York: Basic Books.

Hediger, H. (1950). *Wild Animals in Captivity*. London: Butterworth.

Holt-Lunstad, J. (2017). The potential public health relevance of social isolation and loneliness: Prevalence, epidemiology, and risk factors. *Public Policy & Aging Report*, 27(4), 127–130.

Holt-Lunstad, J., Smith, T. B., Baker, M., Harris, T., & Stephenson, D. (2015). Loneliness and social isolation as risk factors for mortality: A meta-analytic review. *Perspectives on Psychological Science*, 10(2), 227–237.

Joinson, A. N., & Paine, C. B. (2007). Self-disclosure, privacy and the Internet. In A. Joinson. K. McKenna, T. Postmes, & E. D. Reips (eds.), *The Oxford Handbook of Internet Psychology* (pp. 237–251). Oxford: Oxford University Press.

Kennedy, D. P., Gläscher, J., Tyszka, J. M., & Adolphs, R. (2009). Personal space regulation by the human amygdala. *Nature Neuroscience*, 12, 1226–1227.

Lawson, B. (2001). *The Language of Space.* London: Architectural Press.

Lyman, S. M. & Scott, M. B. (1967). Territoriality. A neglected sociological dimension. *Social Problems*, 15, 236–249.

Meagher, B. & Marsh, K. (2017). Seeking the safety of sociofugal space: Environmental design preferences following social ostracism. *Journal of Experimental Social Psychology*, 68, 192–199.

Neave, N. & Wolfson, S. (2003). Testosterone, territoriality, and the 'home advantage'. *Physiology and Behaviour,* 78(2), 269–275.

Novelli, D., Drury, J., & Reicher, S. (2010). Come together: Two studies concerning the impact of group relations on 'personal space'. *British Journal of Social Psychology*, 49, 223–236.

Osmond, H. (1959). The relationship between architect and psychiatrist. In C. Goshen (ed.), *Psychiatric Architecture.* Washington, DC: American Psychiatric Association.

Pedersen, D. M. (1979). Dimensions of privacy. *Perceptual and Motor Skills*, 48, 1291–1297.

Pedersen, D. M. (1997). Psychological functions of privacy. *Journal of Environmental Psychology*, 17, 147–156.

Pedersen, D. M. (1999). Model for types of privacy by privacy functions. *Journal of Environmental Psychology*, 19, 397–405.

Proshansky, H. M., Ittelson, W. H., & Rivlin, L. G. (1972). Freedom of choice and behavior in a physical setting. In J. F. Wohlwill & D. H. Carson (eds.), *Environment and the Social Sciences: Perspectives and Applications* (pp. 29–43). American Psychological Association.

Sommer, R. (1959). Studies in personal space. *Sociometry*, 22, 247–260.

Sommer, R. (1969). *Personal Space: The Behavioral Basis of Design*. Englewood Cliff, NJ: Prentice Hall.

Sommer, R. (2002). Personal space in a digital age. In R. B. Bechtel & A. Churchman (eds.), *Handbook of Environmental Psychology* (pp. 647–660). Chichester: Wiley.

Sommer, R. & Ross, H. (1958). Social interaction on a geriatrics ward. *International Journal of Social Psychiatry*, 4, 128–133.

Stokols, D. (1972). On the distinction between density and crowding: Some implications for future research. *Psychological Review*, 79(3), 275–277.

Szlemko, W. J., Benfield, J. A., Bell, P. A., Deffenbacher, J. L., & Troup, L. (2008). Territorial markings as a predictor of driver aggression and road rage. *Journal of Applied Social Psychology*, 38, 1664–1688.

Uzzell, D. & Horne, N. (2006). The influence of biological sex, sexuality and gender role on interpersonal distance. *British Journal of Social Psychology*, 45, 579–597.

Woolf, V. (1929). *A Room of One's Own*. London: Hogarth Press.

SUGGESTED READING

Sommer, R. (2002). Personal space in a digital age. In R. B. Bechtel & A. Churchman (eds.), *Handbook of Environmental Psychology* (pp. 647–660). Chichester: Wiley.

Most comprehensive environmental psychology texts, and especially those by North American authors devote considerable space to the topic. Particularly useful is Gifford's text, in whichever edition is most readily available.

Gifford, R. (2002). *Environmental Psychology: Principles and Practice, Third Edition.* Colville, WA: Optimal Books.

An interesting book on spatial behaviour is by Brian Lawson, a British Architect.

Lawson, B. (2001). *The Language of Space.* London: Architectural Press.

If a copy is available it is worthwhile looking at Altman's seminal book which brings all of these concepts together.

Altman, I. (1975). *The Environment and Social Behavior.* Monterey: Brooks/Cole.

4

BEHAVIOUR DURING DISASTERS AND EMERGENCIES

INTRODUCTION

Environmental psychologists have an important role advising on place design and management as ways to mitigate the loss of life and injury from major incidents and emergencies. By researching and understanding what people typically do as an incident unfolds, they can provide guidance based on empirical evidence rather than assumption and stereotype. Insights gained into what people do *during* life-threatening emergencies can also be used by clinical and counselling psychologists helping survivors make sense of their own behaviour.

Potentially life-threatening incidents vary in cause, for example, *natural events* including tsunamis, landslides, earthquakes, and volcanic eruptions, *intentional human action*, including terrorist attacks, or *unintentional action*, which might be the case with fires caused by a dropped match, a crowd crush at an entertainment event, or an industrial gas release. This chapter will primarily focus on behaviour in fires, but people caught up in different types of incidents show a remarkable consistency in the way they behave; therefore, lessons learnt in one type of event often can be broadly applied to another, although as with any generalisations, caution should be exercised. The chapter will include consideration of both relatively small-scale events, such as domestic fires, and much larger incidents that become multi-fatality disasters.

DOI: 10.4324/9780429274541-4

PANIC AND DISASTER MYTHS

We all tend to have an image of how others will behave if their life is threatened or if they are involved in a disaster. But these events are quite rare, so few of us will have had first-hand experience of them, or even know someone who have been directly involved. In fact, it is unlikely that most people have even been involved in more frequently occurring smaller events such as domestic fires. The image we have is therefore likely to fit one of the stereotypes of behaviour under threat. Because these images tend to be inaccurate, the term 'disaster myths' has been applied to these behavioural scenarios. The myths include the belief that people panic, engage in looting or other criminal behaviour, or that they will freeze, and become helpless. Probably, the most widely held belief is that people will panic. Because it is so pervasive, and potentially dangerous, we will examine it in detail later. We will briefly look at the other myths first.

The idea that people freeze is often referred to as 'disaster syndrome' or 'disaster shock'. Auf der Heide describes the response as, "*a state of stunned psychological incapacitation that results in the inability to take care of oneself or others*" (Auf der Heide, 2004, p. 350). Although there is widespread belief that such a reaction is common (Nogami, 2018), empirical evidence and case studies show that it is in fact rare (Drury et al. 2019; Leach, 2004) and confined to very specific conditions (Auf der Heide, 2004). Far from people freezing and becoming helpless, objective evidence is clear that people involved in an emergency or disaster are the first to give aid and assistance during the emergency and in its aftermath.

The expectation that there will be widespread looting or other criminal activity also fails to gain support in data from real emergencies and disasters. Although there are sometimes media reports of crimes during a disaster, they usually turn out to lack validity. For instance, *The Sun*, a tabloid newspaper in the UK, reported that during the 1989 Hillsborough disaster, in which 96 people died, Liverpool football fans had stolen from the victims. Members of the police repeated the same allegations. During the subsequent inquest, which concluded that no such thefts happened, Michael Mansfield QC describes the accusation as "a blatant lie". Not only is crime and looting rare *during* an emergency, there is little evidence to suggest crime is a common response in the aftermath of an incident. In many cases crime rates can reduce following a disaster, as happened throughout New York after the terrorist attacks on the World Trade Centre in 2001 (Auf de Heide, 2004). These myths will crop up again in this chapter, but as panic is the behaviour most often expected in an emergency, we will now spend a little more time on that.

Quarantelli and Dynes (1970) provide a more graphic image portraying the common view of people's behaviour in fires. They observe that

> The popular image of disaster has often centered on the theme of personal chaos. Such an image is frequently documented by isolated anecdotes used to prove the universality of such behavior. This image suggests that individuals panic and that individuals lose their concern for others. . .They act irrationally in terms of their own self-interest. Also, as the result of the disaster experience, it is suggested that people become hostile and take aggressive action toward others. People, hysterical and helpless, gradually shed the thin veneer of civilization and exploit others. It is assumed that many will flee from the disaster area in mass panic. . .
>
> (Quarantelli & Dynes, 1970, pp. 325–326)

The behaviour described by Quarantelli and Dynes is what most people assume is accurate. There are several qualities that make up the concept of panic so it is worth deconstructing the idea a little. Sime (1980, 1990) conducted extensive research looking at the concept of panic – how it is used and what its characteristics are supposed to be. He examined previous research as well as behaviour reported in news media. His results confirm that panic is the most frequently used description of behaviour in emergencies. When panic is reported, the characteristics that typify the behaviour are that it is irrational and makes no logical sense. That the behaviour results from an involuntary instinct, people are unable to control what they do themselves, and it is impossible for others to control them while they are panicking. Importantly, panic is thought to be infectious or contagious, and consequently, once one person has succumbed, others will 'catch' and spread panic themselves. Finally, it is a highly emotional state. Behaviour of this sort is, of course, outside the usual conventions that guide behaviour, with normal social functioning breaking down along with people's control of their actions.

Despite the widespread use of panic as an explanation of people's behaviour, empirical research shows that it does not reflect what happens in an emergency. Instead, within its context, behaviour is rational, happens within the framework of everyday behaviour, with the usual rules of behaviour and place continuing to apply and be followed. In an emergency people generally behave normally and, to a significant degree, consistently with what they would usually do if there were no emergency. Naturally, there will be some change in behaviour as people deal with the situation, but it will not be outside the realm of normal behaviour.

Sime (1990) also identified the stimuli or cues that have been reported to trigger panic during fires. These are people shouting either 'panic', 'don't panic', or 'fire'; physical evidence of fires such as smelling or seeing smoke; the sound of an alarm; having to travel long distances to evacuate a building; limited access to exits; the number and size of exits; widely spaced stairs; being unfamiliar with a building; large numbers of people; different types of people; and the presence of children. Even though they are wrong, some of these seem quite plausible. However, when examined more carefully they make much less sense. When looking at these supposed panic triggers it is worth keeping in mind that it is claimed that these factors will make people involuntarily switch immediately from normal to uncontrollable behaviour.

Throughout our lives we will hear the words 'panic', 'don't panic' or 'fire' many times with little if any reaction. So what is it that makes a word harmless in one context and likely trigger panic in another? If smelling smoke or seeing flames trigger a panic reaction, why does that not happen at, for instance, bonfire parties or when people have open fires in their homes? In fact the same question arises for all the other triggers. We experience most of them on a regular basis and do not respond to them by losing control. Therefore, there must be something in the context that accounts for the difference. If there is, then people must be working out that there is a problem. That is, there must be active, cognitive processes underlying the interpretation of the context by the person involved so that they establish that there is a threat. That then becomes a problem for the ability of the myth to account for behaviour. The idea of a conscious cognitive process goes against the notion of instinctive, immediate loss of control and so undermines the explanatory power and concept of panic.

The idea that an alarm is a trigger for panic is particularly interesting. While most psychologists would caution again drawing on individual anecdote as evidence, most people have been in situations where an alarm has sounded. What the majority of people will probably have experienced is that the alarm usually triggers slight awareness, often irritation, and regularly indifference; often the most that happens is people ask each other if they should do something. Knowing people's response to an alarm is a bit more than personal anecdote however. There has been evidence from social psychology studies as far back as the 1960s that even when smoke is blown under the door of an experimental room people do not leave, especially when they are with others, and they certainly do not panic (Latané & Darley, 1968). The real difficulty with alarms is not stopping people from panicking; it is getting people to react urgently or even at all. As Auf de Heide points out in relation to getting people to leave generally, there is often a hesitancy to evacuate (2004).

WHERE MYTHS COME FROM

There is some evidence that people's understanding of disasters and emergencies come from news reports and fictional accounts given in the cinema or on television. These sources tend to be inaccurate and misleading, portraying and reinforcing disaster myths, particularly the idea of panic. This is important not only because the misrepresentation of people's behaviour has consequences for the design and the management of disasters, but also because they could also stop us from recognising when we ourselves are involved in a life-threatening event. To deal effectively with an emergency, we need to know what a disaster looks like, and in the early stages, when it is still possible to escape; initially disasters tend to look little different from normal. Because the events do not fit the images they are used to in fictional accounts, people will often interpret them as non-threatening (Donald & Canter, 1992).

Newspaper and other reports of disasters make interesting reading, especially when compared to factual accounts of what happened. Media reports refer to panic even though there is little, if any, evidence to support the claims. Although dated, Sime (1990) provides a good illustration of this from the Beverly Hills Supper Club fire in the USA. The disaster was reported around the world. In the UK the headlines emphasised panic: The Sun, *Panic Kills 300*; Daily Mail, *Panic and 300 Stampede to Death*; Daily Express, *A killer Called Panic*. In these accounts not only is panic reported as taking place but is also blamed for killing or significantly contributing to the deaths of 300 people.

Not untypical for media reports, the number of fatalities was exaggerated. The real number killed was 167, not 300. Rather than a stampede being the cause of death, the formal report into the disaster made clear that the building design led to the rapid spread of the fire, and that the room capacity where the fire happened was 536 but the number of people in the room was 1,350. Importantly, there was a delay of two minutes between when the fire was noticed and any alarm or warning being given. Finally, most fatalities resulted from smoke inhalation; there was no evidence of panic.

Sime (1990) provides analysis of several other newspaper reports that interpret people's behaviour as panic. The accounts given in the media tend to share some characteristics. They often use the location of the victims as the evidence for irrational behaviour. They also interpret behaviour from an outsider's perspective rather than from the victims' experience during the emergency. In doing this, journalists have the advantage of retrospect; knowledge of the outcome, a lot of time to think about possible alternate actions, and details of how the fire spread and how other circumstances unfolded. In contrast, those caught up in the emergency must think very quickly with limited information. People are in circumstances that are highly constrained, where they often have limited if any prior experience of the environment they are in, and they lack knowledge of alternative routes and other possibilities. So, for instance, if a person jumps from a window it is seen as panic rather than a rational option given their understanding of the situation they are in.

Empirical research has demonstrated for over 70 years that people do not panic when faced by life-threatening emergencies (Quarantelli, 1954, 1960). Writing half a century ago Quarantelli and Dynes (1970) explain, "*Disaster victims act positively, not irrationally or passively. Mutual help and self-help are frequent. Psychological disturbances do not render the impacted population helpless*" (p. 326). The expectation that people will panic is especially problematic if it becomes the basis on which environments are designed, emergency preparedness is planned, and incidents are managed (Auf der Heide, 2004; Cole, Walters & Lynch 2011; Donald & Canter, 1990; Drury et al., 2019).

There is strong evidence that people involved in planning for and managing emergencies also often hold the view that people will panic (Auf der Heide, 2004; Drury, Novelli & Stott, 2013; Nogami, 2018, 2020; Wenger, James & Faupel, 1985), and that those who are involved in an emergency expect others to panic (Nogami & Yoshida, 2014). Research shows that there is still a lot of work to do in dispelling misunderstanding of people's behaviour. John Drury and his colleagues (2013), for instance, examined the beliefs of police officers, safety professionals, sports events stewards, and members of the public. Their research looked at the beliefs the groups held about what people would do in an emergency incident. They examined belief in the three myths of mass panic, civil disorder, and helplessness. Those responsible for managing emergencies believed that there *would be* panic and disorder in an emergency. The emergency managers as a result thought that incident management should be coercive and paternalistic. The *police* thought that the emotions and instincts of crowd would overcome rational thought. They also believed there would be 'contagion' of those emotions and instincts. It is surprising that police officers would hold these beliefs as they are trained in controlling crowds. *Civilian safety professionals* held similar views to the police. Football *stewards* endorsed most characteristics of mass panic as being likely. The only part they did not agree with was that people's behaviour would be characterised by selfishness. The *public*, however, agreed with every aspect of the idea of mass panic. Interestingly, all the groups agreed that members of the emergency services do not panic. These results show that people's beliefs are inaccurate compared to what research has told us happens in an emergency. Those inaccurate beliefs have the potential to lead to dysfunctional emergency management, which can make the difference between life and death.

Doing things that are aimed at trying to stop panic that can cost lives. Mitigation attempts can include delaying notifying people of the potential threat, reducing the information given to them, and attempting to reduce the sense of emergency. A consequence of panic mitigation can also include reliance on building design and technology that fails to recognise what people will do, and so can increase the difficulties they face (Sime, 1985). Over-reliance on these techniques means there is an absence of the information that people need to understand and interpret what is happening so that they can make decisions and take effective action. Research has shown that interpretation and decision-making are crucial to people when facing an emergency (Canter, 1990).

Assuming that people will panic means that a vital resource at the scene is not exploited. Consistently, a characteristic behaviour seen during emergencies is people coming to one another's aid. Authors have begun to refer to those who help as 'zero responders', because they are, of course, at the scene and available to assist before first responders can get to the location (Cole et al., 2011; Drury et al., 2019). Believing people caught up in an incident will act dysfunctionally, and so perceiving them as part of the problem or threat rather than as able to contribute to the solution, can delay victims receiving assistance. There are several incidents where that type of assistance has been important, including the 2005 terrorist bombs on the London Underground and the 2017 attack on the Manchester Arena.

UNDERSTANDING BEHAVIOUR IN EMERGENCIES

To understand people's behaviour in emergencies we need to consider how they are experienced. Emergencies and incidents that become disasters are of course dangerous situations. But they are also rare events, so most people have little experience to draw on, other than inaccurate portrayals found in the news media, dramas, and films. Most emergencies are complex, ambiguous, and rapidly changing. To avoid serious injury or loss of life, people must act rapidly. One difficulty they face is that the early stages of an emergency can look quite normal or ambiguous, and so are not interpreted as anything requiring action. Then, in the later stages as the incident develops, it can be fast changing and different from anything people have experienced before, meaning that people do not know what to do. They know action is needed but not necessarily what it should be. People do not have an appropriate *behaviour scripts* that they can follow to deal with the circumstances they are in.

As well as problems with ambiguity and interpreting what is going on, and a lack of scripts to guide behaviour, people often lack knowledge and understanding of fire growth dynamics, which means they are not very good at estimating the speed with which fires will grow (Fridolf & Nilsson, 2011) and so the need for early rapid action. People often wrongly assume that there is time to engage in various activities, such as paying their bill, collecting belongings, finding things to fight the fire, or stopping to use the toilets on the way out. By the time they have completed their activity they are often in considerable danger. In real emergencies, making inaccurate estimates can easily be the difference between a successful or tragic evacuation attempt. The nature of fire growth means that information should be provided clearly and rapidly, and alarms sounded without delay, the opposite of what is done when the aim is to prevent panic.

BEHAVIOURAL CONTINUITY IN EMERGENCIES

In the next sections the concepts that help explain behaviour and its underlying cognitive processes will be outlined. We will then use those conceptual tools to look at and understand people's behaviour during life-threatening incidents in different settings, including during a major disaster.

There are three approaches to explaining behaviour under life-threatening circumstances that we will look at. These include *affiliative* concepts (e.g., Sime, 1985), others drawing on theory and ideas from *social identity* (Drury, Cocking & Richer, 2009a), in particular self-categorisation theory (Turner, 1981), and *normative* explanations (e.g., Donald & Canter, 1992). Although there are differences between the theories, they all demonstrate the importance of cognitive and social psychological processes on guiding action. Each provides an explanation of some aspect of behaviour in emergencies and they should perhaps be seen as complementary rather than alternatives.

Affiliative Approaches

Affiliative approaches provide a useful framework for understanding how people behave when they are with others, or in groups. It shows how they tend to seek each other out once they have realised that they are facing some form of threat. Trying to find others and move with members of a group can delay evacuation and ultimately to people being injured or losing their life. Sime (1985) extends this idea to the environment, using the term *place affiliation*. In the same way that people will gravitate to members of their group in an emergency, they will also move towards parts of the environment with which they are familiar. This idea is used to explain why people often evacuate via an exit that they have used before and that they are familiar with, sometimes passing closer means of egress on their way to it. If the concept of panic were valid, you would expect that social ties would break down and people would not seek each other out or attempt to escape together.

Identity and Self-Categorisation

Identity and self-categorisation theory also demonstrate that social cognition and interaction do not break down under external threat, and on the contrary, the shared nature of external threat can help to bring people together to support and help one another. In a sense people identify with others as a group because they face a common threat. Therefore, rather than behaviour being competitive, as would be predicted by a panic model, people are supportive. As Drury et al. (2019) state, "*shared identity provides individuals with strengths and abilities that they do not have alone...*" (p. 2). The basic idea is that when caught in an incident people will develop a shared identity via a process of self-categorisation. They will categorise themselves and others as sharing that experience while it is still ongoing, and afterwards. As people with shared identities are more likely to support each other, there will be some mutual help by those involved. Drury and his colleagues suggest that authorities and incident management should identify ways of facilitating that behaviour and community resilience under threat. The approach is particularly productive in explaining mutual helping during an incident, and has found support in data from fires, bombings, crush events, train crashes, and a ship sinking (Drury et al., 2009a, 2009b).

Normative: Roles and Rules

From environmental psychology, we know that behaviour can be predicted from knowing the type of place someone is in, the role they have there, and what their goals or purposes are (see Chapters 1 and 2). This is important because the way a place is used under normal circumstances will have a significant impact on how people respond in an emergency. The clear structure to people's behaviour in emergencies shows that place-related cognitive processes play a role in shaping their actions. To understand emergency behaviour it is therefore necessary to understand those processes (Donald & Canter, 1992; Mintz, 1951).

The purposes people have in a place do not disappear when an emergency starts to unfold. The research evidence shows that people will tend to continue to pursue their original goals often until late in the incident timeline, even up until the loss of life. As we know, goals are associated with the roles a person plays in a setting, and further, that settings come with associated rules. There are also rules, or at least expectations that are attached to roles. The roles and rules associated with a place might be explicit or implicit, but they tend to be well understood and generally followed under normal circumstances. If the people using a place did not follow the place rules, it would hardly be able to function. In that sense, the idea of roles and rules continuing to shape action in emergencies fits within an approach that has been characterised as *normative*. In the next paragraphs we will elaborate on this basic idea.

The role a person has in an environment, for instance, shopper, waitress, lecturer, or student, will still be in place during an emergency and they will usually continue to be guided by it. The same can be said of place rules. Because the rules are so central to the use and functioning of a place and are ingrained, they are often not broken even when maintaining them puts the person's life in danger. There are many examples of people continuing with place rules. For instance, as we noted when discussing Sime's idea of place affiliation, people tend to leave by the way they came into a building, often passing emergency exits on the way. If, under normal circumstances, the use of emergency exits is not allowed, in an emergency they may well continue to be perceived as out of bounds (Canter, Comber & Uzzell, 1989; Donald & Canter, 1990). The norm of not using an exit may be stronger than the exception to that rule. Studies going back to the 1960s demonstrate that when people are in the presence of others, they are slower to respond to indications of an incident than if they were on their own. The explanation is that people do not want to be seen to even break implicit (place) rules. They also do not want to look foolish by 'overreacting' (Latané & Darley, 1968).

We noted previously that people are not passive responders to the environment, they actively read and interpret their surroundings, assessing what is happening and how it might affect them. Under normal circumstances, people might not be aware of the process, but when something unusual happens, they will consciously try to make sense of it. Their interpretation will be based on what they know tends to happen in that place and their previous experiences. As most people have little exposure to real emergencies they do not have much that they can draw on, in which case they will be guided by their assumptions and expectations about what will happen, what it will look like, and how they ought to behave. All this links together to provide a framework that usually works, but unfortunately it does not necessarily help them deal with an unfolding incident. That is one reason why emergency planning, management, and support are important.

Place Schema and Scripts

Two concepts from the field of social cognition that help us to understand people's behaviour in emergencies are the idea of *scripts* and *event schemas*. The concepts were originally developed to explain social interaction, but they can readily be applied to understanding how the environment is used and comprehended (Donald & Canter, 1992). Social scripts are "*coherent sequence of events expected by the individual, involving him either as a participant or an observer*" *(Abelson, 1976, p. 33)*. "*Event schemas or scripts. . .describe appropriate sequences of events in well-known situations. . .(they) serve to organize people's expectations regarding a likely sequence of events*" (Fiske & Taylor, 1991, pp. 119–120). As well as guiding behaviour, scripts also help us to understand and interpret other people's behaviour (Fayol & Monteil, 1988). In social psychology writers identify different components that are part of event schemas, including people's roles, sequence rules, such as whether you pay for food before you consume it (a fast food restaurant) or after you have eaten it (most decent restaurants), and props, such as timetables in a train station or menu in a restaurant. Within environmental psychology those components are extended to include the environment or place, in the sense of the concept we discussed in Chapter 2.

There are some points to emphasise in the previous quotes. We can note that scripts are complex sequences of behaviours over time rather than single acts. Scripts guide our own behaviour *and* shape how we interpret and understand other people's. When we see people behave in a particular way, we know what it is they are doing and what it is they will probably do next. This is important when we are trying to make sense of what is happening in an evolving emergency. For instance, if we see people going about their normal activity, what we recognise as the appropriate scripts, we are likely to assume everything is normal. It is when we see people deviate significantly from those scripts that we start to think something is wrong. There are at least two problems that arise from that. First, if you expect behaviour in an emergency to look like panic, and follow a 'panic script', you will assume everything is normal when you do not see anyone panicking. The second problem is that people will also be watching what you do, and interpreting your behaviour as evidence that all is well. In this way, it might be thought that *inaction* is contagious rather than panic being so. Later we will look at some examples of these from statements given by people involved in a major incident, but for now we will consider studies of fires in different settings.

STUDIES OF BEHAVIOUR IN FIRES

There has been a growing interest in academic research into behaviour in fires, which is often carried out in simulations. Research on real fires and emergencies is less common. In a series of studies, Canter, Breaux, and Sime (1990) carried out detailed examination of the behaviours of people that had been involved in fires in different occupancies: domestic buildings, multiple occupancies (hostels and hotels), and hospitals. Using people's accounts and questionnaires they were able to study the *sequence* of behaviour of people involved in fires. Analysing sequences rather than single actions is important, because, as fires are dynamic and changing, what is important is not just the frequency of behaviours, but when they occur and the order in which they occur. This approach also fits with the idea of scripts and event schema. Using this method their research revealed a coherent model of behaviour consistent across different settings.

DOMESTIC SETTINGS

Canter et al. (1990) examined 14 *Domestic Fires* involving 41 people and 1,189 behaviours. Although there is some variation in each incident, the pattern is remarkably consistent. They found that, typically, occupants were in bed when the fire began. Like many emergencies, the start of the incident tended to be ambiguous, with occupants hearing noises. The ambiguity of the initial cues led to delays in anyone acting. Eventually, the occupant or one of the occupants would investigate. Usually, they would enter the room the noise was coming from and encounter the fire. Of course, once a fire is generating enough heat to create loud sounds, it is usually dangerous to enter the room and too late to fight the fire.

The research revealed clear gender role-related differences in behaviour. Men were the most likely to misinterpret the initial fire cues, and delay taking action. Women responded more quickly, except if they were with a male, in which case they were be delayed by their interaction with him. Once the occupants decided there was a problem, males and females were equally likely to investigate. On being informed of the fire there was tendency for the other person to check the situation; however, if the male was informed of the fire by a female, he was more likely to go to the site of the fire himself than would a female informed by a male.

From the point that the fire is encountered there is greater variability in behaviour, which is partly a consequence of the stage of the fire's development. What people do then also depends on their gender. Women tend to warn others, wait for help, or seek assistance. They are also more likely to close the door where the fire is and leave the house, after informing others if they are there. Men, however, are more likely to attempt to fight the fire. Interestingly, the behaviour of neighbours is also gender related with males being more likely to attempt to search the building, even moving through smoke, and will try to rescue anyone that is there.

The conclusions drawn by Canter and his colleagues confirmed research by Wood (1990), who examined nearly a thousand fires, 50% of which were in dwellings. He identified the three most frequent reactions to a fire were evacuation, fire-fighting, and warning and alerting others or the fire service. When the fire was most serious people would tend to leave the building, if less serious they would attempt to fight it. He also found gender differences in people's first action on finding the fire, with women being more likely to warn others, leave the building immediately, ask for help, or evacuate their family. Women were less likely to fight the fire or minimise the risk. Men were also more likely to go into smoke in a building.

What is already clear from the description of domestic fires is that there is a logical sequence of events, which involves interpretation, decision-making, and action. The behaviour also maintains its connections with behaviour under normal circumstances, for instance with gender roles being continued throughout the incident. In the next section we will consider multiple occupancy buildings, such as hotels, which show how people behave in different, but still coherent ways.

MULTIPLE OCCUPANCY PROPERTIES

Behaviour in multiple occupancies becomes slightly more complex because of the greater number of people who are potentially involved and the greater range of relationships there are with the environment. Canter and his colleagues (1990) examined eight multiple occupancy fires, involving 96 people. The start of an incident is again characterised by ambiguity and misinterpretation resulting in delayed action. Eventually someone will investigate the source of the fire cues and encounter the fire. The typical response is for that person to return to their original room. Once there, they will either wait, or dress and gather any valuables they have.

While that is the typical sequence, there is more variety than in domestic fires. That is because there is a greater number of possibilities for action, ways in which the fire can be detected, and the variety of roles occupied by the people involved. The presence of staff means that guests hearing noises might assume it is something usual or is being dealt with and so not investigate. If they do encounter the fire they will be unaware of whether it has already been reported and they may be reluctant to set off a fire alarm at night. Those concerns are not relevant in domestic fires. The presence of other people can explain why someone would return to get dressed and to collect their valuables. They might wait because they expect the staff are managing the response to the fire and that they will be informed if it is necessary to evacuate. In domestic fires returning to the original room only happened if there was someone else there to warn. Occupants in domestic fires did not return to their bedroom and wait. In the multiple occupancies there is no attempt to fight the fire. Compared to other settings, it tended to take longer for people in multiple occupancies to be alerted to the fire.

HOSPITALS

Before moving on to look at one disaster in more detail, it is interesting to consider hospitals. In their 1990 study Canter and colleagues examined six hospital fires. The detection of a fire in a hospital is usually early compared to domestic and multiple occupancies. This is probably because there is staff on duty 24 hours a day who tend to move around the building. Once a fire is detected in a hospital, the transfer of information is highly specified. For example, senior nurses are informed, they then typically investigate further. Information is rapidly relayed to more junior staff, who carry out their directed actions. While the organisational structure and clear roles in hospitals can help to manage a fire, delays can occur because of the hierarchy. There is also a greater complexity because of organisational factors, but that complexity does not seem to increase threat – probably because of design and training. Danger can be a function of communication levels and members of staff who have a pivotal role. Failure at a senior level can result in an inadequate response and delay, potentially leading to catastrophic outcomes. Comparing hospitals with multiple occupancies shows how, in hospitals, there are clear, specified functional communications between roles that are not present in the other settings.

Training is one reason hospital fires are usually dealt with effectively. One way of thinking about that training is in terms the concepts of scripts and schema. What in effect people are doing is developing event-appropriate behavioural scripts that can be applied to an incident rather than relying on everyday scripts. Once the staff switches from its everyday script to one appropriate for emergencies there is a clear pattern of behaviours for them to follow.

GENERAL MODEL OF BEHAVIOUR IN FIRES

Although there are clear differences between all these settings in how people behave, it is possible to propose a general model of

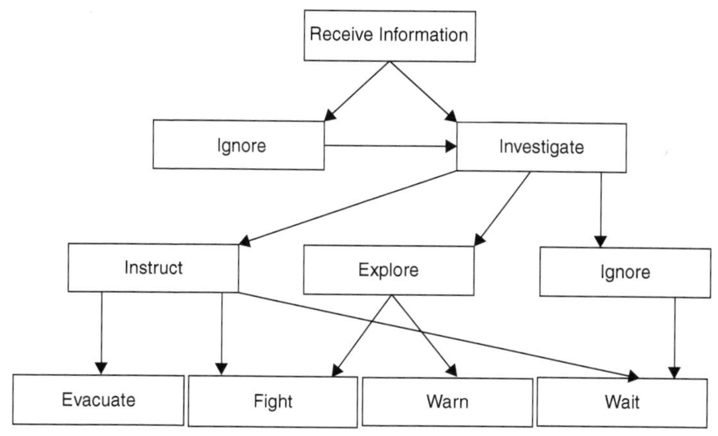

Figure 4.1 General Model of Behaviour during Fires (from Canter et al., 1990).

behaviour in fires, which can, with minor modification, be applied to other incidents. The model is shown in Figure 4.1. It is possible that it also applies to how people deal with terrorist attacks, which is a fruitful avenue for further research. There are three stages to the model proposed by Canter et al. (1990): interpret, prepare, and act. All behaviour in fires begins with the *interpret* stage and with receiving information, which can be fire cues such as smoke, an alarm, or instructions from another person. Once cues are detected they will be ignored or investigated. Of course, if ignoring the cues is the first action, it will at some point change to investigation. The time between receiving information and acting can be crucial in defining the outcome.

At the next stage, people *prepare*. They will instruct others, explore further, or leave. Which action they take will depend on the individual circumstance, including whether a person is alone. The path a person follows at this point onwards will be influenced by their role. In the final stage people *act*. They either evacuate, fight the fire (then evacuate), warn, or wait before engaging in one of the other actions. Again, circumstances will influence these options. For instance, the longer it takes to become aware of the fire, the less likely it is that there will be an option to fight the fire (Wood, 1990). Role and occupancy are relevant to the *act* stage. For instance, as mentioned above, a person who is a guest in a hotel is more likely to wait for further instructions than they would be in a domestic house fire.

Naturally the model does not capture the complexities and subtleties of individual fires, but it does provide a structure for understanding behaviour. Which options a person takes through the routes in the model will depend on the context of the fire. It can also be seen from the model that as the sequence of behaviours develops, along with the fire's progression, the number of options and the complexity increases. Importantly, the model emphasises that behaviour has a clear structure and is therefore not irrational and uncontrolled. That is further demonstrated in the complex example of the King's Cross Underground fire, which we will look at now, in the final part of the chapter.

KINGS CROSS UNDERGROUND STATION FIRE: A CASE STUDY

A major fire took place in King's Cross underground station in London in November 1987. The fire killed 31 people and caused injury, including some which were life changing, to over a hundred others. The subsequent inquiry into the disaster was unusual in commissioning evidence from psychologists, asking them to examine people's behaviour before, during, and after the fire (Canter, Donald & Wood, 1988). This gave rare access to witness statements, expert testimony, and the witnesses themselves. The examination of the data confirmed the findings of previous research, as well as providing some new insights. It allowed psychologists to piece together the behaviour of those caught up in the fire, including that of those who lost their lives. In the next sections we will look at first-hand narratives given by people shortly after being involved in the fire. They provide a case study and illustration of some of the concepts that have been used to explain people's behaviour in a way that adds some reality to the theory.

King's Cross underground station is one of the largest and most complex on the London Underground system. At the time of the fire, it had five underground lines feeding into it, along with two major main line stations and what was then called the Midland over ground line, now Thames Link. To accommodate all these lines, the station is built on five levels. In 1987 around 250,000 passengers passed through the main ticket hall each day. The station had no evacuation plan, most staff had no emergency training, and communications technology was rudimentary. For instance, British Transport Police had to return to the surface to use their radios to communicate during the incident. There were of course no mobile 'phones' in 1987. The fire started on an escalator from the Piccadilly line that went up into the ticket hall. It is thought that a dropped match or cigarette igniting oil, grease, and debris beneath the wooden escalator was the cause.

Because of the numbers of people involved and the complexity of the setting, there were several different types of cues to the fire, which people considered when deciding what to do. Some of these are mentioned in the statements reproduced here. The statements show that people actively interpret their surroundings, and that cues go beyond the direct physical products of the fire, demonstrating a detailed and complex decision-making process. Indicators of the fire included the behaviour of other people, changes in the environment not directly associated with the fire (e.g., gates being closed), presence of specialised staff (e.g., police), what other people said, physical products of the fire, and instructions given by authority figures (Donald & Canter, 1990, 1992).

FIRE CHRONOLOGY

Because of the complexity of the station, a description of the dynamics of the event is also complicated. It is therefore worth reading fuller accounts of the disaster and people's behaviour (Donald & Canter, 1990, 1992). It is nonetheless useful to have a summary to at least provide a little context and a timeline.

7.29 PM	Passengers alert a booking clerk to the fire on an escalator, he alerts the station inspector. Flames are only inches above the treads of the escalator.
7.30	Passenger presses the escalator stop button. A ticket inspector and two transport police investigate.
7.32	The fire brigade is called.

7.36	Passengers are diverted away from the burning escalator, up another bank of escalators, which also go into the ticket hall.
7.39	Police decide to evacuate the ticket hall (ten minutes after initial alert).
7.40	Top of the burning escalator is cordoned off. Passengers are still entering ticket hall.
7.41	Staff stop selling tickets. Staff told to 'non-stop' trains.
7.42	Some gates in ticket hall are closed. A Northern Line train lets off over 50 passengers.
7.43	People are being directed off the platforms and up alternative escalators, into the ticket hall. Piccadilly line train lets off passengers (last to do so).
7.44	Booking staff leave the ticket hall. Not all workers are evacuated.
7.45	**FLASHOVER**. Ticket hall and underground passages engulfed in smoke and flame. People are still going up via escalators into ticket hall.
7.48	Northern Line trains are no longer stopping at the station.

We can see that there is early action by the public, but quite slow action by officials after the initial examination of the fire and after calling the fire brigade. It is ten minutes after the alert is given that the evacuation begins. As fires develop very quickly, that delay is significant. People are evacuated from the ticket hall and station, but at no point are people stopped from entering, making evacuation pointless except for staff. Trains continue to drop off passengers until after the fire explodes. In effect, with relatively minor adjustments, the station runs almost normally while officials are dealing with the evacuation and fire. The station is an interesting setting, in that with the exception of those who work there, if people are stopped from entering, the station will quite quickly empty naturally by passengers catching trains.

BEHAVIOUR AT KING'S CROSS UNDERGROUND FIRE

In this section we will consider excerpts from the accounts of witness to the disaster, some of whom escaped with just seconds to spare. The accounts are people's own words as given in statements to the British Transport Police and the Inquiry. They illustrate some of the points already made, and others will introduce issues not yet covered.

This first account shows the remarkable persistence people will display in the face of fire cues, and the thought processes as they try to interpret the cues and understand what is happening. We can see from this that the witness continues his original intentions in the face of growing evidence of a problem. We can also see how he tries to interpret what is happening. There are two further points worth noting from this. One is that he describes other's behaviour as panic, but does not say what they are actually doing. There were no examples of people panicking. He also looks to see what other people are doing. He notes that no one looked concerned. So, he is looking to others to decide how serious the incident is and what he should be doing. Presumably others are looking at him for the same reason.

This account is not atypical and is representative of what most people would do.

> . . .I became aware of smoke. It was a thin grey layer . . .clearly visible. At this point people did not seem too concerned . . . on turning left it was quite apparent that there (was) a more serious problem ahead of me. Smoke was certainly thicker and more dense ahead. I kept walking still intent on making my way to St. Pancras . . .As I walked along this subway, smoke was getting thicker and more dense. I began to feel that the smoke was affecting my eyes and getting into my throat. At this stage I could hear a lot of general shouting and general panic coming from the booking hall ahead. I stopped and quickly considered what I was going to do. The situation was getting worse and worse. . .the area of the main booking hall was dense with thick black smoke. I did not see any flame at any time. People were hurrying to exit the booking hall area. I decided to quickly walk back the way I had come. . .I would say the area was fairly crowded. People had begun to run past me. . .there may have been upwards of fifty or sixty people in the area at this time. I turned and exited the subway via the steps leading up to the front of the main station. . .I waited around . . .at the top of these steps. . .Smoke was literally billowing out from the exit. . .

In the next illustration we can again see cue interpretation and conversations around decision-making. As we know, research often shows that, when evacuated, people will attempt to leave by the way they entered a setting, even if that is not the closest route. This witness gives his thinking behind making that choice. The statement also shows us that people will consider, as part of their interpretation, the possibility that the emergency had passed.

> We got to the entrance, there was absolutely no indication of anything wrong. . .it was not until we had nearly reached the semi-circular passage that I realised that things were not normal as it was here that I smelt smoke. . .I looked to my left along the passageway towards King's Cross Station and I saw the smoke I had smelt. . .I could see four or five people . . .they seemed stationary as if trying to make up their minds about what to do. . .it was quite obvious that there was, or there had been very recently, a small fire. I went down the steps to the closed gates with (a friend) flowing closely behind, to try and work out what was happening and where the fire had been or might be, in order to take the appropriate action. . .(a period of time elapses) I said to (his friend) 'this is obviously more serious than we thought' and we agreed that we should get out as quickly as possible. . .it was a conscious decision on my part to go back to the surface the way we came in as I knew this way was clear of locked gates etc, and I said to (friend) 'it would be best to go the way we came' or words to that effect.

In the next statement the witness explicitly mentions people's lack of panic, which she sees as supporting her conclusion that everything is normal. Again, the witness assumes the incident has passed.

> As I entered the ticket hall the atmosphere was hazy with what appeared to be grey smoke. The whole ticket hall was covered in this hazy smoke, but visibility wasn't impaired. Everything looked normal and there were no signs of panic. I was going to go down the Piccadilly line escalator, but, decided that there must have been a fire somewhere below. So I decided not to use the underground. . . when I decided not to travel, I turned around and made my way to the St Pancras Road exit. As I walked along this passageway 4 or 5 people passed me going into the booking hall. . .nobody followed me out of that subway.

The evidence given by another witness who is told there is a fire in the station shows the idea that people continue to follow their routine behaviour and intentions even in the face of a clear incident. The passage in which he stops to make the phone call is part of the station and is where several people died moments later.

> The police officer said words to the effect 'could you please get off the platform, there is a fire on the station.' Upon hearing this I picked up

> my bag and left the platform. . .while walking across the ticket hall I felt large gusts of heat although the heat was not immense. There were a lot of people both in front and behind me. Whilst in this passage I picked up one of the wall 'phones intending to 'phone my wife. I put a 10p piece into the slot but left the 'phone because the smoke became thicker. The visibility became like dense fog.

The final example comes from one of the female toilet attendants in the station. This demonstrates the informality of the communications, and the way in which she continues to perform her role and fulfil its obligations. She also, as most people would, takes the time to collect her belongings. This witness avoided being trapped in the fire by a matter of seconds.

> One of the male attendants came to me and said . . .'I think we may need to get out." Mr . . .then turned around, and walked out. He didn't say where we should get out. I got up and followed him, and he went back to the male toilet. Whilst at the entrance to the female toilets I saw smoke and people coming up from the direction of the tube station. On seeing this I went back inside the female toilets, and got my coat and my bag, locked my locker, and then came out. I was going to lock up, but changed my mind. At this time there was no smoke in the toilets, and there were no persons in the toilets. When I came out of the toilets into the main corridor leading to the surface, I couldn't see a thing. The smoke was thick and pitch black. I joined the crowd making their way to the surface.

FATALITIES OF THE DISASTER

The access researchers had to the information around the fire allowed them to examine the actions of the fatalities (Donald & Canter, 1992). From cross-referencing witness statements, forensic details, and knowledge of the initial intentions of those who were killed, it was possible to put together a reasonable account of what they were likely to have been doing when they died. This is useful because it allows us to know if there is anything about the behaviour of those who died, which might be distinct from those who survived. The research showed that there is a clear pattern to the location in which people died and what they were originally intending to do in the station. It reveals most people continued with their original intention even up until the point of death. Locations also suggest that some of the people who died were queuing in an orderly way to exit the station though the ticket barriers. People tended to continue to their originally intended destination via their intended route. Finally, it is also apparent that victims working in the station continued to fulfil their roles and obligations. None of the evidence shows any indication of panic amongst the victims. Like the survivors, those who died behaved in a structured and controlled way that had continuity with their normal behaviour. The difference between survivors and victims was not different behaviour, just the time that it was carried out.

MEDIA REPORTS

It is interesting to contrast the witness statements from the disaster with media accounts. It is particularly instructive to read those that were given after the initial shock of the fire and after the findings of the inquiry were known and had been much discussed. *The Guardian*, 16 years after the fire, for instance, describes "*panic-stricken commuters*" showing the insistence of media reports in describing panic behaviour, when the official inquiry clearly shows that no such behaviour took place. There was also no evidence of panicking people hammering on the doors of trains hurriedly moving through the station, as the media describe, although some trains did stop at the station and not open their doors. Others did pass through the station without stopping, some after the main fire had engulfed the ticket hall. At least two people who died in the fire had alighted from trains that had stopped after the underground management had been alerted to the fire.

FINALLY

A number of general conclusions can be drawn about people's behaviour when facing life-threatening incidents. People often fail to recognise danger and often delay in taking action. The idea of people panicking and being uncontrollable does not fit the data; instead, it is evident that people will maintain what they *perceive* to be appropriate behaviour during an emergency, and although people's behaviour may seem bizarre and inappropriate from the outside, it nonetheless emerges from a coherent and socially supported framework. Socially understood roles and rules are followed even in extreme conditions. A person's importance in an event is often a function of their organisational position or role. Finally, as we have seen already, and will see again in future chapters, people do not passively respond to the environment, they actively interpret what is happening around them and behave on that basis.

REFERENCES

Abelson, R. P. (1976). Script processing in attitude formation and decision making. In J. S. Carroll & J.W. Payne (eds.), *Cognition and Social Behavior.* Hillsdale: Erlbaum.

Auf der Heide, E. (2004). Common misconceptions about disasters: Panic, the "Disaster Syndrome," and looting. In M. R. O'Leary (ed.), *The First 72 Hours: A Community Approach to Disaster Preparedness* (pp. 340–380). New York: iUniverse, Inc.

Canter, D., Breaux J., & Sime J. (1990). Domestic, multiple occupancy and hospital fires. In D. Canter (ed.), *Fires and Human Behaviour: Second Edition* (pp. 117–136). London: David Fulton.

Canter, D., Comber, M., & Uzzell, D.L. (1989). *Football in Its Place: An Environmental Psychology of Football Grounds.* London: Routledge.

Canter, D., Donald, I., & Wood, P. (1988). *Behavioural and psychological aspects of the fire at King's Cross Station.* Invited report to the Fennell Investigation into the King's Cross Underground Fire. University of Surrey, Guildford.

Cole, J., Walters, M., & Lynch, M. (2011). Part of the solution, not the problem: The crowd's role in emergency response. *Journal of the Academy of Social Sciences*, 6(3), 361–375.

Donald, I., & Canter, D. (1990). Behavioural aspects of the King's Cross disaster. In D. Canter (ed.), *Fires and Human Behaviour: Second Edition* (pp. 15–30). London: David Fulton.

Donald, I., & Canter, D. (1992). Intentionality and fatality during the King's Cross Underground fire. *European Journal of Social Psychology*, 22, 203–218.

Drury, J., Carter, H., Cocking, C., Ntontis, E., Guven, S., & Amlot, R. (2019). Facilitating collective psychosocial resilience in the public in emergencies: Twelve recommendations based on the Social Identity approach. *Frontiers in Public Health,* 7, June, 1–21.

Drury, J., Cocking, C., & Richer, S. (2009a). Everyone for themselves? A comparative study of crowd solidarity among emergency survivors. *British Journal of Social Psychology*, 48, 487–506.

Drury, J., Cocking, C., & Richer, S. (2009b). The nature of collective resilience: Survivor reactions to the 2005 London bombings. *International Journal of Mass Emergencies and Disasters*, 27(1), 66–95.

Drury, J., Novelli, D., & Stott, C. (2013). Psychological disaster myths in the perception and management of mass emergencies. *Journal of Applied Social Psychology*, 43(11), 2259–2270.

Fayol, M., & Monteil, J-M. (1988). The notion of script: From general to developmental psychology. *Cahiers de Psychologie Cognitive*, 8, 335–361.

Fiske, S. T., & Taylor, S. E. (1991). *Social Cognition: Second Edition*. London: McGraw-Hill.

Fridolf, K., & Nilsson, D. (2011). People's subjective estimation of fire growth: An experimental study of young adults. *Fire Safety Science – Proceedings of the Tenth International Symposium*, (pp. 161–172). International Association for Fire Safety Science.

Latané, B. & Darley, J. M. (1968). Group inhibition of bystander intervention in emergencies. *Journal of Personality and Social Psychology*, 10, 215–221.

Leach, J. (2004). Why people "freeze" in an emergency: Temporal and cognitive constraints on survival responses. *Aviation, Space, and Environmental Medicine*, 75, 539–42.

Mintz, A. (1951). Non-adaptive group behaviour. *Journal of Abnormal and Social Psychology*, 46, 150–159.

Nogami, T. (2018). Disaster myths among disaster response professionals and the source of such misconceptions. *Journal of Contingencies and Crisis Management*, 26, 491–498.

Nogami, T. (2020). Negative misconceptions about disaster behaviour through availability cascades: An examination of secondhand information and the moderating effect of trait anxiety on disaster myths. *Journal of Community and Applied Social Psychology*, 30, 369–380.

Nogami, T. & Yoshida, F. (2014). Disaster myths after the Great East Japan Disaster and the effects of information sources on belief in such myths. *Disasters*, 38(2), 190–205.

Quarantelli, E. L. (1954). The nature and conditions of panic. *American Journal of Sociology*, 60(3), 267–275.

Quarantelli, E. L. (1960). Images of withdrawal behavior in disasters: Some basic misconceptions. *Social Problems*, 8, 68–79.

Quarantelli, E. L. & Dynes, R. R. (1970). Introduction: Special issue on organizational and group behavior in disaster. *American Behavioral Scientist*, 13(3), 325–330.

Sime, J. (1980). The concept of panic. In D. Canter (ed.), *Fires and Human Behaviour* (pp. 63–81). Chichester: Wiley.

Sime, J. (1985). Designing for people or bal-bearings?. *Design Studies*, 6(3), 163–168.

Sime, J. (1990). The concept of panic. In D. Canter (ed.), *Fires and Human Behaviour: Second Edition* (pp. 63–82). London: David Fulton.

Turner, J. C. (1981). Towards a cognitive redefinition of the social group. *Cahiers de Psychologie Cognitive*, 1(2), 93–118.

Wenger, D. E., James, T. F., & Faupel, C. E. (1985). *Disaster Beliefs and Emergency Planning*. New York: Irvington.

Wood, P. G. (1990). A survey of behaviour in fries. In D. Canter (ed.), *Fires and Human Behaviour: Second Edition* (pp. 83–96). London: David Fulton.

FURTHER READING

The classic book on behaviour in fires is Canter's edited volume,

Canter, D. (Ed.) (1990). *Fires and Human Behaviour: Second Edition*. London: David Fulton.

A good overview of myths about disaster behaviour and accounts from disasters can be found in Auf der Heide's chapter, which can, at the time of writing, be downloaded from the internet: https://www.atsdr.cdc.gov/emergency_response/common_misconceptions.pdf

Auf der Heide, E. (2004). Common misconceptions about disasters: Panic, the "Disaster Syndrome," and looting. In M. R. O'Leary (ed.), *The First 72 Hours: A Community Approach to Disaster Preparedness* (pp. 340–380). New York: iUniverse, Inc.

5

CRIME, ENVIRONMENT, AND GEOGRAPHICAL PROFILING

INTRODUCTION

In this chapter we will consider three main themes: the weather and crime; built environment, design, and crime; and serial offenders' spatial behaviour, often used in geographical profiling. These three areas are useful to look at as they represent different ways in which the environment is linked to crime. In the first, crime is generally seen as being, in some way, caused by the environment. In the second example, there may be causal elements, but in the main the environment is seen as offering opportunities for crime. In this case, the environment facilitates or inhibits the commission of an offence. The third theme looks at the way criminals use the environment and how this can give clues that can help police and other agencies with their investigation and possible apprehension of the perpetrator.

CRIME AND THE WEATHER

Although the twentieth century began with some historically important sociological work on crime and the environment (Burgess, 1925; Shaw & McKay, 1942), it was in the 1960s that significant and widespread interest in the relationship between crime and the environment grew. A series of riots in the USA sparked curiosity about the role of the environment in generating crime. From 1965, and peaking in 1967, there were 159 riots in cities across the country. The unrest was primarily related to race, but because the most serious riots took place at the height of summer, interest grew in

DOI: 10.4324/9780429274541-5

the influence of weather on crime. The period of the riots became known as the long hot summer.

So fascinated were the public that the official report from the National Advisory Commission on Civil Disorders (The Kerner Commission), which investigated the riots, sold more than two million copies. The Commission blamed social and economic conditions and white racism for the riots. It also briefly noted in the report that most riots began on days with a temperature of over 80 degrees Fahrenheit (27°C); but it also concluded that there was no strong evidence that the weather had played a significant part in causing the riots. Despite that, a popular belief developed that the weather played a causal role. The legacy of that view still has currency today. For instance, the weather was also speculated on as a factor in the riots in UK cities during August 2011. As with the US riots 50 years earlier, giving the weather a role in triggering the riots provided a useful distraction from the social and economic explanations. In 2020 there was also some conjecture that people would break the Covid-19 lockdown rules in the UK if the summer were hot. Although it was a hot summer, most people continued to follow the rules.

The implications of there being a link between warmer weather and crime are going to gain more significance with global warming and climate change. If the predictions from some areas of research on weather and crime are correct, projected warming will cause a significant increase in crime. The research estimates, made for the USA, result in an *additional* 22,000 murders, 180,000 rapes, 1.2 million assaults, 1.3 million burglaries, and 2.2 million larceny cases (Ranson, 2014). It is likely that this calculation over-estimates the relationships between crime and the weather; nonetheless, even if the parameters are adjusted, there will still be a significant effect that will require resource and resilience.

When suggesting a link between crime and the environment, including the weather, it is important that there is a strong and convincing explanation or theory to account for the relationship. This is especially the case when studies are correlational, as many are. Several broad theories have been proposed to explain a possible relationship between the weather and offending. Environmental economists Horrocks and Menclova (2011) provide a concise and useful summary of these. Generally though, we can divide theories or models into those looking at some form of causal basis of behaviour, so for instance temperature causing arousal which, in turn, leads to violent acts, and theories that can be considered situational, where the environment provides opportunities for crime. Causal theories usually look for some form of underlying mechanism for behaviour, such as physiological arousal. The situational theories examine the context of crimes and how that provides the conditions for people to offend.

The *Negative Affect Escape (NAE) Model* (Bell & Baron, 1976) specifically focuses on the relationship between temperature and behaviour, primarily violent crime. In the model, increasing heat leads to increased aggression and violence. However, once the temperature and discomfort reach a high level, the motive to be aggressive is replaced by a motive to get away, to escape. This relationship between temperature and crime is described as an inverted-U curve, with temperature being on the x-axis and aggression on the y-axis. There has been a long-running discussion about whether the curve is this shape, or whether it is linear, which would show that people keep getting more aggressive as temperature rises. The linear idea can be found in the *General Affect Model (GAM)* proposed (Cohn & Rotton, 2000), which is in essence the same as Bell and Baron's (1976), but with a continued positive temperature-aggression relationship; it never gets too hot to be aggressive.

One of the problems with both the GAM and the NAE models is that they do not explain *why* people get more aggressive as temperature rises, other than, for instance, hot weather creates discomfort, which facilitates aggression. Anderson (2001) states that the most powerful explanations "*all revolve around the 'crankiness' notion. Being uncomfortable colors the way people see things*" (p. 36). It is likely that some form of stress is involved, but how that might work has not yet clearly been shown. Currently, both the NAE model and GAM lack a more robust explanation of the underlying psychological or biological mechanisms linking temperature and behaviour.

Despite a lot of research testing these models, it remains unclear whether aggression increases in a linear way or rises to a maximum level after which it falls off. More fundamentally, it is not clear that there is any relationship at all between temperature and *crime*, as opposed to feelings of aggression. Some studies support a temperature-crime link while others do not. Even overviews of the research draw different conclusions, some saying that the evidence is clear that there is a relationship, and that it is causal (Anderson, 2001), with others concluding that the evidence is unclear. In her overview of relevant research, Cohn (1990) found five studies that showed a relationship between temperature and crime and 15 that did not. The explanation for the contradictory findings is most likely methodological differences.

The methodological weaknesses identified in the studies include a lack of precision in defining different variables, poor measurement, and inappropriate or inadequate statistical analysis (Cohn, 1990). Different studies define the weather using different metrics, some for instance use a simple binary system of, in essence, hot-not hot, while others use more precise temperatures. The time scales over which measurements are made also vary a lot, occasionally being so large that they are psychologically, almost meaningless. For example, in one study, Michael and Zumpe (1983a, b) looked at the relationship between temperature and murder in 16 locations in the USA. Although they found a positive, significant correlation between temperature and crime, the data were for annual mean temperature and annual homicide rate at city and state levels; consequently, we have no detail about the nature and circumstances of the crimes. They also report that the three locations with the highest temperature (Los Angeles, Puerto Rico, and Texas) also had the highest homicide rates, but there was no significant relationship between *monthly* temperature and homicides in 13 of the 16 locations they looked at. Despite this, the study is often presented as supporting an environment-crime relationship without comment or a caveat. In another example, DeFronzo (1984) also took a very broad approach, correlating the annual number homicides rates with the number of 'days hot' in those years (Cohn, 1990).

The difficulty these and some other studies using gross measurement give us is that we do not know if the crimes actually took place on the hottest days, or at the hottest times of day or during the cooler evenings. Looking at homicide, even when committed on the same day there might be time lags between an offender deciding to murder someone and them doing it. In that process, it is not clear where or when the weather would be having the decisive effect. Of course, this also assumes the person committing crime is exposed to the heat and not inside a well air-conditioned building.

There can also be issues with the statistics used in weather–crime research. For instance, with a lot of variables in an analysis we would expect some statistically significant relationships to appear by chance rather than because of a genuine link. Banziger and Owens (1978) found a correlation between weather and dysfunctional behaviour, but out of 128 correlations, only 13 were statistically significant, some of which would be expected by chance. Further, the variables that predicted crime were not consistent and were different in each city. The authors themselves acknowledge the difficulties of weather research, writing, "predicting. . .from weather data. . .cannot be done in any useful way with the available tools and information" (p. 433).

The research leaves us with quite an ambiguous picture on the causal relationship between weather and crime. Overall, there is *probably* some relationship between temperature and interpersonal crime. In summarising her assessment of studies of crime and the weather, Cohn (1990) concludes that

> It appears that assaults, burglary, collective violence, domestic violence and rape tend to increase with ambient temperature . . .High temperatures do not appear to be correlated with robbery, larceny, and motor vehicle theft . . .property crimes are not strongly related to temperature changes.
>
> (p. 61)

She goes on to add that there may be mediating variables that explain the relationships. For instance, alcohol consumption increases in warm weather, and people take more vacation and leisure time, which might be contributing factors. The role of alcohol is obvious, but that of leisure and vacation is less so; however, it usually means spending time with family and friends, and as Cohn points out, the majority of violent crimes occur between or within these groups.

The variables mediating between weather and crime, which Cohn refers to in her review, indicate *situational* explanations of the link (Clarke & Cornish, 1985; Smith & Clarke, 2012). These approaches emphasise the social and environmental conditions that facilitate crime rather than direct psychological or physiological changes that might be brought about by the weather. There are several situational theories or approaches, including crime prevention through environmental design, which we consider in more detail later. One of the most useful theories for thinking about weather and crime is Routine Activity Theory (RAT) (Cohen & Felson 1979). This approach emphasises the social context of crime and sees lawbreaking as arising out of normal behaviour. It proposes that because more people are out and on the streets during warm weather, there are likely to be more encounters and more opportunity for interpersonal and other crime. Add to that the possibility that people might be drinking more alcohol outside during warm weather, and it is easy to see how there could be an increase in crime, and especially violent offences. There could also be an effect on property crime because people are outside and so there are more empty properties, providing more burglary opportunities.

Within the framework of RAT, a crime requires three things: a motivated offender, a suitable target, and the absence of a suitable 'guardian' (Cohen & Felson 1979). Note that the offender already must be motivated to commit a crime. The weather does not turn a non-criminal into a criminal. There is some natural balance in this system that results in checks or breaks on crime too. The increased number of potential guardians, or witnesses, who will also be outside, will counter the increased opportunity resulting from the greater availability of potential victims. Consequently, the possibility for crime increases, but so does the chances of being caught, or at least observed. Another way of looking at this is as costs and benefits, which is the final model we will look at.

These theories attempt to explain crime in general rather than specifically linking crime and weather. The *cost-benefit model* proposed by Becker (1968) and Rational Choice Theory (RCT) (Cornish & Clarke, 1986, 2006) argue that a criminal will weigh the benefits of committing a crime, such as gaining money, against the costs of committing that crime. Included in those costs will be, for instance, the chances of being caught and the kind of sentence they might get if they are. Benefits can include the amount of money they might make or the pleasure they derive from the act. If the perceived benefits are greater than the perceived loss, the potential offender will, logically, commit the crime. Of course, there are moral issues involved in making those decisions too (Mehlkop & Graeff, 2010). Within this theory the environment is significant to the extent it facilitates benefit or influences cost. One suggested flaw is that the theory is quite limited in explaining crime that does not result in reward, such as assault, other violent crimes, and vandalism. However, it could be argued that the perpetrator might gain pleasure from committing a violent act and that the intrinsic reward is sufficient to motivate them (Anderson, 1989).

There are several other characteristics of weather that have been explored in relation to crime. These have included the amount of sunlight, atmospheric temperature, barometric pressure, relative humidity, wind velocity, cloudiness, change in temperature, snow, rain, visibility, sky cover, and fog. The relationship between these factors and crime tends to be even more ambiguous than that of temperature. They also often suffer similar methodological weaknesses. One of the issues with some of the research is not taking context sufficiently into account. Experience of environmental conditions will vary over time and context. The same objective weather condition will be experienced differently at different times and in different situations. For instance, wind speed might be positive in the summer (a cooling breeze), yet the same wind velocity might be negative in the winter (a cutting chill). This emphasises that it is not the absolute environmental stimulus that matters, but rather the context of the stimulus and how it is experienced. In other words, assuming a reasonably simple deterministic relationship between weather conditions and crime is not likely to yield definitive or valid results.

What we can say about the weather and crime is that some temperature effect is found for interpersonal crimes such as homicide, rape, domestic violence, and assault. The same effects tend not to be found for property crimes such as burglary or theft. Despite the origins of interest in the weather-crime relationship being in riots and protest, effects are not found for political action, uprisings, assassinations, and political coups. Interpersonal crime is likely to be affected because, generally, people interact more when it is warm, which provides more opportunity for something to go wrong. However, this may be exacerbated by other factors related to the physiological impact of heat on our biological systems.

CRIME AND ENVIRONMENTAL DESIGN

Situational crime prevention is a fruitful and interesting area of inquiry that examines the designed environment and crime, and includes practical solutions to crime. The idea that the built environment causes, or at least encourages, crime has held quite a lot of currency, and still underlies some government policy and research. The opposite side of that coin is the idea that you can use the environment for preventing crime. In effect, that you can 'design crime away'. When looking at this area the focus is on crime being facilitated or inhibited by the environment. Naturally, the aim of crime prevention is to inhibit criminal action.

A lot of what is included in crime and design can be conceptualised as *target hardening*. This way of stopping crime has been popular with policy makers and organisations, as well individuals in domestic surroundings. Target hardening mainly consists of installing environmental features that make committing a crime more difficult or detection more likely. It can include locks, gates, barriers, CCTV, and alarms. Many of these measures also make people feel secure, though they do not necessarily make them safer.

Target hardening is sometimes discreet, especially in public places. In other circumstances it is much more obvious. There are many reasons for preferring one over the other. The obvious presence of protection can make people feel more secure, or more threatened if they think they are in a target area. Discreet measures are less likely to result in that kind of fear and may well be aesthetically more pleasing in some contexts. However, if the aim is to discourage would-be criminals or terrorists from even attempting an offence, very discreet measures might lose their deterrent role.

Many public places have been hardened to prevent terrorist attacks, particularly those involving the driving of vehicles into pedestrians or buildings. Some of these are obvious, as well as aesthetically unattractive. For instance, the barriers along Westminster Bridge in London, installed after a terrorist attack, or those in front of the Houses of Parliament are unsightly with no attempt to disguise their purpose. Examples of subtler, discreet, hardening can also be found in other public places. An international train station in Kent, which serves the line from London to continental Europe, for instance, has several hardening measures. The surrounding landscaping includes pleasant undulating lawn areas in front of the station building that would prevent vehicles from being driven at speed towards the station. Attractive planters that are substantial, and spaced less than a vehicle width apart are also found on site. All of these environmental features harden the environment and increase the effort required for criminals. There are also other subtler, related approaches to reducing crime through design.

DEFENSIBLE SPACE

Oscar Newman's ideas on 'defensible space' have been influential in thinking about the built environment and crime. Drawing on ideas such as territoriality, which we discussed in Chapter 3, Newman (1973) proposed that there are a range of design features that could reduce crime and people's fear of crime. The basic idea is that the use of real and symbolic barriers and indicators of ownership will deter potential criminals. The symbols can include small or large fences, tidy well-kept gardens, toys in the garden, and a well-maintained property. While some of these might be considered target hardening, such as a high fence, most are not. They do not physically prevent access; rather, they are symbols of possession and territory. Further, Newman proposed that increasing the possibility of surveillance would enhance the deterrent nature of the environment. The forms of surveillance could include a property that can be seen by community members from the street, or one that is overlooked by neighbours. Together, Newman argued, these features would "bring the environment under the control of its residents" (Newman, 1973, p. 3).

Areas around homes, including streets, gardens, the outside of buildings and entrance halls, and corridors within apartment buildings, are considered to be included in defensible space (Newman, 1996). Four distinct physical areas are demarcated in the theory: private, semi-private, semi-public, and public space represent the main zones of ownership and provide a continuum of space that runs from private to public. The aim of defensible space is partly to clearly demarcate each of the zones. Private space might include the inside of a house and the rear garden. Semi-private could be the front garden, and public might be the street. When looking at a block of flats (or apartments), the flats themselves are private but the remainder of the building can be semi-public or public, if there is no clear transition space from the public street to the private apartment.

Without a semi-private area it is difficult for the residents to have ownership and, importantly, to distinguish between those who have legitimate reasons to be in the building and those who do not. The markers of the owned but semi-public areas could be as simple as flowers in an apartment block entrance hall, which signify a sense of ownership of the environment by the residents.

Newman's ideas clearly draw on Jacobs' writing (Jacobs, 1961), and have come under some criticism. Mawby (1977) criticises the work on the basis of what he considers insufficient research and contradictory recommendations made by Newman. For instance, some of the territorial features can prevent observation by neighbours or others. In a study carried out on a Sheffield estate, Mawby noted that some of the concepts were sufficiently vague that some of the same sites could be described as both high and low in defensible space. Forty years later, Mawby (2017) seems to have softened his view on Newman's work, acknowledging its significant influence and contribution to stimulating thinking about environmental design and crime, although he still describes the original work as "essentially, a series of imaginative, exploratory propositions about the influence of design on crime patterns" (Mawby, 2017). Leaving those criticisms aside, in evaluating the concept it would seem that overall, empirically, there is moderate or mild research support for Newman's ideas (Gifford, 2002).

Some interesting research has examined burgled and non-burgled houses as well as burglars' perceptions of properties and their defensible space qualities. In one of these studies Brown and Altman (1983) compared properties that had been burgled and those that had not. They found that those houses that had been burgled had territorial characteristics suggesting openness and the appearance of not being occupied, fitting with Newman's description of vulnerable properties. Those houses that had not been burgled had territorial qualities indicating that they were private, or semi-private, including territorial markers indicating privacy and individuality. The non-burgled houses also had greater visual contact with neighbouring houses, allowing surveillance. The study does seem at least in part to support the ideas of defensible space, but there are significant problems with the research methodology, including up to more than a year delay between the burglary and the defensible space cues being measured.

Brown and Bentley (1993) asked incarcerated burglars to rate pictures of houses that they thought had or had not been burgled. They found that generally burglars could not identify which was which. They did find, however, that the ratings burglars used to classify properties were mainly related to territorial cues and other features of house appearances. Across all homes, the ones perceived as unlikely to be burgled were judged as occupied, difficult to enter, with neighbours who would react, and with residents showing territorial concern. This fits with the ideas of Becker's (1968) cost-benefit model and Cornish and Clarke's (1986) RCT, and reflects some of Newman's ideas. In keeping with RCT the researchers found a small group of burglars explicitly rated houses on a risk to profit ratio. They were more prepared to burgle properties that displayed characteristics that suggested it might be risky if they thought that a successful burglary would result in a significant profit.

The idea that a property displaying characteristics that suggest it is cared for and can result in burglars assessing the property as worth burglarising supports some previous research findings. MacDonald and Gifford (1989) found that while surveillance opportunity was something that burglars' thought would deter them from breaking in, many perceived territorial and symbolic markers that made the property look well cared for also indicate that it might be a high value target. Consequently, they assessed those properties as highly likely to be burgled.

Overall, there is some support for Newman's ideas, primarily for the idea that when passers-by and owners can readily observe a property, it is less likely to be a target for a burglar. Those showing pride of ownership and other symbolic territorial markers might not have a deterrent effect, and may well increase the likelihood that they will be targeted. Despite the mixed results, Newman's research remains influential, and its value is perhaps, as Mawby (2017) suggests, in the debate and interest it has stimulated, particularly through an approach called crime prevention through environmental design.

CRIME PREVENTION THROUGH ENVIRONMENTAL DESIGN

Crime prevention through environmental design (CPTED) can be thought of as a descendant of defensible space. A strong advocate of CPTED, Crowe (2000), has argued that "*the proper design and effective use of the built environment...can lead to a reduction in the fear of crime and the incidence of crime, and to an improvement in the quality of life*" (Crowe, 2000, p. 1). Cozens (2002) directly links CPTED to defensible space saying that they have, however, refined it into a more holistic approach, with CPTED being community based, rather than individualistic. The approach builds on four key strategies of territoriality: natural surveillance, activity support, access control, and effective and continuous maintenance and management. This latter strategy prevents areas becoming derelict and consequently vacant and open to antisocial use. The four components aim to create a community level sense of shared territory around the neighbourhood. The basic ideas of CPTED are found in other approaches beyond defensible space, including target hardening, and broken window theory. An interesting and relatively detailed account of the development of CPTED is given by Cozens (2002), and Reynald (2015), in her review of crime and environmental design, provides an overview including CPTED in the context of other approaches.

The efficacy of CPTED has been researched, with several reviews summarising the findings. An examination of 28 studies of pre- and post-interventions concluded that it is an effective approach to reducing robbery (Casteel & Peek-Asa, 2000). However, a difficulty in assessing the success is that many of the interventions were implemented amongst a number of initiatives, and CPTED was not evaluated independently of other factors that were potentially contributing to robbery risk. Nonetheless, there is sufficient evidence for Reynard (2015) to suggest that the evaluations are promising.

To summarise this section, we can conclude from defensible space theory and CPTED that a property that can be observed by the residents and neighbours is probably less likely to be the subject of burglary, which is also perhaps why houses in cul-de-sacs experience lower burglary risk (Johnson & Bowers, 2010). A property that shows territorial markers and high maintenance is unlikely to deter a burglar but may well signal that the property contains something that they may consider worth taking a risk to break into for. Although defensible space theory has a lot of weaknesses, the related concept of CPTED has potential, but that is hard to assess as long as it is part of multiple initiative interventions.

GEOGRAPHICAL PROFILING

We have seen that ordinary, day-to-day environmental interactions and the everyday use of buildings can shape people's expectations and interpretations of the environment and so their behaviour. For instance, we saw that behaviour in emergencies reflects people's normal daily activities prior to the emergency. If ordinary environmental interactions shape behaviour, you would expect the way a crime is committed, and the place and setting in which it is committed can potentially tell us something about the person who commits the crime and something about their everyday life and environment. It should therefore be possible to work backwards from the features of a crime to the characteristics of the person, or type of person, that is likely to have committed that crime. At a general level that is the essence of criminal offender profiling. Geographical profiling is a subset of offender profiling and is the making of predictions about offenders based on information about the location and timing of the offences. The reliability and validity of criminal profiling in general is debated and sometimes questionable (Alison, 2005). Geographical profiling seems to hold more promise and has a stronger theoretical base, drawing on theories that we have considered already, including RAT and RCT.

HOW LOCATIONS ARE CHOSEN

Underlying the notion of geographical profiling is the idea that the crimes are not random. If an act is not random it is likely to be the result of an internally rational cognitive process (Cornish & Clarke, 1986). Once the assumption is made that criminals are acting rationally, we can start to form ideas about how they decide on the locations of their crimes. When offenders make decisions about where they will commit crimes, they might, for instance, include where they think risks are lowest, or where potential gains are likely to be the highest, as previously discussed in relation to burglary. Whatever the basis of those decisions, it is likely that they will reflect something about the individual and their life. Environmental psychologist working with others including law enforcement agencies have been identifying which aspects of a person's life are most useful in geographical profiling.

As a person travels through familiar places, they gather information and form a cognitive map, a mental representation of the spatial environment and its organisation. That map will help them navigate places making them easier to move around as they become more familiar. As a criminal develops their cognitive maps, they will also gather and store other information that they can potentially use to carry out or plan their crimes. An offender can only do this effectively in areas with which they have some form of familiarity and so connection. The more often the offender interacts with a particular environment, the more detailed their knowledge or map of that place will be. It is also likely that with increased use of an area will come increased opportunities to commit their crime. Because of opportunity and familiarity, an offender is consequently most likely engage in criminal activity around their home or in some systematic relationship to it.

However, one problem with committing crimes around a home area is that if they remain close to where they live, the offender might be recognised. This is particularly the case with interpersonal crimes, such as assault or rape, which have much more potential for recognition, chance meeting, and identification. Those who do not bring the criminal into contact with their victim, such as burglary, will suffer less from issues of identification, unless they have been caught on CCTV. For the purposes of anonymity, therefore, it makes sense for offenders to go to locations where they are not liable to be identified and where they are unlikely to bump into a victim afterwards. Despite this, the security offered by familiarity with a well 'mapped' area often outweighs the risks of being recognised while committing an offence (Brantingham & Brantingham, 1981). Taking these two forces together, it suggests that there will be a minimum distance from the home in which the offender would tend not to offend, to maintain anonymity, and a maximum distance that they are likely to feel comfortable to travel. Supporting this are consistent findings over more than 80 years that offenders usually do not travel very far from home to commit crimes (Shaw & McKay, 1942; Snook et al., 2005).

It is worth highlighting that home is not the only anchor point relevant to crimes. Other significant places in a person's life can play a similar role. For example, where a person works, the places they socialise, and where friends or relatives live all potentially provide areas around which they may have familiarity and opportunity and so the possibility to commit crimes. Even though these other possibilities exist, the dominant anchor point is likely to be home (Brantingham & Brantingham, 1981; Canter & Gregory, 1994). Nevertheless, importantly, what all of these places have in common is that they are related to the offender in some way, are areas that an offender has a cognitive map of, and they all have the potential to betray something about the perpetrator that might help lead to their identification.

ENVIRONMENTAL RANGE OF SERIAL CRIMINALS

In this section we will consider a selection of studies that have looked at serial offenders. In choosing those studies the aim is to include different offences, from rape and murder to burglary, which show the applicability of geographical profiling to a range of crimes. They also demonstrate how some crimes involves more than one location and that each location can say something about the offender. We will start with the development of a general model of criminal geographical behaviour that is the basis for many of the studies in the field.

Our understanding of geographical profiling has been greatly extended by the work of environmental and investigative psychologist Canter (Canter, 2003). In one of his early studies, he and Larkin examined the extent to which a general model can be developed that is applicable to the majority of offenders' spatial activity (Canter & Larkin, 1993). Their hypothesis was that the choice of crime venues relates to the home or base from which an individual operates. The area within which the offences are committed is the offender's 'criminal range'. Canter and Larkin distinguished between 'criminal range', which can include many significant places, and 'home range', which is simply the area around where they live.

Canter and Larkin (1993) identified two patterns of spatial behaviour, which they used to categorise offenders as either 'commuters' or 'marauders'. If the region covered by the crimes includes the location of the residence, offenders are 'marauders'; they maraud around their home area. However, if the offender's home is outside of the region in which the crimes take place, they are 'commuters'; the offender commutes to an area away from their home to commit crimes.

Their study of 45 people convicted of multiple sexual assaults revealed that 39 (87%) of the offenders fell into the marauder category. They committed crimes around their home area. Of the six offenders who did not show that pattern, all commuted to a specific area to offend, so their site selection was not of random places away from their home. Two of those six picked up their victims in a car in their home area, and then commuted away to a different region where they carried out the assault. The initial part of the offence was therefore committed within the home area, though the final offence of rape took place outside of it. Another two offenders targeted a specific street away from where they lived. Overall, what comes across very clearly from the study is that offenders do not choose random locations, and, significantly for investigators, a very substantial proportion of offenders will be found living within an area defined by a circle around their crimes.

SPATIAL PATTERN CONSISTENCY: TYPE OF CRIME AND CRIMINAL EXPERIENCE

An important question that arises from Canter and Larkin's model is whether there is consistency across different types of crime and criminals. Research shows differences in offenders' spatial patterns depending on the *type* of crime and the *experience* of the criminal. Looking at types of crime, both serial rapists and serial arsonists tend to follow the marauder pattern of crimes (Kocsis & Irwin, 1997; Meaney, 2004). For serial burglary, however, they are equally likely to follow the commuter or marauder spatial patterns (Kocsis & Irwin, 1997; Kocsis et al., 2002), though in one study the commuter distribution was found to be slightly more frequent (Meaney, 2004).

It is not clear why these differences exist. However, sex offending, and in some instances arson, can be thought of as mainly motivated by some form of interpersonal violence, while burglary may be more likely to be motivated by instrumental, personal economic gain. It is possible that the more interpersonally motivated a crime, the more likely it is to happen nearer to the offender's home base. Research supports that idea. Arsonists that are motivated by instrumental gain, for instance, tend to move further from their homes, while those with emotional, interpersonal motives remain closer to their home (Fritzon, 2001).

It is possible that the more interpersonal and potentially visible an offence, the more an offender will carry out their crimes purposefully moving in different directions around their home, inadvertently creating a circle containing it. Burglars might show a similar pattern some of the time, but other burglars or the same burglar on other occasions might have target places away from their home area, for instance a neighbourhood of high value houses, which are in a single area some way from where they live.

The criminological concept of 'criminal career' recognises that as an offender becomes more experienced, they develop skills, techniques, and approaches that are different from those of a novice. This raises the question of whether we might expect the spatial patterns of offences to change as serial offenders develop. The research evidence from burglars provides mixed results, with some research showing no variation over time (Kocsis et al., 2002), while others indicate that the first offences burglars commit tend to show a marauder pattern, and for later offences the perpetrator becomes a spatial commuter (Barker, 2000; Meaney, 2004). In displaying these patterns, the burglars moved from offending close to home to extending their range further in later offences, with travel distance increasing with experience.

The change in the spatial pattern followed by offenders might be a reflection of relatively random acts that are opportune in the early days of a burglar's career, which are close to their home. As they become more professional, they may seek out more wealthy neighbourhoods or other 'specialised' targets and different opportunities, which require them to travel further distances (Meaney, 2004). Crimes involving an emotional content are likely to be conducted closer to home because that is where emotionally related interactions are likely to be generated. Burglars characteristically do not select targets for either personal or emotional reasons, Experience therefore opens up potential targets in areas that have no personal attachment. Burglars attempt to operate within areas where they will maximise take and minimise problems rather than experience emotional gain (Meaney, 2004).

MULTI-LOCATION CRIMES

The evidence we have looked at shows that within crime types there is a relatively consistent set of spatial patterns. The final question we will look at is whether the patterns hold for crimes that involve several geographical components. For instance, in the case of rape, a person might be met in one place and then taken some distance to where the rape is committed. In the case of murder, there can be a place where the victim is picked up, another where they are murdered, and yet another where the body is disposed of. Each of the multiple sites will provide indicators that may point to a specific individual if we know how the sites relate to an offender.

Lundrigan and Canter (2001) looked at the slightly gruesome question of where serial killers dispose of their victim's bodies. Examining data from 120 US serial murderers, they found that the offenders home base was central to the spatial patterns of body disposal sites. Further, each disposal site was usually in a different direction from the previous one, with those changes in direction being strongest for offenders travelling the shortest (<10 km) distances and weakest for those travelling the furthest (>30 km). This change in direction of the disposal of a body makes sense if we consider the likely thought processes of the serial murder. The first disposal is most probably a site with which they are familiar, or because it is a place they know they will not be observed. When it comes to the second site, the offender might view the first location as now too risky, so choose somewhere else in a different direction. That place then becomes risky, so they select a third, and so on. At some point, if they have committed sufficient murders without being caught, they will run out of sites and need to return to earlier areas. There is an irony that the murderer's attempts to reduce risk of detection provide a stronger and stronger indication of where they live.

OTHER ENVIRONMENTAL QUALITIES

In this section we have focused on geographical profiling based on spatial patterns. Now we will address the question of whether there is consistency in the environmental qualities of selected crime site. The type of area, land use type, socio-economic characteristics, and temporal dynamics are less consistent in offender behaviour and tend to be less useful to investigators. However, although these variables do not give very clear indicators of the offender, they are more consistent than would be expected by chance, with the crimes of one offender being more similar to each other than they are to the crimes of another offender (Lundrigan, Czarnomski, & Wilson, 2010). All of this suggests that the environments selected for criminal purposes are a result of some psychological processes, which might be deliberate or unconscious. The greater the extent to which the offender thinks them through, the more their environmental choices provide potential for application to apprehending them. The key is to identify better predictors, allowing more accurate targeting. That is something for the future of research on the environmental psychology of crime.

USING GEOGRAPHICAL PROFILING

The way in which a marauder circle is calculated is relatively simple and can easily be undertaken by investigators. It is achieved by taking the two offences furthest from each other as the diameter of a circle. All the other offences committed by the offender will usually fall within that area. If the offender has adopted a marauder pattern, their home will also be within it. The approach will be likely to be valid for a significant number of offenders, but there are two weaknesses. When working backwards from the offences of a convicted offender it is relatively easy to establish the furthest two offences, because you usually know what offences they have committed. When the offender is not known, that becomes more challenging. First the offences need to be established and linked to the same offender. Making these attributions is not an easy task, but fortunately police forces are reasonably good at it, and there are approaches to identifying a series based on DNA or behavioural characteristics. The second weakness is that the offender might be committing crimes with a commuter spatial pattern and so lives outside the range of their crimes. If that option is not kept in mind the investigators could spend a long time looking in the wrong place, allowing the offender to continue with their activities. This highlights the need to use geographical profiling with caution and in the context of other intelligence.

When a crime or series of crimes is committed, the number of possible offenders is likely to be large. To investigate effectively and quickly the police need to narrow the pool of suspects. There are many ways in which they can do that, for instance, paying attention to known offenders who have committed similar crimes, and whose general offence style is similar. There might also be a description or partial description of the offender given by the victim or witnesses. Although these will help narrow down the list of potential offenders, there can still be a significant number of suspects, especially in a high-density urban area. Being able to reduce the number of suspects by establishing a geographical area within which the offender is likely to live, will help to focus an investigation. Even if there are several suspects within the radius of a particular location it is a significant help to the police to reduce suspects down to that number. If none of those suspects could have committed the crimes, the investigators know that either the offender is not on their suspect list, or they could be using a commuter spatial pattern. The investigator can then look at what might be attracting a person to the area, such as specialist targets, for example prostitutes, or look for other associations, like the offender's workplace.

Using geographical profiling to narrow down suspects of sexual assault has the potential to lead to the apprehension of the offender. But there are behavioural differences related to different types of crime. We know that there is a broad and significant difference between interpersonal crimes, like assault and sexual assault, and non-interpersonal crimes such as burglary. Of course, some burglaries become interpersonal, but that is rarely the intent, and target choice is often influenced by a desire to avoid interaction.

FINALLY

In this chapter we have seen several ways in which the environment and crime can be linked. Some of these ideas and approaches are inconclusive. Perhaps that is because they fail to take into account the complexity of the relationship between people, crime, and the environment. This was captured by the Brantingham's when they wrote,

> While much of the general public and many criminologists . . . still seem to believe in simple physical determinism, most current researchers and theoreticians . . .(now) view crime occurrence as the result of an individual's perception of and knowledge about the surrounding environment, and are paying particular attention to how this perception and knowledge is shaped by underlying states of criminal motivation and the actual presence of criminal opportunities. . .Crime must be thought of as a broad range of actual behaviours, which, while sometimes appearing similar, may be the result of many different incentives or etiological processes (p. 5).
>
> (Brantingham & Brantingham, 1993, pp. 4–5)

There are then many routes to the same (criminal) behaviour, and thinking about crime needs to reflect that. As well as different motivations, crimes occur in diverse situations under highly varied circumstances. If we consider the weather or defensible space, it could be that the concepts do not adequately reflect the complexity of crime. Overall, the conclusion that can be drawn is that the solutions to crime problems will often need to reflect complexity yet also be focused and specialised.

REFERENCES

Alison, L. (2005). From trait-based profiling to psychological contributions to apprehension methods. In L. Alison (ed.), *The Forensic Psychologist's Casebook: Psychological Profiling and Criminal Investigation* (pp. 3–22). Cullompton: Willan Publishing

Anderson, C. A. (1989). Temperature and aggression: Ubiquitous effects of heat on occurrence of human violence. *Psychological Bulletin*, 106, 17–96.

Anderson, C. A. (2001). Heat and violence. *Current Directions in Psychological Science*, 10(1), 33–38.

Banziger, G., & Owens, K. (1978). Geophysical variables and behavior: II. Weather factors as predictors of local social indicators of maladaptation in two non-urban areas. *Psychological Reports*, 43, 427–434.

Barker, M. (2000). The criminal range of small-town burglars. In D. Canter & L. Alison (eds.), *Profiling Property Crimes* (pp. 59–73). Aldershot: Ashgate.

Becker, G. S. (1968), Crime and punishment: An economic approach. *Journal of Political Economy*, 76, 169–217.

Bell, P. A., & Baron, R. A. (1976). Aggression and heat: The mediating role of negative affect. *Journal of Applied Social Psychology*, 6, 18–30.

Brantingham, P. J. & Brantingham, P. L. (1981). Notes on the geometry of crime. In P. J. Brantingham & P. L. Brantingham (eds.), *Environmental Criminology* (pp. 27–54). Beverley Hills: Sage Publications.

Brantingham, P. J., & Brantingham, P. L. (1984). *Patterns in Crime*. New York: Macmillan.

Brantingham, P. J., & Brantingham, P. L. (1993). Nodes paths and edges: Considerations and the complexity of crime and the physical environment. *Journal of Environmental Psychology*, 13, 3–28.

Brown, B. B., & Altman, I. (1983). Territoriality, defensible space and residential burglary: An environmental analysis. *Journal of Environmental Psychology*, 3, 203–220.

Brown, B. B., & Bentley, D. L. (1993). Residential burglars judge risk: The role of territoriality. *Journal of Environmental Psychology*, 13, 51–61.

Burgess, E. W. (1925). The growth of the city: An Introduction to a research project. In R. E. Park, W. E. Burgess, & R. D. McKenzie (eds.), *The City* (pp. 47–62). Chicago, IL: Chicago University Press.

Canter, D. (1995). Psychology of offender profiling. In R. Bull & D. Carson (eds.), *Handbook of Psychology in Legal Contexts* (pp. 343–355). Chichester, West Sussex: John Wiley & Sons.

Canter, D. (2003). *Mapping Murder: The Secrets of Geographical Profiling*. London: Virgin Books.

Canter, D., & Larkin, P. (1993). The environmental range of serial rapists. *Journal of Environmental Psychology*, 13, 63–69.

Canter, D.V. & Gregory, A. (1994). Identifying the residential location of rapists. *Journal of the Forensic Science Society*, 34, 169–175.

Casteel, C., & Peek-Asa, C. (2000). Effective crime prevention through environmental design (CPTED) in reducing robberies. *American Journal of Preventative Medicine*, 18, (4 Supplement), 99–115.

Clarke, R.V. G. & Cornish, D. B. (1985). Modelling offender decisions: A framework for research and policy. In M. Tonry & N. Morris (eds.), *Crime and Justice, iv* (pp. 147–185). Chicago, IL: Chicago University Press.

Cohen, L. E., & Felson, M. (1979). Social change and crime rate trends: A routine activity approach. *American Sociological Review*, 44, 588–608.

Cohn, E. (1990). Weather and crime. *British Journal of Criminology*, 30(1), 51–64.

Cohn, E., & Rotton, J. (2000). Violence is a curvilinear function of temperature in Dallas: A replication. *Journal of Personality and Social Psychology*, 78, 1074–1081.

Cornish, D. B., & Clarke, R. V. (1986). *The Reasoning Criminal.* New York: Springer-Verlag.

Cornish, D. B., & Clarke, R.V. (2006). Understanding crime displacement: An application of Rational Choice Theory. *Criminology*, 25, 933–948.

Cozens, P. M. (2002). Sustainable urban development and crime prevention through environmental design for the British city. Towards and effective urban environmentalism for the 21st Century. *Cities*, 19(2), 129–137.

Crowe, T. D. (2000). *Crime Prevention through Environmental Design: Applications of Architectural Design and Space Management Concepts, Second Edition.* Oxford: Butterworth-Heinemann.

DeFronzo, J. (1984). Climate and crime: Tests of an FBI assumption. *Environment and Behavior*, 16, 185–210.

Fritzon, K. (2001). An examination of the relationship between distance travelled and motivational aspects of fire setting behaviour. *Journal of Environmental Psychology*, 21, 45–60.

Gifford, R. (2002). *Environmental Psychology: Principles and Practice, Third Edition.* Colville, WA: Optimal Books.

Horrocks, J. & Menclova, A. K. (2011). The effects of weather on crime. *New Zealand Economic Papers*, 45(3), 231–254.

Jacobs, J. (1961). *The Death and Life of Great American Cities.* New York: Random House.

Johnson, S. D. & Bowers, K. J. (2010). Permeability and burglary risk: Are cul-de-sacs safer? *Journal of Quantitative Criminology*, 26, 89–111.

Kocsis, R. N., Cooksey, R. W., Irwin, H. J., & Allen, G. (2002). A further assessment of "circle theory" for geographical profiling. *Australian and New Zealand Journal of Criminology*, 35(1), 43–62.

Kocsis, R. N. & Irwin, H. J. (1997). An analysis of spatial patterns in serial rape, arson, and burglary: The utility of the circle theory of environmental range of psychological profiling. *Psychiatry, Psychology and Law*, 4(2), 195–206.

Lundrigan, S. & Canter, D. (2001). A multivariate analysis of serial murderers' disposal site location choice. *Journal of Environmental Psychology*, 21, 423–432.

Lundrigan, S., Czarnomski, S., & Wilson, M. (2010). Spatial and environmental consistency in serial sexual assault. *Journal of Investigative Psychology and Offender Profiling*, 7, 15–30.

MacDonald, J. E., & Gifford, R. (1989). Territorial cues and defensible space theory: The Burglar's point of view. *Journal of Environmental Psychology*, 9, 193–205.

Mawby, R. (2017). Defensible space. *Oxford Research Encyclopaedia of Criminology*. Retrieved 6 October 2021, from https://doi.org/10.1093/acrefore/9780190264079.013.6

Mawby, R. I. (1977). Defensible space: A theoretical and empirical appraisal. *Urban Studies*, 14, 169–179.

Meaney, R. (2004). Commuters and marauders: An examination of the spatial behaviour of serial criminals. *Journal of Investigative Psychology and Offender Profiling*, 1, 121–137.

Mehlkop, G., & Graeff, P. (2010). Modelling a rational choice theory of criminal action: Subjective expected utilities, norms, and interactions. *Rationality and Society*, 22(2), 189–222.

Michael, R. P., & Zumpe, D. (1983a). Annual rhythms in human violence and sexual aggression in the United States and the role of temperature. *Social Biology*, 30, 263–278.

Michael, R. P., & Zumpe, D. (1983b). Sexual violence in the United States and the role of season. *American Journal of Psychiatry*, 140, 883–886.

Newman, O. (1996). *Creating Defensible Space*. Darby, PA: Diane Publishing Co.

Newman, O. (1973). *Defensible Space: People and Design in the Violent City*. London: Architectural Press.

Ranson, M. (2014). Crime, weather, and climate change. *Journal of Environmental Economics and Management*, 67, 274–302.

Reynald, D. M. (2015). Environmental design and crime events. *Journal of Contemporary Criminal Justice*, 31, 71–89.

Shaw, C. R., & McKay, H. D. (1942). *Juvenile Delinquency and Urban Areas.* Chicago, IL: University of Chicago Press.

Smith, J. M. & Clarke, R. V. (2012). Situational crime prevention: Classifying techniques using "Good Enough" theory. In B. C. Welsh & D. P. Farringdon (eds.), *The Oxford Handbook of Crime Prevention* (pp. 291–315). Oxford: Oxford University Press.

Snook, B., Cullen, R., Mokros, A., & Harbort, S. (2005). Serial murderers' spatial decisions: Factors that influence crime location choice. *Journal of Investigative Psychology and Offender Profiling*, 2, 147–164.

SUGGESTED READING

There are several publications that have been referred to in the chapter that are worth consulting. In particular:

Canter, D. (2003). *Mapping Murder: The Secrets of Geographical Profiling.* London: Virgin Books.

The article by Canter and Larkin lays a lot of the groundwork for subsequent studies.

Canter, D., & Larkin, P. (1993). The environmental range of serial rapists. *Journal of Environmental Psychology*, 13, 63–69.

In relation to CPTED it is worth looking at

Cozens, P. M. (2002). Sustainable urban development and crime prevention through environmental design for the British city. Towards and effective urban environmentalism for the 21st Century. *Cities*, 19(2), 129–137.

Crowe, T. D. (2000). *Crime Prevention through Environmental Design: Applications of Architectural Design and Space Management Concepts, Second Edition.* Oxford: Butterworth-Heinemann.

THERAPEUTIC, SUPPORTIVE, AND RESTORATIVE ENVIRONMENTS

INTRODUCTION

There are many ways in which the environment and environmental psychology are relevant to therapy, in its widest sense. That can include, for instance, mental and physical health, mobility, social relations, stress reduction, and our feelings of general well-being. We can think of the therapeutic and restorative role of the environment in two overarching categories: environments *for* therapy, and environments that *are* therapy. Environments *for* therapy provide the surroundings in which therapy takes place. In some ways they are, in effect, the container for therapy. Environments that *are* therapy make a more active contribution to the therapeutic process or play a significant, supportive part in it.

These two types of environments are usually not mutually exclusive. An environment *for* therapy can also have its own direct therapeutic effects or may indirectly make the therapy more effective. Environments that are therapy will often also contain other contributions to therapy. Overall, then, the role of the setting is a matter of emphasis.

As all therapy is situated in an environment, the setting always plays some part, as it would in any other situation. With therapeutic environments the physical context is usually consciously designed for that process. Restorative environments, which we consider in the second part of the chapter, are different in not being necessarily designed to 'restore' but they are often visited for that purpose. Of all the environments that *are* therapy, they probably provide the clearest example.

DOI: 10.4324/9780429274541-6

ENVIRONMENTAL AND CLINICAL PSYCHOLOGY

The environment is relevant to mental health issues and clinical psychology in other ways as well. While we will not be discussing all of those in any detail, it is worth drawing attention to them. In an interesting exploration of the relationship between clinical and environmental psychology, Anthony and Watkins (2002) identify several areas in which the environment is linked to mental health issues. These can broadly be divided into two, one of which overlaps with the dichotomy of environments for and as therapy that we have just discussed. The other, with which we are less concerned in this chapter, but which we should mention, is the ways in which the environment can contribute to the aetiology and development of mental health issues and can exacerbate existing ones.

The environment can act as a trigger to past traumatic events in a person's life. For instance, someone who has experienced an assault in a particular locale might have a traumatic response triggered by similar environments, or even elements that were present in the environment in which they were assaulted. The authors point to similar, but psychologically different reactions related to PTSD (Post-Traumatic Stress Disorder). The initial exposure to traumatic events can relate to environmental psychology concepts such as place attachment. We saw in Chapter 2 that place attachment can lead people to remain in or return to high-risk areas, increasing their potential exposure to traumatic events and subsequent PTSD. As well as its triggering role, the environment is relevant to some phobias, the most obvious being agoraphobia. Anthony and Watkins (2002) also note that the environment is strongly related to Obsessive Compulsive Disorder (OCD), for instance in relation to obsessive cleaning and organisation.

They further echo work by Stokols and colleagues that examines the role of the environment in the aetiology of issues including those related to physical activity such as obesity or maintaining general health in older age (King et al., 2002). These can generally be conceptualised as *health supportive environments* (Stokols, Grzywacz, & McMahan, 2003). The idea includes the notion that the environment and the ways in which it is structured, resourced, and built can contribute to health outcomes. For instance, research has examined the way in which the environment contributes to obesity. Traditionally, treatments and interventions have focused on behavioural and educational initiatives as well as the use of drugs. Lake and Townsend (2006), among others, argue that a fruitful approach is to examine how the environment shapes and supports health-related behaviour. In particular they point to physical design, land use patterns, and transportation systems. Environmental characteristics can be from small scale – such as ensuring that there is adequate provision and maintenance of pavements, or ensuring that people feel safe outside – to larger scale issues – for example, separating facilities such as shops from residential areas, and encouraging walking. Wilding et al. (2020) identify several factors associated with childhood obesity, including air pollution, neighbourhood disturbances (e.g., vandalism), traffic, green space, walkability, and the presence of fast food outlets. As the authors note, the role of the environment in obesity is complex but our everyday environments have a part to play, and that the therapeutic role of setting is not confined to specialist facilities.

Another example is how the environment can relate to child sex abuse (Anthony & Watkins, 2002; Holman & Stokols, 1994). It is suggested that the socio-spatial structuring of the environment can facilitate abuse by providing opportunities. In some ways this is similar to the discussion we had in Chapter 5 on design and crime. Although Anthony and Watkins mention the environment motivating abuse, it is likely that an abuser has their intentions independent of the environment, but likely enough, certain environments may allow them more easily to perpetrate the offence. Equally they suggest that environmental design can provide some form of protection.

The final relationship between clinical psychology and the environment is the design and layout of the clinical setting itself. Anthony and Watkins (2002) make the point that the environment is rarely considered in the clinical psychology literature. Although a small number of articles do address the subject, the environment does seem to play little more than the role of a neutral backdrop in clinical psychology. They argue however that the therapist's environment may "significantly influence the attitudes and behaviour of clients, and the success or failure of the therapeutic process itself. It may exacerbate client's preexisting conditions – for better or for worse" (p. 140). There is some indication that therapy offices do represent a medically orientated aesthetic (Anthony & Watkins, 2002), which implies a particular orientation to therapy based around a medical model. In the next section we will consider the models that underlie the provision and nurture of therapeutic environments. Further, research has shown that it is not only the internal conditions of clinical and counselling settings that are important. Ito-Alpturer and Uslu (2010) have demonstrated the importance of the location of counselling offices and the potential conflict between accessibility and privacy. Balancing the needs of users in important when making location decisions, as might be expected from the discussion in Chapter 3.

THERAPEUTIC SETTINGS AND MODELS OF THERAPY

The role given to therapeutic or supportive environments is often dependent on the model or conceptualisation of the needs being addressed and of the therapeutic setting (Canter & Canter, 1979). The model shapes the approach to the setting, the user and their needs, and the way in which the setting and user relate. In this section of the chapter, to provide a reasonable range of settings, we will briefly look at prisons, inpatient mental health facilities, design for dementia, and the design of schools for children with autism. In each case we will consider the setting in terms of its design and characteristics and the aim of the setting. The models we will use as part of our understanding of the settings and their goals will include the custodial, medical, prosthetic, normalisation, enhancement, and individual growth models (Canter & Canter, 1979). As we will see, while a setting might relate to or support its users in one dominant mode, increasingly two or more models will apply to a therapeutic environment.

PRISONS

The dominant role or model for prisons is custodial. The primary purpose is separating people and society, often to protect the community from the residents. In keeping with that role, the environment emphasises security and containment; occasionally, there is also an element of punishment.

Although prisons have a long history, there is relatively little environmental psychology research carried out in them, primarily because of issues of access (Wener, 2012). Underlying prison design are the goals of the institution. Wener notes that the names given to prisons reflect the different approaches to incarceration. For instance, in the USA, penitentiaries are, theoretically at least, for reflection and *penitence*; correctional facilities suggest an attempt to change or 'correct' behaviour; detention centres, jails, or prisons are for detaining people (Wener, 2012). In these latter cases, the building has the primary aim of secure 'storage' or warehousing (Canter & Canter, 1979).

Much environmental psychology research on prisons has been concerned with the spatial environment, including the concepts discussed in Chapter 3 (privacy, crowding, personal space, and territoriality), along with issues of isolation, noise, and ambient conditions. Overall, the results of studies have shown that most prison environments have a negative effect on their inmates by, for instance, being crowded and lacking privacy. In describing prisons, Wener summarises the setting:

> Even when inmates are unthreatening, the staff professional, and when designers have strived for 'normalization' of the setting, the noise levels; odors; lack of access to light, air and nature; the uncertain temperature control; and lack of privacy – for sleeping, sitting, using the toilet or shower – make these the kind of settings that few go to willingly.
>
> (Wener, 2012, p. 4)

Recently there has been a growing interest in the potential impact of nature and natural environments on prisoners (Söderlund & Newman, 2017). We will very briefly mention this again when we look at the role of the natural environment in stress and restoration in the second part of this chapter, but the basic idea is that exposure to nature improves mental health and general well-being. A recent initiative in UK prisons uses gardens and gardening as a way of enhancing well-being and reducing recidivism, thus bringing into custodial environments the ethos of green prescribing and restoration (see below).

There is a long history of gardening in prisons. Up until around 20 years ago, UK prisons were self-sufficient in food, with their needs being met by their own gardens. In that sense, they represent a sustainable model with implications outside of prisons

(Devine-Wright, Baybutt, & Meek, 2019). Additionally, however, research is showing that access to gardens and engaging in gardening have direct mental health benefits for prisoners (Farrier, Baybutt & Dooris, 2019). Further, the presence of green space within prisons fosters lower levels of violence and self-harm (Moran et al., 2021). Within the models listed previously, the provision of green spaces and gardens can be thought of as an *enhancement* goal, in which the designs counteract the deficiencies inherent in the institutions and their environments providing an enriched or supportive setting for the users. This shift away from storage and security to enhancement has been gradual. As Wener (2012) hints at in the earlier quote, there are also attempts to make prison environments more 'normal'. The *normalisation* model aims to make settings like 'normal' everyday environments as possible, often making them appear more domestic (Chrysikou, 2014). Both normalisation and enhancement goals aim to improve the well-being of prisoners for their and society's benefit. This is a significant contrast to the warehousing, purely custodial idea described earlier.

MENTAL HEALTH FACILITIES

The custodial model usually refers to prisons, but also can include mental health facilities. When used in a contemporary psychiatric context, a custodial approach is used for people who are either dangerous to themselves or others. In the UK, when people are high risk to the public, they may be confined to high security psychiatric hospitals such as Broadmoor, Rampton, and Ashworth (Boyd-Caine, 2012).

High security hospitals are under the administration of the National Health Service (NHS). As hospitals, they operate within a medical model of treatment. This model came to prominence with our increased knowledge of pathology, disease and infection, and their application to physical conditions. While the approach works well when dealing with disease and infection, the application of a medical model to psychiatric 'illnesses' has been controversial since around the 1960s, when a series of publications attacked the approach to mental 'illness' (e.g., Clare, 1976; Laing & Esterson, 1964; Szasz, 1972). That debate continues today (e.g., Bentall, 1990,

2009). The corollary of this is that the type of environment appropriate for treating physical diseases is not necessarily appropriate for treating 'diseases of the mind', a point we will return to later.

Because of the dual role of treating and containing, high security hospitals span more than one therapeutic model, which, in this case, has the potential to create conflict. In the *medical model* of therapeutic environments, a key element is treatment and making better. However, as Holley, Weaver, and Völlm (2020) observe in relation to high security hospitals,

> . . .the tension between the requirements of treatment and security has long been recognised. These services are extremely restrictive for those detained within them and it is well established that the highly restrictive nature of secure care services can impact negatively upon quality of life. (p. 2)

The conflict of two goals, drawn from different models and roles of therapeutic settings, is not confined to high security environments.

Although there has been a move towards care in the community, partly driven by the questioning of the medical model and its appropriateness for mental health, treatment in hospitals remains a substantial part of psychiatric provision (Papoulias et al., 2014). A significant problem in mental health in-patient facilities in general is the levels of aggression. In fact, levels of violence in general psychiatric hospitals are greater than those found in high security units. In the UK NHS, the majority of attacks on staff happen in mental health settings (Rogerson et al., 2021). The challenge of violence in these environments is not confined to the UK either, with studies showing that it is a worldwide phenomenon (Bowers et al., 2011). Although the physical environments of hospital wards are considered by staff to be a core contributing factor in the violence (Rogerson, et al., 2021), most of the research has examined patient characteristics, staff training, and care processes, with few considering the impact of the physical setting (Ulrich et al., 2018). Nonetheless, a small number of studies have looked at the relationship between ward designs and aggression (Jenkins, Dye & Foy, 2015; Rogerson et al., 2021; Ulrich et al., 2018; van der Schaaf et al., 2013).

In one of the more comprehensive studies, the authors suggested a set of physical design interventions that they hypothesised would reduce aggression in a facility (Ulrich et al., 2018). They argued that by reducing users' stress, the design could result in less aggression. The researchers proposed four main categories of design aims. The first aim was to reduce crowding stress by, for example, providing single patient rooms with private bathrooms, and having communal areas with moveable seating and space to regulate interaction and lower social density. We saw in Chapter 3 that the ability to control privacy is important for social interaction and well-being. The second aim was to reduce environmental stress buy reducing noise and increasing control over noise. There is extensive research in environmental psychology that shows that one of the factors that make noise stressful and annoying is not having control of the sound as well as sounds being intermittent (Evans & Cohen, 1987). The third part of the design was reducing stress through the inclusion of distractions, such as gardens, views and pictures of nature, and daylight exposure. We will cover how that might be beneficial in the second part of the chapter when we look at restoration. The final aspect of design was observation, which translates to good visibility of communal areas and bedroom doors.

In their study, Ulrich and his colleagues compared a new hospital, which had almost all the design features, with the old hospital that it had replaced, using previously collected data from that hospital. Data were also obtained from a control setting that had not been refurbished and which only included one of the design features. Using levels of chemical and physical restraint as indicators of aggression, they found a significant fall in their use in the new facility. Importantly, unlike other studies, Ulrich et al.'s research controlled for organisational and non-environmental factors, so we have a good idea that the differences can probably be attributed to the environments. However, as the authors note, it is not clear whether the fall in the use of restraints was because the patients experienced reduced stress, or whether it was because the staff felt less stressed. That is something future work can explore, but either way, the study is a good indication of the positive influence of design in a therapeutic setting.

A more recent study of inpatient mental health facilities in seven NHS trusts across England produced results that are in stark contrast to Ulrich et al.'s (2018) study. In this case, the researchers found a positive relationship between aggression and the dimensions of higher staffing and greater space availability, and increased comfort and facilities (Rogerson et al., 2021). The results were consistent for the dependent measures of physical aggression, verbal aggression, and property damage. Why aggression should increase with higher staffing levels, lower density, and greater comfort is unclear. There are, however, some difficulties with the study from an environmental perspective. For instance, the situational dimensions used by the researchers comprised both physical and organisational variables, which makes disentangling the role played by the environment very difficult. There were also other confounding issues discussed by the authors, which potentially weakened the study. Nonetheless, given the number of hospitals included in the research and the consistency of their findings, the results suggest that we need to investigate the role of the environment in aggression in mental health facilities further.

As well as considering aggression, there have been several studies looking more broadly at well-being in general psychiatric inpatient settings. A systematic review of the literature found that those studies that have been carried out tend to suffer methodological weaknesses making the drawing firm conclusion difficult (Papoulias et al., 2014). Notwithstanding those issues, the authors conclude that there is a positive relationship between private spaces and 'home-like' features and increases in interaction and well-being. The idea that creating a more 'normal' home-like environment improves mental health and well-being is in keeping with moves away from the medical model towards a normalisation model that attempts to provide support for its users while at the same time remaining as 'normal' as possible, avoiding the problems of large-scale environments and institutions that can hinder rather than help therapy.

DESIGNING FOR DEMENTIA

The prevalence of dementia in those over 60 is between 6% and 7% in most regions of the world, though it is higher in parts of South America and lower in some African countries. In 2010, there were 36.5 million dementia sufferers worldwide, with the number expected to double every 20 years (Prince et al., 2013). The majority of people with dementia in the West live in their own homes and remain there for as long as possible (van Hoof et al., 2010). Despite that, most research on dementia in environmental psychology and design is carried out in institutional settings (Day & Calkins, 2003).

The main symptoms of dementia comprise a collection of cognitive deficits. They include memory impairment, and, variously, inability to speak, disorder of motor planning, a reduction in executive cognition (loss of planning ability, reduced complex behaviour, difficulty following sequences), and/or inability to recognise objects, shapes, or people. The cognitive deficits manifest in several behavioural difficulties and conditions, including wandering, confusion, and wayfinding problems.

Wayfinding, both within buildings such as care homes and outside of buildings, is fundamental to normal, everyday functioning, including social interaction. Understanding people's ability to find their way is an area related directly to environmental psychology and suggests that the discipline has a role to play in improving the lives of those with the condition.

There are several stages involved in the process of wayfinding, including knowing the starting point, knowing the route to the destination, and knowing the destination and when it has been reached (Brush & Calkins, 2008). A person with dementia can struggle with each stage of that process. Although building configuration or floor plans can potentially help with orientation, wandering, and social interaction, the conclusions of research to identify which are the best designs are unclear (Day & Calkins, 2002).

Examining wayfinding in nursing homes, Marquardt and colleagues observe that even residents in the advanced stages of dementia can find destinations if there are supportive design features (Marquardt, 2011; Marquardt & Schmieg, 2009). Overall, those features can be categorised as floor plan configurations and environmental cues (Marquardt, 2011). From a review of five studies, Marquardt (2011) and others (e.g., Mitchell et al., 2003) have identified design configurations that support or hinder wayfinding. The supportive features are (a) environments that are small scale; (b) unobstructed views of relevant places; (c) simple decision and reference points; (d) places with different and clear functions; and (e) spatial closeness of kitchen, dining room, and activity rooms. In the latter case, groupings of spaces benefit the residents by not being separated by long distances and decision points. Those factors that made orientation more difficult are long corridors, changes of direction, and repetitive elements, that is design features that are the same, or look the same. Marquardt's review of the literature identified facilitative environmental cues, including signage using residents' names or portrait photographs, or photographic labels and personal items on doors. The main cues interfering with the residents' orientation was information clutter, which could include too many signs, such as posting meal plans, and staff rotas (Passini et al., 1998).

Since most people with dementia live at home, it also means that they live in the community and will often need to navigate outside, for practical reasons, leisure, quality of life, and well-being. However, there is relatively little research that has looked at orientation in the outside world for people with dementia. It does seem that the same design cues and characteristics relevant to buildings should apply to more general environments, as perhaps you might expect. Mitchell et al.'s (2003) review of the literature on dementia and navigating outdoor space identifies design aims as being to ensure that the outdoor environment is familiar, legible (e.g., few turns, clear lines of sight), distinctive, accessible, comfortable, and safe.

For those sufferers who remain in their own homes, the changes to cognitive function brought about by dementia means that the domestic environment is unlikely to meet the needs of the person with symptoms (Desai & Grossberg, 2001). Eventually there is a point at which the dementia user can no longer adapt to their environment and therefore the environment must change to meet their needs (Desai & Grossberg, 2001). Therefore, while caring for people with dementia in their home is very strongly within the normalisation approach to therapy and support, provision based on the prosthetic model can potentially provide effective assistance. This approach borrows from the general notion of prosthetics, in which a device or the environment compensates directly for a deficit to help a person achieve their needs. The most obvious examples are, for instance, where physical environmental prostheses enable people to cope with physical challenges using ramps or stair lifts.

As well as design changes, assistive technologies can potentially help support people in their homes (Ludden et al., 2019). Assistive technologies are devices or systems that can support someone in their day-to-day activities. While they can be used in all settings, they are particularly useful at home where assistance from carers can be more limited than in a care home. There have been several reviews of the use of assistive technology to aid people with dementia. Worryingly, one systematic review of the efficacy of assistive technologies to support memory was unable to find any high-quality evidence that they significantly support people with dementia-related memory loss (Van der Roest et al., 2017). Several existing reviews were brought together by Ludden et al. (2019). They identified numerous areas in which assistive technology is used to facilitate daily activities, such as eating and bathing, safety monitoring, and helping with physical and cognitive tasks. These included cognitive assistants and memory aids. Following their review, they concluded that whether assistive technologies are proving effective is unclear. It remains uncertain the extent to which assistive technology is helpful in mitigating the symptoms of dementia. There is, however, a wide variation in the technologies. It is likely that there are instances in which they are supportive and occasions when they are not. Further, it will be important that the technology is matched to the user's changing needs, making evaluation difficult. Van Hoof et al. (2010) provide an extensive and useful review of assistive technologies as well as environmental design and how they can be used to support daily activities.

An important point made by Ludden et al. (2019) is that there is little research exploring uses of technology to support leisure and recreational uses and to help social engagement. Further, there appears to be little participatory involvement in design and development of technologies by users, which is a comment made by Day and Calkins (2003) about participation in environmental research in general. As a result, many of the technologies are targeted at heterogeneous populations even though the users are in very different stages of dementia (Ludden et al., 2019).

This overview of environmental support for people with dementia indicates areas where there is potential for environmental psychology and other disciplines to play an important part in improving people's lives. One conclusion that researchers and reviewers often draw is that there is uncertain evidence for the degree of benefit offered by many of the proposed interventions. This might be explained by the fact that it is difficult to accommodate user participation because of the nature of their symptoms. Further, as we have seen before, it can be difficult to isolate the impact of an intervention from other activities in a setting. Another issue is that those designing environments, or developing assistive products, psychologists and nursing professions have different perspectives that need to be integrated in producing and assessing environments for the mitigation of dementia.

DESIGNING FOR AUTISM

Recent work has been examining and developing environments for autistic children. Mostafa, an architect whose work has led to the proposal of several design guidelines, leads much of this and will provide the focus for this section. As she has noted, the frequency of autism amongst children is estimated to be 1% in the UK (Bancroft et al., 2012), which makes it one of the most prevalent special needs in children of school age, with an incidence rate above visual, hearing, and physical impairment (Mostafa, 2020).

There are several ways in which the environment can be thought of in relation to autism. An influential perspective, which has been referred to as the *neuro-typical approach*, is that the environment should remain unchanged with the person on the autism spectrum adapting their behaviour to fit the setting. One rationale for this approach, especially amongst children, is that by experiencing the challenges they will face in everyday environments children with autism will develop the skills they will need in later life (Henry, 2011). This, it is further argued, is particularly important as some people with autism have difficulties generalising from one environment to another (Marion, 2006).

An alternate, *sensory-centric* approach to design is based on the idea that a significant part of autism is a "*sensory malfunction when assimilating stimulatory information from the surrounding environment*" (Mostafa, 2008, p. 191). From this perspective, the environment becomes central and has a major role to play in allowing children with autism to improve their everyday life by making changes to the sensory input they experience from the setting. Rather than focusing on the child adapting to the environment, improvements to their learning experience can be achieved by changing the sensory *output* of the environment, placing the children's surroundings at the centre of change.

The aim of Mostafa's work has been to reduce sensory input and thereby modify autistic behaviour and facilitate skill development and learning. She proposed environmental features conducive to those aims: "*one must calm it down, break it down into manageable experiences in discrete spaces, organize those spaces in a sensory and temporally logical flow, and accommodate for sensory overload escape*" (Mostafa, 2020, p. 482). These can be translated into design strategies to reduce the overwhelming amount of sensory input that some autistic children experience, make spatial organisation predictable, and give them environmental spaces that allow them to manage times of sensory imbalance. That, in turn, enables the child to engage in learning activities and facilitates their social interactions and learning.

Within that overall strategy, Mostafa (2008, 2020) proposes seven design tactics: *acoustics* (reduction in noise), *spatial sequencing* (spaces are organised in the same sequence as daily activities), *escape space* (small spaces the users can go to when feeling social or sensory overload), *compartmentalisation* (spaces dedicated to single activities), *transition spaces* (spaces that facilitate the sensory movement from one activity to another), *sensory zoning* (grouping spaces of similar sensory levels), *safety*, taking into account different perceptual experiences and proprioception (kinaesthesia) and behaviour that could result in injury through the use of design and materials.

Applying these and other tactics to the design of environments for autistic children has led to many benefits (Mostafa, 2020). For instance, increased attention span, improved temperament, and reduced time for children to respond to teachers were all associated with changes to the settings. Comparing the sensory-centric approach with a neuro-typical approach, including medical models, we see the environment being used to enhance people's ability to live and learn rather than attempting to change or 'treat' the children and expecting them to adapt to the environment. In terms of the models we discussed earlier, the neuro-typical approach would fit with a normalisation framework. The sensory approach, however, seeks *enhancement* of the environment in ways that allow the children to learn.

MULTI-SUPPORT AND THERAPEUTIC MODEL SETTINGS

The design of many therapeutic environments now includes characteristics that draw on more than one of the models identified earlier. For instance, the provision of gardens, views, and art included as part of the new design of the hospital in Ulrich et al.'s (2018) study falls within the enhancement model, but also has elements of normalisation. The enhancement model has some clear similarities to the prosthetic model. However, in enhanced environments there is not a direct compensation for a particular condition. Rather than counteracting 'deficiencies' in users, the designs counteract the deficiencies inherent in the institutions and their environments. The deficit is considered to be with the environment rather than the users of the setting.

The idea that relying on a single model for a therapeutic setting is inadequate was made by Chrysikou (2014), who argued that they

> should be a hybrid of a domestic and a health care environment, which also takes into account the rehabilitation procedures at the earliest possible stages of their involvement in the mental health system and where a domestic atmosphere and organisation plays a key role, but where also the three parameters model of safety, competence and personalization and choice is taken into account as a basic therapeutic element.
>
> (p. 183)

The provision of facilities for people with dementia drawn on prosthetic, enhancement, and normalisation ideas both in their homes and in care homes. Much the same can be said for designs for autistic children, although there is less evidence of prosthetic support than for those with dementia. However, there is a strong orientation towards an individual growth model, in which the environment provides the conditions for its users to develop and grow, and the setting can also develop with the needs of its users.

Comparing where we began with custodial environments that contain and control individuals, therapeutic and supporting settings have come a very long way. We have ended this section with a positive role for the environment, enhancing personal development and growth. Perhaps the shift that we have seen in settings for therapy is most importantly a shift away from users adapting to the environment towards a position where the setting adapts to the specific needs of the user.

In the next section we will consider a body of work that has looked at how the environment can contribute to restoring our health and well-being. As part of that we will again see some examples of the impact of environment characteristics on people in different therapeutic contexts including hospitals.

RESTORATION

The idea of environments restoring our well-being is not a new one. For instance, holidays usually involve going to a different environment, with a change of setting being an essential part of the vacation, itself often designed to 'recharge our batteries'. Someone feeling stressed may be *restored* to his or her non-stressed state by a 'change of scenery'. In recent years, the idea of environments restoring our well-being has gathered a lot of new interest. The concept of *green prescribing* has received attention from health care providers and interest from governments, including in the UK where they have funded research into how the natural environment can be used to improve mental health and well-being. These examples all reflect restoration, which is about psychological or physiological recovery and the restoring of a state of well-being, and in particular the role of the environment in that process.

In the remaining sections of the chapter, we will look at the major theories of restoration and the research that has tested their ideas. The key theories that underlie the concept of restorative environments were initially developed in the 1980s. The two most influential of these are *Attention Restoration Theory (ART)* developed primarily by the Kaplans (Kaplan, 1995; Kaplan & Kaplan, 1989), and *Stress Recovery Theory (SRT)* (Ulrich, 1983). Although different theories, they do have some things in common, and there have been attempts to integrate them (Kaplan, 1995).

ATTENTION RESTORATION THEORY (ART)

The basic idea of ART is that some activities require a lot of attention or concentration. After a while, the energy that takes results in fatigue, which can then lead to a variety of outcomes, some of which can be detrimental. To recover from this effort, to be restored, people need to engage in an activity or an environment that does not need their attention. The proposition is that some environments demand concentration, adding to our tiredness, while others are restorative environment because they allow us to relax, daydream, and think without effort.

An important conceptual distinction in ART is between *directed attention*, which is consciously directed and under a person's control, and the more relaxed *fascination*, which is not. Directed attention includes attention that is given to performing a task or solving a problem, as well as the attention used for dealing with distractions in the environment, which require a person to filter what is important from what is unimportant. As attention is directed, rather than being thoughts that are freely wandering, it requires effort to maintain focus, which makes us susceptible to fatigue or, more precisely, *directed attention fatigue (DAF).*

Directed attention fatigue occurs in many people's lives. Some jobs are particularly prone to fatigue, especially if they require constant monitoring and decision-making, such as air traffic control. Other jobs needing prolonged directed attention include surgery, which can require concentration for several hours, or long-distance lorry driving, where the driver must stay alert for significant periods of time. Most students will experience DAF by the end of a period of exams, during which they have been highly focused for unusually long hours. Any activity that requires significant directed attention can lead to fatigue.

There are costs that accrue from DAF. Amongst the consequences are increased errors, which are particularly problematic for roles such as air traffic controllers, physicians, pilots, and drivers, where mistakes have potentially serious consequences. Another outcome, which most people will have experienced, or witnessed in others, is a greater level of irritability and aggressiveness along with reduced socially appropriate behaviour (Kaplan & Kaplan, 1989).

In contrast to directed attention, *fascination* is thoughtfulness that is not really under conscious control. It is relatively involuntary, freewheeling, daydreaming, or going with the flow of our thoughts (Kaplan & Kaplan, 1989). Its closest contemporary manifestation is probably found in mindfulness activities. Because we are not directing and holding attention on a particular subject, involuntary attention requires little if any effort and so is resistant to fatigue. In fascination there is therefore an opportunity for cognitive rest.

These ART ideas can be tied to the environment by the idea that fatigue can be reduced by exposure to settings that have restorative qualities. Those qualities include *being away*, *fascination*, *extent*, and *compatibility* (Kaplan, 1991). Being away is being absent from the everyday environment. This might be physical absence, such as when we go on holiday, or conceptual, when we daydream, and our thoughts are allowed to wander. Fascination can be facilitated when an environment contains patterns that hold our interest and attention, without us having to expend effort. Fascination can be achieved by looking at a static environment or object, but also by a dynamic process, such as a sunset, clouds moving across the sky, or slowly running water. These gentle scenes, *soft fascination*, are the more restorative. Dramatic scenes, like waves crashing against cliffs, are *hard fascination* and have less of a restorative affect (Kaplan, 1991).

An environment that allows fascination does not necessarily allow for restoration if it does not also have *extent* because it would not have enough 'scope', to occupy a person's thoughts. By 'extent' Kaplan describes an environment that allows an observer to remain engaged with it. To have extent, the environment needs to be rich and coherent; the environment must be sufficient to create 'another world'. To be restorative the environment must be able to effortlessly occupy most of a person's thoughts.

Finally, 'compatibility' is the environment's ability to support what a person wants or is inclined to do in that setting with little effort and in a way that is appropriate for the setting. Because different people have very different purposes, the extent to which an environment is compatible will vary, depending on the person and their goals or purposes. Like much in environmental psychology, the goals and aims a person has in the setting will influence the experience of that setting and the impact it will have on them. Compatibility is another example of person-environment relations being a transaction.

STRESS RECOVERY THEORY (SRT)

We saw earlier that Ulrich et al. (2018) put stress reduction at the centre of suggestions to reduce aggression in mental health facilities. Those ideas grew from Ulrich's earlier work, in which he proposed a stress-based theory of restoration. In essence his argument is that when people find events threatening or when conditions place too great a demand on them, they experience stress. If they are subsequently exposed to restorative environments their stress will be reduced and their normal, non-stressed state will be restored (Ulrich, 1983).

Both Ulrich and the Kaplans thought that experiencing natural rather built environments could help overcome the effect of stress or fatigue. However, they disagree on the nature of the outcome of the demands people's daily lives place upon them. The mental fatigue described in ART is not equivalent to stress in SRT. The Kaplans have clarified the difference between the two writing, "*Stress involves the preparation for an anticipated event that has been evaluated as being threatening or harmful. Though mental fatigue may well result from such circumstances, it also arises out of hard work on a project one enjoys*" (Kaplan & Kaplan, 1989, p. 178). They make their point with the analogy that being chased by a bear can be very stressful but need not cause mental fatigue. In some senses, with ART it is possible to enjoy the process of becoming fatigued.

Drawing on the work of psychologists before him, Ulrich takes a *psycho-evolutionary* perspective. Which, simply put, means those factors that aided our evolution still impact on our behaviour, even though we may not be aware of them. The argument continues that because language is necessary for thought, before we had language humans could only respond directly, immediately, and emotionally to their surroundings. They did not and could not consciously think about them. This leads to a key part of SRT, which is that people's first immediate response to an environment is emotional. It is central to the theory that affect is *precognitive.* Once an affective response has been made, there may or may not be an additional cognitive process, but if there is, it will follow the emotion rather than vice versa.

The argument behind SRT holds that our distant ancestors had to make relatively rapid decisions about whether to approach a setting or fear it and run. Because they were making quick decisions, they would have had to make them based on ambiguous and general characteristics of the environment. The cues that they would have had would not contain enough information for complex cognitive decision-making. Decisions were therefore made on a place's *ambience* (cf. Ittleson, 1973), or as Ulrich refers to them, *preferenda* (Ulrich, 1983; Zajonc, 1980), which he describes as, "*gross, often vague, configural aspects that may be insufficient as a basis for cognitive judgements but can be highly effective in eliciting affect*" (Ulrich, 1983, p. 89). The person's subsequent behaviour would therefore be determined by this emotional response.

In evolutionary terms, preferenda are important features of the environment that were central to our species' survival, alerting us to danger or inviting us to approach. Ulrich (1983) has translated these ideas into environmental characteristics, describing them as gross *configurational* or *structural features* (symmetrical elements, spatial cues, the 'texture' of surfaces, and absence of threat), *gross depth properties* (ability to see into a moderate or long distance), and *general classes of environmental content* (plants, types of vegetation, water).

Together, these characteristics can provide a sketch of the sort of view a person would, in evolutionary terms, consider approachable rather than threatening, and so would be preferred (Ulrich, 1983). The environment should have a moderate to high level of complexity, a good view with a focal point, it should include order and patterning, so the complexity has structural properties that establish a focal point. The scene should have a high level of depth, which can be perceived unambiguously, as Ulrich describes it. The ground surface texture will be quite uniform and 'conducive to movement', and finally, there would be a deflected outlook (for instance a curved path moving out of the picture or view), absent or minimal threat, and preferably some water. This is, of course, rather reminiscent of many traditional Western landscape paintings.

The preferred environment can be contrasted to what would be hypothesised to be the least preferred. According to Ulrich's theory, the least preferred would have little complexity or structure and no focal point. The ground would be difficult to walk across, probably be rough and uneven, with objects obstructing the way. There would be restricted view, and an absence of water. Their potential for danger, which it is hypothesised, would also add to people's dislike of the scene.

Ulrich (1983) acknowledges that there are similarities and links with a significant body of research on landscape preference. In particular echoes of Appleton's evolution-based prospect-refuge theory are relevant (Appleton, 1975). As the name suggests that theory sees preference based in characteristics that would have given an advantage. Refuge would allow early humans to hide either from their pursuers or from what they are hunting. Prospect would allow them to see across the space, again providing advantages.

While aesthetic preference is interesting, the importance of preferred environments in this context is their relationship to stress. Within SRT, the premise is that if a person finds a view pleasant, it can reduce their stress. As Ulrich writes,

> Many aesthetic and affective reactions to natural environments are assumed to motivate behaviours that are not necessarily expressed as

> observable actions, but which nonetheless qualify as adaptive functioning. For example, if an observer's state prior to a visual encounter is one of stress and excessive arousal, an attractive natural view might elicit feelings of pleasantness, hold interest and block or reduce stressful thoughts, and therefore foster psychophysiological restoration.
>
> (Ulrich, 1983, pp. 94–95)

One question this statement raises is that if stress reduction results from viewing perceived pleasantness, will a cityscape that is perceived as pleasant, or more pleasant than a rural landscape reduce stress equally, or perhaps even further?

The main emphasis of research on restorative environments, including for both ART and SRT, has been on the natural environment, with urban environments seen at best as less restorative, and at worst as adding to stress and fatigue. Ulrich refers to the idea that the natural environment has superior restorative qualities as the *nature benefit assumption* (Ulrich, 1981). Although Ulrich (1983) has written that much of his SRT framework applies to urban environments as well, he and others argue most strongly that natural environments are preferable. Some early studies appear to support the greater positive impact of natural settings.

One of the most widely known studies of the influence of the environment on physical and mental health and well-being examined the impact of having a view from a window in a hospital recovery room (Ulrich, 1984). The researchers compared surgical patients in small double occupancy rooms, who had a view of either a small group of trees or brick wall. The results showed that those with a tree view spent less time in hospital – took fewer painkillers and fewer narcotic analgesics. All three differences were statistically significant. A lot of the literature that references this study suggests that many other associations were found. However, none of those were statistically significant and so could have been the result of chance. Generally, it appears that subsequent accounts of the study tend to exaggerate the findings, and so it is worth considering the original source publication in more detail.

Because trees are natural and a brick wall is not, the findings of the study have been said to support the view that natural environments are better for our health. However, overall, what the research shows is that having a view more interesting than a brick wall had positive outcomes for patients. It does not show that a natural scene *per se* is important. A view of a brick wall is much less interesting than trees, and it is possible that the outcomes were a result of having an interesting view rather than a natural view. It is possible that a similar positive result could have been achieved if the view had looked out over an interesting built scene. Nonetheless, the study does show that the view someone has in hospital can impact on his or her experience, treatment, and length of stay. That is an important finding and as we saw when we discussed mental health facilities earlier, designs that are incorporating views of and access to nature are successful in reducing stress (Ulrich, 2018).

Rachel Kaplan addressed the question of whether the important feature of a view is nature or just something interesting. She was focused on ART rather that attempting to clarify Ulrich's findings, but her research has relevance to SRT as well. Kaplan (2001) argued that windows, and especially a room with a view, are important because many people do not have regular, easy access to natural environments. Therefore, windows can provide some contact as *micro-restorative settings.* The research compared windows with different views in relation to several outcomes. The results showed that nature played a significant role in people's satisfaction with their residence, and an important role in their well-being. Trees were the most important element of a view that contributed to well-being and of feeling of being *restored*. Conversely, the built components of the views significantly detracted from residential satisfaction, although they did not have an impact on well-being, so were not detrimental. In other words, residents preferred a natural view, which also improved their feeling of well-being and restoration.

In an unusual break with studying natural environments, Stephen Kaplan and colleagues examined an art museum, arguing that it has the qualities of a restorative environment, despite being a man-made setting. From an ART perspective, the gallery has *extent, being away, fascination, and compatibility* (Kaplan et al., 1993). As might be expected they found that, in general, visitors did have a restorative experience, supporting the idea that built environments can, for some, have restorative qualities. The restorative effect varied with the amount of time spent in the museum, with those who spent more than three hours there experiencing the most restoration. Interestingly the researchers found that knowledge of art and visit frequency did not have a significant effect on restoration. Hardly surprisingly, whether people felt comfortable and whether they got lost did have an impact of restoration, in the direction that would be expected; those with the highest levels of confusion and 'being lost' scores also scored lowest on restoration.

Most of us will have experienced, either directly or via horror films and thrillers, that the natural environment can also sometimes generate feelings of foreboding and fear, as would be anticipated from evolutionary theories of landscape preference such as Ulrich's (Ulrich, 1983). More systematic research has examined the circumstances under which natural environments evoke fear or stress, and when they might require directed attention rather than fascination (Gatersleben & Andrews, 2013).

Using pictures of dense wooded areas of natural settings and walks in real outdoor settings with different levels of accessibility, prospect (clear field of vision), and refuge (places to hide), Gatersleben and Andrews (2013) showed that exposure to natural environments with high levels of prospect (visibility) and low levels of refuge (places for a potential threat to hide) is restorative. However, exposure to natural environments low in prospect (visibility) and high in refuge (places to hide) is not restorative and *increases* levels of stress and attention fatigue.

These few studies show us that even just having a window to a pleasant environment can have a restorative impact on us. They also show that some natural environments can be stressful, while Kaplan et al.'s (1993) study of the museum shows that potentially some built environments can be restorative. Beyond the few investigations described here, however, there are reviews of the literature on restorative environments that provide an overall conclusion about the different impacts of different settings. While authors informally examining the relevant research literature have often concluded, "There is a lot of research evidence showing that natural environments are more restorative than urban environments" (Berto, 2005. P. 249), it is useful to look at the systematic reviews that have been undertaken.

There are two well-conducted, relatively recent systematic reviews of the research on restorative environments. The earliest of these (Bowler et al., 2010) looked at studies of the relationship between *health and well-being* and natural and built environments, rather than restoration. They also included activities within the natural environment rather than only exposure to nature. Meta-analysis revealed some evidence of a positive benefit of a walk or run in a natural environment compared to activity in a synthetic environment, demonstrating that being in a natural environment is better than seeing pictures or videos of it. They initially found some support for the idea that people can concentrate or show greater attention after experiencing a natural environment. However, when adjustments were made for pre-test differences, the effects disappeared. In other words, they did not find evidence to support the view that natural environments will facilitate concentration. When a person is stressed their blood pressure can increase and they are likely to have elevated levels of the hormone cortisol in their blood. Bowler et al. (2010) found that there was less evidence of a consistent difference between the impact of urban and rural environments on cortisol levels, which is an objective level of stress, than on self-reports of stress. The authors found relatively weak evidence supporting the restorative quality of natural environments, although they do conclude that studies are "suggestive that natural environments may have direct and positive impacts on well-being" (Bowler et al., 2010, p. 9).

Ohly and her colleagues' review was slightly more supportive of the impact of natural environments on attention restoration (Ohly et al., 2016). The researchers did look specifically at restoration, and they confined their review to studies that used objective measures. They found that the studies they considered used a variety of outcome measures to assess the restorative quality of environments, each attempting to measure some aspect of cognitive or other functions. Ohly et al.'s review revealed three measures on abstract cognitive tasks that demonstrated beneficial effects. They also found task performance on another increased significantly following exposure to *non-natural* settings. The authors report that there were no differences between non-natural and natural settings on ten other attention measures. Commenting on the cognitive performance measures that had been used in the studies that they reviewed, the authors noted that while some of the measures show a statistically significant improvement, how that translates to practical significance in everyday life is not clear. Which is to say, significant laboratory-based results on abstract tasks might not be associated with meaningful change in everyday life. Notwithstanding that cautionary comment, it seems that some aspects of cognitive functioning might be improved or restored by exposure to natural environments, but at this point it is not clear exactly which aspects of cognition are improved. Further, it is quite possible that some people might find non-natural settings restorative too.

Interestingly, adolescents tend to have a preference for more urban settings compared to natural environments (Kaplan & Kaplan, 1989). Studies have shown that teenagers display negative reactions to the idea of being in nature (Bixler & Floyd, 1997). A study directly looking at the restorative qualities of environments for teenagers found that natural settings do provide a restorative experience to a greater extent than indoor environments. However, the researchers also found that being with friends improves that experience (Greenwood & Gatersleben, 2016). It is worth noting that the study found that playing games on their phones did not interfere with the teenagers' restorative experiences.

One of the problems with drawing conclusions from the research reviewed is that they often use different outcome measures making them hard to compare. In addition, few studies examine impacts *during* exposure to nature, meaning that there may be benefits in real time that are missed as they do not last beyond the exposure. Finally, Ohly and her colleagues focused on objective measures. It is quite possible that people's subjective experiences have beneficial effects on their health and well-being even if their cognitive performance stays the same. Overall, it can be said that there is some evidence that natural environments have the potential to restore cognitive attention; however, the evidence is not yet as overwhelming as it is sometimes portrayed.

GREEN MEDICINE

One possible reason for the mixed evidence that exposure to natural environments restores cognitive attention is that the impact of the environment varies with life stage. There is an indication that the relationship between green space and mental health may vary over life course, and in ways that are gender related (Astell-Burt, Mitchell, & Hartig, 2014). Nonetheless, the use of natural environments in individual and public health, preventative medicine, and recovery has become part of mainstream medicine. In this case, the primary aims are improving exercise, achieving weight loss, and improving mental health.

Hartig, one of the leading researchers on health and restorative environments, notes that there has been a shift in the way in which health is thought about. In many ways that change reflects the different therapeutic models we looked at earlier. Resulting from the significant increase in long-term, lifestyle-related diseases as the major cause of death, *biopsychosocial* models have been seen as an alternative to *biomedical* approaches. Consequently, concepts such as psychological stress and social support have become more significant in relation to people's physical well-being (Hartig et al., 2014).

On reviewing the environment and health literature, Hartig and his colleagues contend that there are not enough research studies to be able to be sure of a causal relationship between exposure to the natural environment and health, or how that might differ between subgroups or between different kinds of natural environment (Hartig, Baybutt, & Dooris, 2014). They conclude that there is agreement that there are beneficial effects, but that these benefits are related to intermediate outcomes including physical and physiological activity, and changes in emotional states and cognitive functioning. Exposure to the natural environment does not show benefits based on measures of a direct impact on disease or death rates. The view they came to was that "*the evidence is not yet good enough to say when, where, and for whom given effects will occur or how large or long-lasting they will be*" (Hartig et al. 2014. p. 211).

Despite conclusions showing only moderate relationships between the environment and restoration, the intermediate states, such as increased physical activity, are nonetheless important. For instance, increased exercise has the potential for reducing the current obesity epidemic in many Western countries and improving cardiovascular conditions. Whether that exercise is taken in an urban setting, a green space within an urban setting or a rural environment is secondary to it taking place, notwithstanding issues of air quality.

The potential health impacts of natural environments point to the need to ensure that all people have access to green space, especially in cities. The importance of this is emphasised by research that has shown that availability of green space can reduce health inequalities between different income groups (Mitchell & Popham, 2008). Research has shown that there is a greater inequality between income groups in areas where groups have less access to green environments. It is possible that in areas that lack green space, those who can afford it can gain access more distant spaces and enjoy their benefits. Further, in populations who have access to green environments, inequality of income is less reflected in the inequality in levels of health (Mitchell & Popham, 2008). In other words, income deprivation is less related to lower relative levels of health in people with access to green space. These finding hold for death from circulatory disease as well as for all-cause mortality.

FINALLY

There is a long and diverse history of therapeutic and restorative environments. The extent to which they have been beneficial has varied considerably. The models used to conceptualise the environment and service user needs will impact the way in which the settings are designed. We started the chapter by looking at models of therapy beginning with custodial models that were applied to prisons, and later psychiatric asylums. In those institutions inmates were often warehoused and stored, without regard for rehabilitation or well-being. Recent development of therapeutic environments often use multiple models which act to enhance the environment, provide prosthetic support, and promote development, as we have seen with dementia, autism, and to some extent mental 'illnesses'. Like other areas of environmental psychology, the role of the environment is complex and can be subtle. Therapeutic environments are also drawing on the ideas of restoration, incorporating green spaces and images into their designs. As we have seen, even in prisons gardens and gardening are a way of enhancing well-being and reducing recidivism, thus bringing into custodial environments the ethos of green prescribing and restoration, with research is showing that access to gardens and engaging in gardening have direct mental health benefits for prisoners (Farrier et al., 2019). The longstanding interest in restorative settings and in particular the role of the natural environment is also seeing fruit in the form of green prescribing and the wider use of the environment for health benefits for the general population. The mechanisms that link green spaces and health are not yet fully understood, but it is quite clear there are few if any downsides from these initiatives.

REFERENCES

Anthony, K. H., & Watkins, N. J. (2002). Exploring pathology: Relationships between clinical and environmental psychology. In R. B. Bechtel & A. Churchman (eds.), *Handbook of Environmental Psychology* (pp. 129–146). Chichester: Wiley.

Appleton, J. (1975). *The Experience of Landscape.* Chichester: Wiley.

Astell-Burt, T., Mitchell, R. & Hartig, T. (2014). The association between green space and mental health varies across the lifecourse. A longitudinal study. *Journal of Epidemiological and Community Health*, 68, 578–583.

Bancroft, K., Batten, A., Lambert, S., & Madders, T. (2012). *The Way We Are: Autism in 2012.* London: The National Autistic Society.

Bentall, R. (1990). *Reconstructing Schizophrenia.* London: Routledge.

Bentall, R. (2009). *Doctoring the Mind: Why Psychiatric Treatments Fail.* London. Allen Lane.

Berto, R. (2005). Exposure to restorative environments helps restore attentional capacity. *Journal of Environmental Psychology*, 25, 249–259.

Bixler, R. D. & Floyd, M. F. (1997). Nature is scary, disgusting, and uncomfortable. *Environment and Behavior*, 29, 443–467.

Bowers, L., Stewart, D., Papadopulos, C., Dack, C, Ross, J., Khanom, H., & Jerrery, D. (2011). *Inpatient violence and aggression: A literature review. Report from the Conflict Containment Reduction Research Programme.* Institute of Psychiatry, Kings College London. Retrieved from https://www.kcl.ac.uk/ioppn/depts/hspr/archive/mhn/projects/litreview/litrevagg.pdf

Bowler, D. E., Buyung-Ali, L. M., Knight, T. M., & Pullin, A. S. (2010). A systematic review of evidence for the added benefits to health of exposure to natural environments. *BMC Public Health*, 10, 456.

Boyd-Caine, T. (2012). *Protecting the Public? Detention and Release of Mentally Disordered Offenders.* Oxford: Routledge.

Brush, J. A. & Calkins, M. P. (2008). Cognitive impairment, way-finding, and the long-term care environment. *Perspectives on Gerontology*, 13(2), 65–73.

Canter, S. & Canter, D. (1979). Building for therapy. In D. Canter & S. Canter (eds.), *Designing for Therapeutic Environments: A Review of Research* (pp. 1–28). Chichester: Wiley.

Chrysikou, E. (2014). *Architecture for Psychiatric Environments and Therapeutic Spaces.* Amsterdam: IOS Press.

Clare, A. (1976). *Psychiatry in Dissent: Controversial Issues in Thought and Practice.* London: Tavistock Publications.

Day, K. & Calkins, M. P. (2003). Design and dementia. In R. B. Bechtel & A. Churchman. *Handbook of Environmental Psychology* (pp. 374–393). Chichester: Wiley.

Desai, A. K. & Grossberg, G. T. (2001). Recognition and management of behavioral disturbances in dementia. *Primary Care Companion to the Journal of Clinical Psychiatry*, 3(3), 93–109.

Devine-Wright, H., Baybutt, M., & Meek, R. (2019). Producing food in English and Welsh prisons. *Appetite*, 143, https://doi.org/10.1016/j.appet.2019.104433

Evans, G. W. & Cohen, S. (1987). Environmental stress. In D. Stokols & I. Altman (eds.), *Handbook of Environmental Psychology, Volume 1* (pp. 571–610). Chichester: Wiley.

Gatersleben, B. & Andrews, M. (2013). When walking in nature is not restorative: The role of prospect and refuge. *Health & Place*, 20, 91–101.

Greenwood, A. & Gatersleben, B. (2016). Let's go outside! Environmental restoration amongst adolescents and the impact of friends and phones. *Journal of Environmental Psychology*, 48, 131–139.

Farrier, A., Baybutt, M., & Dooris, M. (2019). Mental health and wellbeing benefits from a prisons horticultural programme. *International Journal of Prisoner Health*, 15(1), 91–104.

Hartig, T., Mitchell, R., de Vries, S., & Frumkin, H. (2014). Nature and health. *Annual Review of Public Health*, 35, 207–228.

Henry, C. N. (2011). Designing for Autism: The 'Neuro-Typical' Approach. *ArchDaily 3 November.* Accessed 25 August 2021. https://www.archdaily.com/181402/designing-for-autism-the-neuro-typical-approach. ISSN 0719-8884

Holley, J., Weaver, T., & Völlm, B. (2020). The experience of long stay in high and medium secure psychiatric hospitals in England: Qualitative study of the patient perspective. *International Journal of Mental Health Systems*, 14, 25. https://doi.org/10.1186/s13033-020-00358-7

Holman, E. A. & Stokols, D. (1994). The environmental psychology of child sexual abuse. *Journal of Environmental Psychology*, 14, 237–252.

Ito-Alpturer, M., & Uslu, O. (2010). Accessibility versus privacy: Turkish students' evaluation criteria for the location of university counselling offices. *Procedia Social and Behavioural Science,* 5, 502–506.

Ittelson, W. H. (1973). Environment perception and contemporary perceptual theory. In W. H. Ittelson (ed.), *Environment and Cognition* (pp. 1–19). New York: Seminar.

Jenkins, O., Dye, S., & Foy, C. (2015). A study of agitation, conflict and containment in association with change in ward physical environment. *Journal of Psychiatric Intensive Care,* 11, 27–35.

Kaplan, R. (2001). The nature of the view from home: Psychological Benefits. *Environment and Behaviour*, 33, 507–542.

Kaplan, R. & Kaplan, S. (1989). *The Experience of Nature: A psychological perspective.* New York: Cambridge University Press.

Kaplan, S. (1991). Meditation, restoration and the management of metal fatigue. *Environment and Behaviour*, 33(4), 480–506.

Kaplan, S. (1995). The restorative benefits of nature: Towards an integrative framework. *Journal of Environmental Psychology*, 15, 169–182.

Kaplan, S., Bardwell, L. V., & Slakter, D. B. (1993). The museum as a restorative environment. *Environment and Behaviour*, 25, 725–742.

King, A. C., Stokols, D., Talen, E., Brassington, G. S., & Killingsworth, R. (2002). Theoretical approaches to the promotion of physical activity: Forging a transdisciplinary paradigm. *American Journal of Preventive Medicine*, 23(2), Supplement 1, 15–25.

Laing, R. D., & Esterson, A. (1964). *Sanity, Madness and the Family.* London: Tavistock Publications.

Lake, A., & Townsend, T. (2006). Obesogenic environments: Exploring the built and food environments. *Journal of the Royal Society for the Promotion of Health*, 126(6), 262–267.

Ludden, G. D. S., van Rompay, T. J. L., Niedderer, K., & Tournier, I. (2019). Environmental design for dementia care – Towards more meaningful experiences through design. *Maturitas*, 128, 10–16.

Marion, M. (2006). Bringing the world to the classroom. *The Exceptional Parent*, 36(4), 32–35.

Marquardt, G. (2011). Wayfinding for people with dementia: A review of the role of architectural design. *HERD Health Environments Research Journal*, 4(2), 75–90.

Marquardt, G. & Schmieg, P. (2009). dementia-friendly architecture: Environments that facilitate wayfinding in nursing homes. *American Journal of Alzheimer's Disease and Other Dementias*, 24, 333–340.

Mitchell, L., Burton, E., Raman, S., Blackman, T., Jenks, M., & Williams, K. (2003). Making the outside world dementia-friendly: Design issues and considerations. *Environment and Planning B: Planning and Design*, 30, 605–632.

Mitchell, R., & Popham, F. (2008). Effect of exposure to natural environment on health inequalities: An observational population study. *Lancet*, 372, 1655–1660.

Moran, D., Jones, P. I., Jordan, J. A., & Porter, A. E. (2021). Does nature contact in prison improve well-being? Mapping land cover to identify the effect of greenspace on self-harm and violence in prisons in England and Wales. *Annals of the American Association of Geographers*, 111, 1779–1795.

Mostafa, M. (2008). An architecture for autism: Concepts of design intervention for the autistic user. *Archnet-IJAR: International Journal of Architectural Research*, 2(1), 189–211.

Mostafa, M. (2020) Architecture for autism: Built environment performance in accordance to the autism ASPECTSS design index. In U. Dass, N. Papnaeophytou, & T. El-Kour (eds.), *Autism 360°* (pp. 479–500). London: Academic Press.

Ohly, H., White, M. P., Wheeler, B. W., Bethel, A., Ukoumunne, O. C., Nikolaou, V., & Garside, R. (2016). Attention Restoration Theory: A systematic review of the attention restoration potential of exposure to natural environments. *Journal of Toxicology and Environmental Health, Part B*, 19(7), 305–343.

Papoulias, C., Csipke, W., Rose, D, McKellar, S., & Wykes, T. (2014). The psychiatric ward as a therapeutic space: Systematic review. *British Journal of Psychiatry*, 205, 171–176.

Passini, R., Rainville, C., Marchand, N., & Joanette, Y. (1998). Way- finding with dementia: Some research findings and a new look at design. *Journal of Architectural and Planning Research*, 15, 133–151.

Prince, M., Bryce, R., Albanese, E., Wimo, A., Ribeiro, W., & Ferri, C. P. (2013). The global prevalence of dementia: A systematic review and meta-analysis. *Alzheimer's and Dementia: Journal of the Alzheimer's Association*, 9, 63–75.

Rogerson, M., Haines-Delmont, A., McCabe, R., Brown, A., & Whittington, R. (2021). The relationship between inpatient mental health ward design and aggression. *Journal of Environmental Psychology*, 77. https://doi.org/10.1016/j.jenvp.2021.101670

Söderlund, J. & Newman, P. (2017). Improving mental health in prisons through Biophilic design. *The Prison Journal*, 97, 750–772.

Stokols, D., Grzywacz, J. G., & McManhan, S. (2003). Increasing the health promotive capacity of human environments. *American Journal of Health Promotion*, 18, 4–13.

Szasz, T. S. (1972). *The Myth of Mental Illness*. London: Paladin.

Ulrich, R. S. (1981). Natural versus urban scenes: Some psychophysiological effects. *Environment and Behavior*, 13, 523–556.

Ulrich, R. S. (1983). Aesthetic and affective response to natural environment. In I. Altman & J. Wohlwill (eds.), *Human Behavior and Environment, Vo1.6: Behavior and Natural Environment* (pp. 85–125). New York: Plenum.

Ulrich, R. S. (1984). View through a window may influence recovery from surgery. *Science*, 224(4647), 420–421.

Ulrich, R. S., Bogren, L., Gardiner, S. K., & Lundin, S. (2018). Psychiatric ward design can reduce aggressive behavior. *Journal of Environmental Psychology*, 57, 53–66.

Van Hoof, J., Kort, H. S. M., van Waarde, H., & Blom, M. M. (2010). Environmental interventions and the design of homes for older adults with dementia: An overview. *American Journal of Alzheimer's Disease & Other Dementias*, 25(3), 202–232.

Van der Roest, H. G., Wenborn, J., Pastink, C., Dröes, R. M., & Orrell, M. (2017). Assistive technology for memory support in dementia. *Cochrane Database of Systematic Reviews*, 6. Art. No.: CD009627. https://doi.org/10.1002/14651858.CD009627.pub2.

van der Schaaf, P., Dusseldorp, E., Keuning, E., Janssen, W., & Noorthoorn, E. (2013). Impact of the physical environment of psychiatric wards on the use of seclusion. *British Journal of Psychiatry*, 202, 2, 142–149.

Wener, R. E. (2012). *The Environmental Psychology of Prisons and Jails: Creating Humane Spaces in Secure Settings.* Cambridge: Cambridge University Press.

Wilding, S., Ziauddeen, N., Smith, D., Roderick, P., Chase, D., & Alwan, N. A. (2020). Are environmental area characteristics at birth associated with overweight and obesity in school-age children? Findings from the SLOPE (Studying Lifecourse Obesity PrEdictors) population-based cohort in the south of England. *BMC Medicine*, 18, 43. https://doi.org/10.1186/s12916-020-01513-0

Zajonc, R. B. (1980). Feeling and thinking: Preferences need no inferences. *American Psychologist*, 35, 151–175.

SUGGESTED READING

Chrysikou, E. (2014). *Architecture for Psychiatric Environments and Therapeutic Spaces.* Amsterdam: IOS Press.

Wener, R. E. (2012). *The Environmental Psychology of Prisons and Jails: Creating Humane Spaces in Secure Settings.* Cambridge: Cambridge University Press.

7

OFFICE ENVIRONMENTS

INTRODUCTION

The majority of people spend a very significant amount of their adult life in work environments of one sort or another. That setting could be a shop, a factory, a restaurant, behind the wheel of a bus, on a ship, in an airplane, or any other of the many places people work. However, the current dominant workplace that the majority of people spend their time is an office. In this chapter we will focus on this work setting. We will examine the broad theories that underlie its design, and the research evidence that tests the validity of those ideas. We will also look at how the way office environments are managed impacts on workers, and especially on personalisation and the role it plays in work places. We will begin with setting the scene of the office and office research.

SETTING THE SCENE

Vischer wrote some time ago that

> thirty million adults go to work every day in office building in North America. For white-collar workers who work an average productive lifespan, this means that about one third of their lives between the ages of twenty and sixty is spent in these environments.
>
> (Vischer, 1989, p. 1)

The same pattern is likely to apply to all advanced economies and probably much of the developing world. For the organisations occupying offices, the physical environment is their second highest

DOI: 10.4324/9780429274541-7

financial resource cost after employees (Becker & Steele, 1994; McCoy, 2005). As well as being a major investment, the design of their offices has the potential to impact the company's performance and profitability.

Since the 1960s and 1970s a lot of attention has been paid to the environmental psychology of offices. Interest in the field resulted from social and economic change, design innovation and marketing, theoretical developments, a general increase of interest in the environment, and the emergence of environmental psychology. These and other factors provide the antecedent conditions for office research, and have shaped the nature and focus of those studies. The research has often been concerned with trying to find direct causal links between the environment and responses from office workers. Studies vary from examining individual elements of environmental experience such as lighting, heating, or noise, to looking at settings from a more holistic perspective.

The involvement of psychologists in the systematic study of workplaces is different in each country. In the U.K. it began during the First World War with the work of the Industrial Fatigue Research Board (Vernon, 1919), which represented the start of applied psychology research in the U.K. (Donald & Canter, 1987). A century or so ago the focus was on factory environments along with coalmines and other industrial settings. It was not until the 1960s that psychologists left their own offices to study those of others. One reason offices were drawing attention was the rapid growth in the number of office-based workers, to around three quarters of the workforce in Western developed countries. Although increased homeworking is being predicted for a post Covid-19 pandemic world, it is unlikely there will be a serious fall in the numbers of office workers, but they may use the spaces differently. Any change that does take place will be part of a long evolution going back to Victorian times, which has seen significant transformations in the form of offices and the work carried out within them. The speed of change has also increased. For instance, an office worker from as recently as the 1980s would find many facets of contemporary offices unfamiliar.

Office environments are rich with psychological, functional, work, and organisational issues and implications that are worthy of study. Amongst these are environmental issues of personal space, spatial density and crowding, and personalisation, and related organisational and personal outcomes including identity, and workflow (Ashkanasy, Ayoko, & Jehn, 2014), communication, corporate identity, customer satisfaction, culture, well-being, innovation and creativity, collaboration, and more (Kegel, 2017).

Today much thinking about office environments focuses on the social nature of work. Ayoko and Ashkanasy (2020), for example, explain the role of physical work settings in this way: "*the physical environment is more than just a physical container for social interactions, but also crucial for the nature, quality, and duration of employee social interactions, behaviours, interaction processes, and outcomes*" (Ayoko & Ashkanasy, 2020, p. 3). The emphasis in this chapter will follow this characterisation and focus on the social nature of work and work environments and those factors that impinge upon it. That is not to say, however, that they are the only environmental elements that are worth examining. There are many others facets of office settings that have been investigated beyond socio-spatial issues.

Some flavour of the breadth and content of studies can be seen in Sundstrom's (1986) seminal review of research on work environments, which included whole chapters on lighting and windows, temperature and air, noise, music, colour, and workstations. Other chapters focus more of the issues we look at here and include the experience of people at an interpersonal level and include self-identity and status, communication, privacy, and small groups and group formation. Other research has examined the facets of office design identifying different referents including space, ambient conditions, social and socio-spatial components at different levels; workspace, office and building (Donald, 1994a).

The idea that social interaction is central to work and offices environments has not always been part of the thinking about organisations, employees, or design. To understand why this was, and how that has evolved into today's primary concerns, we need to look at theories of organisation and work and what they meant for workers and their environments.

ORGANISATIONAL THEORY AND OFFICE DESIGN

There have always been psychological assumptions made about the nature of work, workers, and organisations. Those assumptions have, in turn, influenced the design and management of office environments. There are, of course, many organisational theories, but the shift from *classical* to *humanistic* theories is arguably the most fundamental in its implications for work and design. In the next sections we will look at how that change has been integrated into thinking about the environment over the last hundred years.

CLASSICAL ORGANISATIONAL THEORY

Ideas that came to be recognised as classical organisational theory began to coalesce at the beginning of the twentieth century. Two of the most influential contributors to its development were Fredrick Taylor (1911), initially working in industrial production in the USA, and Max Weber (1947) (Although the English translation of Weber's influential book appeared in 1947, it was published in Germany, 1921. Moreover, much of his work and many of his ideas had been published before that date), focusing on administrative work and ideas of bureaucracy in Germany. Both wanted to bring scientific objectivity to workplaces, removing subjectivity in decision-making, and rationalising work and work processes. Their aim was to remove waste, inefficiency, and unpredictability. Taylor, Weber, and their followers had a very mechanistic view of work and workers, reducing the role of a person to being part of a 'machine'. In the factories based on Taylor's work, that idea was almost literal in its manifestation. As part of the objectification of workers, the approach leaves aside psychological and social needs such as job satisfaction. In place of the intrinsic satisfaction people gain from work, the theorists considered money to be the sole motivating force.

Taylor's ideas were presented in his groundbreaking book the *Principles of Scientific Management* (Taylor, 1911). In keeping with the aim of bringing 'science' to management, Taylor placed measurement at the centre of his approach. His aim was for tasks to be completed in the fastest possible time. A derivative of scientific management, *time and motion*, was developed by Gilbreth (1912), with the goal of identifying the most *efficient* way of carrying out a task, reducing unnecessary actions and wasted effort, achieving *economy of motion* (Gilbreth, 1912). The aims of efficiency and economy of motion needed tasks to be broken down into their component parts – *elemental tasks.* Once identified, elements were arranged into the sequence that allowed the task to be completed in the quickest and most efficient way. The approach was readily pioneered in the new factories established by devotee Henry Ford, and others, who demonstrated significant increases in efficiency and the elimination of waste.

Time and motion was so called because measurements were taken of the time it took to perform each task. In factories measuring elemental tasks made some logical sense. It wasn't long, however, before time and motion and the principles of scientific management were applied to office work, with sometimes rather absurd results. For instance, we now know that it takes 0.04 minutes to open and close a file draw, and to get up from a chair takes 0.033 minutes (Braverman, 1974). It is unlikely that in practice this knowledge helped to improve productivity and would have done little for the daily lives of employees, but it was part of the ethos of the day.

At around the same time Taylor was working in the USA, German philosopher and sociologist Max Weber was concerned with the concept of *bureaucracy.* Although not drawing on Taylor's work, Weber's ideas had much in common, especially the belief that it is important for the workplace to be impersonal and rational. Similar to what happened in factories, in an administrative context, Weber's theories introduced clear *division of labour*, in which people repeatedly perform specific small components of an overall task. Taylor had emphasised the division between management and worker; Weber emphasised the importance of a *hierarchy of authority.* As mentioned earlier, both believed that interaction should be based solely on formal *impersonal relations*, with social bonds and informal interaction prohibited. In both theories, emotions including satisfaction, pleasure, pride, and achievement are unimportant and should not be something management should consider in designing work or motivating workers. Finally, Weber thought that both work and behaviour should be prescribed by *extensive and stable rules.*

The main ideas of classical theories have been translated into environmental design to varying degrees, most obviously in factories, but also in offices. Building design elements, for instance, can provide a visible hierarchy with *symbols of office* and other indicators of seniority. The British Civil Service, for example, had symbols of office and a rigid code of extensive rules that specified what different grades of employee were entitled to in their office, including the type of coat rack and the number of windows. Although there has been a shift from obvious indicators of hierarchy today, they are still present, and as we will discuss later, removing them can be problematic.

Rational workflow is aided by the demarcation of different types of employees and the separation of functions using office layout and positioning to improve economy of motion and efficiency. In an insurance firm, for example, when a claim is processed it will go through several stages. Those stages can be separated with different employees dealing with each stage of the process. It then makes sense to locate employees in a way that reflects that process so that papers can be easily passed from one to the next, which was especially important before electronic documents. Because within classical theories workers were not trusted to do their jobs without strict supervision, the designs allowed observation and monitoring of employees, which let managers suppress social interaction and informal conversation.

The Frank Lloyd Wright designed Larkin Building in the USA provides a good example of how the application of scientific management to design could be achieved. While the building included many architectural and engineering innovations, including crude air conditioning, it also shows how design and management practices together can dehumanise and control a workforce (Donald, 2001; Duffy, 1980). In the large open office, rows of workers occupied seats that were attached to their desks and pivoted so that they could move, but only in a limited, prescribed way. The aim of the restriction was to prevent needless and inefficient movement. The building reflected the dominance of the organisation over its employees. It did this in several ways. The first was symbolic and probably better recognised by architects and designers than the employees themselves. The rather cavernous offices in which people work had high, multi-storey ceilings that have been architecturally likened to a cathedral in which the office space was intended to demonstrate the dominance of the organisation. Another less subtle design feature of the Larkin and other buildings was the slogans on the walls extolling the virtues of hard work. The final example was the elevated seating position given to supervisors, which allowed them to observe all the employees and monitor their behaviour in a way that would have been very apparent. From their position, supervisors could control informal conversations and interactions that might interfere with work efficiency.

An office environment in which employees are monitored, not allowed to talk informally, or move from their tethered desks and is arranged as a production line, may sound alienating, but many modern call centres share a lot of similarities. Despite examples of this design still being found, classical theory did eventually lose favour. The seeds of its demise lay within its own methodology. Writers began identifying classical organisations as overly hierarchical, stilted in communication, and dehumanising. The real blow to classical theory, however, came because of what were later collectively known as the *Hawthorne studies*. In essence, the studies led to a shift in perspective: out went the idea of employees as parts of a machine, in came recognition of them as complex social beings.

HAWTHORNE STUDIES: FROM MACHINES TO PEOPLE

Most psychologists have heard of the *Hawthorne Effect*, but do not necessarily know the detail of the original research (Mayo, 1933; Roethlisberger & Dickson, 1949). Although the studies ultimately contributed to the humanising of work environments and the end of 'scientific management' as a major force, the original research was in keeping with the principles of scientific management and conceived of with the aim of discovering the optimal physical conditions for increased productivity. The studies were based on the deterministic belief that there is a direct relationship between elements of the physical environment and performance, and the researchers designed straightforward experiments in which they varied environmental conditions and observed their impact on output. In an experimental room they had workers carrying out tasks under different lighting intensities. First, they increased lighting levels for a group of workers and as expected, their performance improved. However, the researchers were surprised to discover that reducing lighting levels did not result in a decline in performance; it continued to rise, even to the point where lighting levels were so low it was difficult to see the task. When the experiments had finished and the workers returned to their usual working environments, they continued to show improved performance. Even more surprising, employees who were not even part of the experiment also increased their output after the studies.

There is subsequent analysis of the data from the study, using archives at Cornell University, which provide a slightly different picture. The new analysis of the data revealed that there was an effect of lighting on productivity; however, that was only for the first experiment. Subsequent experiments failed to replicate the findings. Further, the researchers found that there were serious flaws in all of the experiments (Izawa, French, & Hedge, 2011). Nonetheless, the work continues to have importance in helping us to understand the nature of work and the environment.

We now know that the results can be explained by the involvement of the employees in the research, which allowed them to develop social relationships, have more freedom, feel 'special', and generally pace their work as a group. Not realising the importance of their findings, one conclusion drawn by the researchers was that the physical environment is irrelevant to performance, which quite possibly led to a delay in the development of environmental psychology by some decades. The US National Academy of Science, which had conducted the research, consequently abandoned further studies. Fortunately for industrial and organisational psychology, the Western Electrical Company, which had participated in the studies, was keen to take the inquiries further in the hope of throwing some light on the intriguing results. Working with Elton Mayo and other psychologists at Harvard University, they undertook a series of different and more sophisticated studies (Roethlisberger & Dickson, 1949). In these studies, employees completed questionnaires, some of the first used in industrial psychology, took part in interviews, and were more actively engaged in the research. The focus this time was on understanding the workers' experience. The studies went beyond the idea of a simple deterministic relationship between people and the environment, to include the impact of frequency of breaks, shift length, hours worked, pay, and other components of a person's working day. They also looked at the factors involved in the formation of social groups and norms.

The studies showed that emotions, job satisfaction, involvement, and, above all, the social relations and the groups that developed around work determined productivity. The essence of what the studies revealed was that factors external to a job were more influential on the way in which work was performed than the characteristics of job itself. The implications of this are wide-ranging for work, management, and organisation, and of course, as we will see, for the design of work environments.

HUMANISTIC THEORIES

The humanistic theories of work and organisations put human qualities at the centre of their ideas, recognising the importance of employees' needs and motivations. Like classical theory, humanist theory is not one single theory, and grew out of the work of several authors including Maslow, McGregor, Schein, and Argyris. The writings that comprise humanistic theory have several characteristics that unite them and reflect the themes that developed from the Hawthorne studies. One of the most obvious characteristics is that they identify non-financial rewards as important to people's motivation and performance. Most psychologists will recognise this in Maslow's (1943) ideas on motivation, which appeared around the same time and was another manifestation of the general thinking during this period. Maslow identifies a hierarchy of different levels of motivation, starting at the basic level of shelter and food – the elements needed for survival – through to self-actualisation, which is the motivation to reach your full potential. Within the doctrines of scientific management, work was designed to meet only the lowest levels of motivation. Humanism was more ambitious, aiming, at least in the ideal, for workers to achieve self-actualisation.

The social nature of work is also emphasised by the humanist writers, who documented the influence of evolving social groupings on the way jobs are done, and recognised that workers themselves define their roles and their work norms. Employees often regulate the level of productivity for themselves and others in their work group, decide on the length of work breaks, establish their own workplace leaders, and develop other practices and 'ways of doing things'. As we will see, the environment is potentially important in its influence on group formation and work collaboration. Further, whether employees work in favour of or against a company will depend on many things, including how they feel about the organisation. That, in turn, we will see, can be influenced by the way in which the environment is managed and experienced (Donald, 2001).

Communication is in many ways the essence of an organisation. Traditionally, communication was vertical from the top of the hierarchy to the bottom, often passing through many intermediary levels, with the assumption that the message and its intention will not change. It is now recognised that a two-way communication is important, with the workforce being able to communicate upwards with management. That can happen as part of general everyday life at work or more formally in scheduled times for meetings and participation. Horizontal communication between employees was also recognised as essential and influential rather than something to be suppressed. A further important insight of the humanist theories is that much, if not most, communication happens informally, via channels and means not prescribed by the formal organisation. This means that there are in effect two organisations. There is the formally defined organisation with official communication channels, rules, job roles, and so on. Alongside, or overlaid on top of the formal structures, is the informal organisation of employee consensual leaders or influencers, informal groupings, norms, and informal channels of communication. These new insights into work and employee experience opened up a much wider set of roles and possibilities for the environment. For instance, the environment has the potential to facilitate communication rather than inhibit it. Settings can also be flexible allowing spatial reconfigurations that follow the patterns of groups and group working, making communication and interaction easier. As we will see as we move through the chapter, the relationship between work and the environment can be more subtle and have a less direct impact on organisational functioning and workers' performance than the limited role evident in classical theory.

BÜROLANDSCHAFT: ROLE OF THE ENVIRONMENT IN HUMANISTIC THEORIES

Once vertical and horizontal communication and social interaction are identified as important for organisational performance, design needs to incorporate features that facilitate them. We have seen in Chapter 3 that some relatively simple environmental design characteristics can encourage and facilitate interaction and group formation, and others can inhibit people getting together. We also know that informal interactions can be supported by the provision of informal meeting places. In an office context, these interactions are sometimes referred to as 'water cooler meetings', after the observation that this is where people often bump into each other and have conversations. Adding places for impromptu meetings and removing physical barriers between people could potentially improve accessibility of colleagues, and so potentially improve communication. Ideas such as these started to be reflected in the form of open plan design, with one design in particular responding to the new understanding of work and organisations.

Bürolandschaft (office landscape) was developed in the early 1950s, as a response to the new thinking about work and the social nature of labour. The proponents of the design were the Quickborner Team led by the Schnelle brothers, who were management consultants rather than designers. Bürolandschaft was in fact something of a marketing exercise, but importantly the design was sold on the basis that it could enhance worker performance and productivity through harnessing the social processes that had been described by organisational and work theorists.

Open plan offices were nothing new. Large open office spaces had been around for many years but tended to be large areas containing rows and rows of desks and little else, earning them the name *bullpen* offices. The new open plan office landscaping was different. British architect Frank Duffy described the impact of the radical layout on design professionals:

> Many architects will remember very well the shock of seeing office landscaping for the first time. In the early '60s the essence of office design was to stack homogenised net lettable areas into Miesian towers. Nothing had prepared us for those curious German drawings which actually showed desks, hundreds of desks, randomly arranged in great open spaces. . .Their look burned itself into the retina, an image never to be forgotten.
>
> (Duffy, 1979, p. 54)

Instead of desks in straight lines, workstations were scattered and grouped in seemingly random configurations around the open space, although placement was far from random with the layout and groupings based on communication flows and work-related interactions. Bürolandschaft encouraged all levels of staff to be accommodated together, on the same open floor, with the same standard furniture, aiming to create a non-hierarchical environment and increased communication and collaboration. In the older style of open plan, more senior staff were separated in private offices, usually around the edges of the buildings with windows for natural light, the best views and often furnished to the individual tastes of the occupants.

Office space was divided with area definers such as curved screens, and large potted plants (giving the 'landscape' to Büro*landschaft*), which aim to create some separation of work zones and provide some privacy. Without walls, zones allow both separation for concentration and permeability to encourage interaction and collaboration. Carpets and on the ceiling sound absorbing panels are used to limit noise. The space is flexible and open to reconfiguring to meet the dynamic needs of the organisation and work. In theory at least, the design allows non-hierarchical chains of command, and addresses the need for face-to-face communication, group formation, and flexibility in management. Similar claims have been made for modern open plan offices in general. As the bürolandschaft concept came with a set of rules and rationales about how and why space, people, workers, groups, and organisations should be arranged and what the outcomes would be, the theoretical claims about the design and the assertions that the design could improve office functioning opened it to research and empirical test. As we will see when we discuss the results of office research shortly, the evidence supporting those claims is sparse, with some being directly contradictory (e.g., Bernstein & Turban, 2018).

Open plan is now the dominant office form for most of the workforce, and has attracted most of the research. But not all open plan offices are created equal. The quality of offices can vary significantly from large open spaces with rows and rows of desks, to luxurious settings, with high-quality systems, furniture, greenery, and low-density calm spaces. This variation presents a problem for comparing the findings of office evaluation studies, because it is often difficult to tell from the research publications where the offices being examined lie on this spectrum. As we will see, much of the research concludes that open plan offices do not function well, especially compared with private offices. However, Morrison and

Smollan's (2020) research suggests that a technically well-designed open plan office can mitigate many of the negative effects that other studies report. In their research they find positive evaluations of aesthetics, collegiality, and communication, which would support the claims made by proponents of open plan designs.

Bürolandschaft and other open plan designs tend to subordinate privacy and status in favour of communication flow and interaction. The implications of this can be thought of in terms of our discussion of social interaction in Chapter 3. There we saw that when there is too much interaction people feel crowded and uncomfortable, when interaction is too little they feel isolated. The same ideas can be applied to work and office environments. People can use the physical environment and non-verbal methods to regulate their level of interaction. In private or cellular offices employees could feel isolated and unable to communicate effectively. Accommodating them in large open spaces has the potential to reduce isolation, and increase interaction and communication. However, the removal of walls and barriers can reduce an employee's ability to regulate interaction, affecting privacy, which also has implications for work and well-being. Further the open plan design could increase noise and other distractions.

Much of the research surrounding open plan offices is about the balance between control of privacy and isolation, and being able to work and concentrate, versus being able to communicate and interact (Kim & de Dear, 2013). Ashkansy et al. (2014) summarise the conflicting work-related outcomes stating that "*. . . results of these studies are equivocal, suggesting that the contemporary physical environment of work (i.e., open-plan offices) may be beneficial (e.g., fostering communication and cohesion; Chigot, 2003) or detrimental (e.g., increase noise, poor privacy; (Regoeczi, 2003)*" (p. 1169).

On the negative side, research supports the view that occupants of open plan offices face problems of distractions, which can be from excess noise (e.g., Haapakangas et al., 2008; Hedge, 1982, 1986; Kim & de Dear, 2013), and visual distractions (Liebl et al., 2012). The distractions from noise have been found to be worse when that noise is meaningful, which is essentially other people's conversations (Smith-Jackson & Klien, 2009) that are, of course, what open plan offices are designed to facilitate. However, Irving (2016) found that at team level under some circumstances groups can overcome distractions. Studies also consistently show that occupants of open plan offices experience a lack of privacy (e.g., Ding, 2008; Kim & de Dear, 2013; Kupritz, 2003). The feeling of being observed, which is one element of privacy, is greater amongst women (Morrison & Smollan, 2020), which raises issues about perceived personal security. Research further shows that these factors can, for instance, contribute to emotional exhaustion at work (Laurence, Fried & Slowik, 2013), perceived reduced productivity (Brand & Smith, 2005; Brennan, Clugh & Kline, 2002), as well as an inability to concentrate (Smith-Jackson & Klien, 2009).

There have been several reviews of research examining office environments, primarily in relation to space, social interaction, and their consequences for work and well-being. Particularly useful are systematic reviews, which use an objective process for gathering, selecting, and analysing the relevant papers based on specified criteria. Those that have been carried out in recent years comparing open plan offices with cellular or private offices have been consistent in concluding that open plan offices perform rather poorly on a number of measures. De Croon et al.'s excellent review looked at several characteristics of office environments, including layout and distance from co-workers, concluding:

> . . .open workplaces and high density offices increase cognitive workload . . .office workers have difficulty concentrating, react negatively to interactions and become dissatisfied with their job . . . the lack of acoustic and visual isolation in open workplaces diminishes the control over interaction with others and hinders workers in discussing personal topics in confidence.
>
> (De Croon et al., 2005, p. 129)

Taking more of a focus on health outcomes, similarly pessimistic evaluations of the benefits of open plan offices were evident in the literature reviewed by Richardson et al. (2017). They conclude that every study they reviewed reported "*deleterious effects on employee health*" (p. 46). They found two positive outcomes associated with moving to open plan working. One was an increase in flexibility of both the times employees work and the location of where they work. The other was improved opportunity for informal conversations, though neither improvement was statistically significant (Richardson, et al., 2017). The most recent systematic review, by James and her colleagues at the University of Adelaide (James, Delfabbro, & King, 2021), similarly failed to support the positive claims that have been made about working in open office environments. Examining research comparing private single occupant offices and open plan offices in relation to outcomes of health, satisfaction, social factors, and productivity, the results overwhelmingly reveal that single occupancy offices function better than open plan spaces. Amongst their key findings was that out of 31 measures of satisfaction with the workplace, all were negative for open plan compared to cellular offices. For productivity, most studies showed negative outcomes from open plan, and for health "findings generally tended toward negative outcomes for open-plan offices" (p. 8).

Since one of the characteristics of open plan offices is the balance between privacy and communication, you would probably expect at least some positive social outcomes, which is what James et al.'s (2021) review shows. They identified encouraging findings for single variables in the studies they reviewed, including communication patterns, connectivity, reinforcing interaction, co-worker visibility and proximity, and the ease with which people can be located. All of these are about accessibility. However, when they combined similar variables to form four overall categories, the findings were not positive. The collaboration and communication category showed mixed results, and the remaining three behaviours were overall negative for open plan offices: relationships and getting along, ease of interaction, and leadership and supervisor.

One of the primary goals and work-related reasons for adopting open plan offices is increased communication and collaboration. Part of that is the idea that conversations will occur spontaneously and serendipitously (e.g., Kabo, 2016), what we have previously called, 'water cooler conversations'. The reviews we have already discussed as well as individual studies (e.g., Ayoko, & Härtel, 2003; Värlander, 2012) point to problems with collaboration and communication in open plan offices, although the research is not unequivocal (e.g., Reagans, 2011). An interesting study by Irving, Ayoko, and Ashkanasy (2020) identifies how employees use strategies to cut down on spontaneous collaboration in open plan offices. They found that people emphasised their existing collaborations, reinforced boundaries by, for instance, sitting separately from other groups, used rules that were in place in their previous work site, and minimised social interactions. It is interesting that the staff used these tactics, which in some ways resemble those used by facilities managers to prevent employee-driven changes to the physical environment (Donald, 1991, 1994b).

The findings of Irving et al. (2020) that people use strategies to control increased collaboration are in keeping with what you might expect from studies of privacy and privacy regulation, as discussed above and in Chapter 3. Later we will look at personalisation in the office, which is another way of responding to open plan and reduced privacy and territory. A further possible means of controlling too much openness could be to change the form of communications. For instance, face-to-face social interaction has been found to fall by 70% following a move to open plan offices, being replaced by email and instant messaging (Bernstein & Turban, 2018). This would suggest that even though people are spatially more available, they find ways to reduce direct interaction.

Taking these reviews and studies together, it seems that the claims for the superior performance of open plan offices are somewhat exaggerated. However, there are instances in which open plan is beneficial to some tasks and types of collaboration, but these are quite specific, for instance open plan facilitates collaboration in those circumstances when most people want to collaborate, and when there are formal task interdependencies (Irving, 2016).

There are also many economic benefits to open plan. Generally, they are cheaper for property developers to build with fewer walls and less need to consider in advance the final use and user. They tend to be lower cost for the organisations that inhabit them as well, with running and maintenance costs being less. They are also more efficient for desk sharing (hot desking) allowing a lower desk to staff ratio (Brennan et al., 2002; James et al., 2021; Kim et al., 2016). However, organisations would perhaps be wise to consider the hidden costs as well as the savings. Increased absence, higher turnover, and lower productivity, which have been associated with open plan, reduce a company's profitability and should be part of the calculation of the cost of the physical environment (Bergström, Miller, & Horneij, 2015; Brennan, et al., 2002; James et al., 2021; Oommen, Knowles, & Zhao, 2008; Mylonas & Carstairs, 2007).

Before moving on to consider the management of environments, it is worth noting that even though we are aware of the interrelated nature of work, organisation, social groupings, and the physical environment, much of the research into office environments still isolates single, or a small number of design elements and observes their effect on a single or small number of dependent variables such as self-reported productivity or satisfaction. In that way, quite a few of the studies are conceptually similar to the initial research carried out at the start of the Hawthorne studies, remaining essentially deterministic. Donald (2001) reviewed the research on office environments published in the *Journal of Environmental Psychology*, writing that

> . . .most articles concerned with offices adopt a deterministic framework, were carried out on student populations, used office simulations rather than real offices, considered basic performance criteria for assessing the impact of offices, and showed few statistically significant relationships.
>
> (Donald, 2001, p. 282)

People's relationships with their work settings develop over time and are part of a wider context. Using simulations or conducting research using students will produce research that is always going to have limited value when generalising to office workers. It may well be the case that studies fail to consider the other psychologically important factors that are involved in people's experience of the environment. Unless that broader context is considered research results will remain of limited value.

ORGANISATIONAL PROCESSES, MANAGEMENT, AND THE ENVIRONMENT

Research has shown that organisational process, and the way that a company is managed, can impact on people's evaluations of their environment (Donald, 2001). These processes are almost impossible to reproduce in simulation studies, and so require more sophisticated research in real office environments.

We can illustrate the importance of management context on workers' evaluations of their physical environment using an interesting study of office lighting. Illumination is relatively easy to control and manipulate and has measureable objective characteristics, making it ideal for experimental research, which is perhaps one reason there have been many studies examining lighting.

Researchers often focus on the functional characteristics of the lighting and its direct impact on work to assess which lighting is better for a particular task. Ellis carried out one of the few early psychological studies that went beyond relatively simple stimulus-response consideration of office lighting (Ellis, 1986). In the study, he examined the introduction of new lighting into two offices (Ellis, 1986). Ellis' work was interesting because he looked at the aesthetic and symbolic qualities of people's experience of workplace lighting. Amongst his findings were that different *groups* had different preferences for different lighting types. Acceptance of the lighting schemes was related to the objective lighting characteristics, but was also a function of processes and events that brought them about. The greater the employees' participation in the process that led to the change to the lighting, the greater was their acceptance of it. The research suggests that some users considered the lighting to be inadequate, not because of its physical characteristics but because of management dynamics (Donald, 2001). Ellis found that the aesthetic judgements of the lighting were important not simply as a matter of preference; interestingly, they also influenced employees' attitudes towards work and were related to absenteeism.

The results further reflect the social nature of environmental perceptions in the workplace, showing that *groups* of users perceived the same lighting differently, developing a 'brand loyalty' to a particular lighting type, and interpreting different objective characteristics in very different ways. One group considered their lighting to be 'bright and business-like', whereas a second group described that same lighting as 'cold and clinical'. The second group described their own lighting as 'warm and homey', but the first group saw it as 'gloomy and boutique-like'. The important point is that the objective characteristics of the physical environment interacted with many components of their social and organisational context, including the processes that brought those characteristics about. The process that brings about a setting can be as important to people's consequent experience of the physical characteristics of that environment. It is the totality of those interactions that define people's experience of their environment and its functionality.

Participation by users in organisations, including in the development of settings, is generally considered to be positive. While that is often the case, if not handled well, increased participation can exacerbate or even create problems and negatively impact people's acceptance of the workspace. An example of this can be found in a study that looked at people's experience of either moving to a new office building or of a major renewal of existing premises (Donald, 1991). In this research, one department manager reported numerous functional problems with his workspace and his department's wider work environment. His complaints were causing a significant amount of tension between him and senior facilities management, which was having a detrimental impact on his and his department's work.

During the research, it became clear that many of the environmental issues he raised were not related to the qualities of the physical setting or to their functionality. Instead, it revealed that the processes that had led to the new environment, rather than the environment itself, were the root of the problems. Prior to the new design being implemented, the manager and members of his department had been extensively involved in consultations about their functional needs. Despite this, the reality of other constraints meant that the final design suggested little attention had been paid to their input. The environment consequently became a medium through which the manager expressed his annoyance and anger with what he saw as their wasted time and the organisation's disregard for their opinions and well-being.

This example, as well as Ellis' research, demonstrates the important issue of the role of worker's experience and affect in work organisations and environments (Donald, 2001). During the era dominated by classical theories, emotion and feelings were not viewed as worth consideration; quite the opposite, they were something to be suppressed or ignored. Within workplace design and office research, employee feelings still receive less attention than it deserves. In the next sections we will look at the management of environmental change, which includes some further examples of emotion at work.

MANAGEMENT AND CHANGE IN THE OFFICE

As we have seen, employee involvement and participation in the creation and maintenance of an office environment can impact on their experience and evaluation of it. The need for continuous management of change in an office setting comes from the natural evolution of work and organisations. Organisations face pressure to change to meet the needs of their business and the external forces upon it. At an everyday level, organisational adaption manifests in changing work practices. The environment is part of that dynamic and consequently, there is increasing pressure on it to adjust to meet those new requirements.

Often research conducted by environmental psychologists on offices focuses almost exclusively on the physical aspects of the environments, to the neglect of the management and organisational processes that shape them and their use (Donald, 1994a). Key to the day-to-day running of physical offices settings are facilities managers who are the primary professionals, aside from architects and designers, who shape office use and experience. Facilities management is the process by which the internal environment of such settings as offices is organised in relation to people, technology, and activities (Becker, 1981). Not all organisations have trained or qualified facilities managers, but they all have someone who manages the environment.

While the day-to-day dynamic nature of work and organisations is important, one of the most critical points at which the environment and environment-related processes need to be managed is before and during a major office development, relocation, or refurbishment when there is usually a lot of time and resource go into its planning. The process and result of the changes are a major investment by a company often costing several millions of pounds and many hours of work.

The aim of that work is to achieve a synergy of physical design and organisational and work processes. However, modern organisations and their environments are often too complex to achieve a perfect initial solution. Further, because of the long time from the design conception to building occupation, the design brief may already be out of date by the time the building or office is occupied. The environment and its management therefore need to adapt to the consequences of that gap. Whether that happens depends not only on the design of the physical environment but also on how the mismatch between the original design and current needs is managed.

A CASE STUDY

A useful case study of the management of change in new environments is a cross-national study by Donald (1994b) and colleagues. This research examined office facilities during the first two to three years of occupation of a new building or refurbishment of an existing one. The focus of the work was on work and organisational change and how the environment responds to it. The researchers identified two distinct types of force for change. They referred to these as *intrinsic* and *extrinsic* pressure. Both forms of pressure challenge the synergy of the environment, work, and organisation, but arise from different sources. Extrinsic pressure results from change to the formal structure of the organisation, whereas intrinsic pressure results from the day-to-day work processes and the psychological needs of the employees. Extrinsic change operates at an organisational level rather than an individual level, tends to be 'top-down', and is larger scale. Intrinsic pressure is usually at the level of individuals and groups as they adapt their working methods and practices. Because the staff generates this force for change, it is less formal, primarily 'bottom-up', and small scale.

On a day-to-day basis, it is small-scale changes that are important for people doing their jobs and are the modifications that could make a positive contribution to their work and well-being. However, the research showed that facilities managers respond to extrinsic pressure most readily, and much less so to intrinsic pressures. It seemed that often the management of the environment intentionally prevented or inhibited responses to intrinsic pressure (Donald, 1994b). The research uncovered a series of beliefs that underpin facilities managers' actions, and were key to understanding their response:

- *Day one design can be perfect*: A lot of effort and planning has gone into the design and layout of the office, which has produced the optimum solution that should be maintained.
- *The original design is the ultimate goal*: If the planned design is not achieved on the first day of occupation, efforts should be directed to working towards it, and preventing or avoiding changes that move away from it.
- *The work aesthetic*: Employees should not display personal items and desks should be cleared every evening. In the absence of any metric to measure performance in the new office, its tidiness and general appearance reflects productivity and the quality of the job done by facilities managers.
- *Chaos theory*: Not controlling change and the efforts of employees to make changes, including personalisation, will undermine the principles of the design.
- *The Trivial*: The changes requested are 'nice to haves' rather than necessary for effective working.

Not all of these views were held by all of the facilities managers. It is likely that there will be many beliefs and practices held by facilities managers that will greatly enhance people's working lives and the functioning of the organisation. The important point here is that such beliefs can mean that the office environment fails to meet the dynamic nature of work, not because of factors inherent in the physical design, but because of its management. Rigid beliefs about the physical environment and how it should be used can reduce the impact of participation by the workforce, which can have a knock-on effect on their feelings and evaluations of their settings as well as their work. In order to understand the relationship between workers and the environment, it is necessary to look beyond the physical setting itself.

PERSONALISATION IN THE OFFICE

In the case study on office design, one of the important beliefs that was highlighted was that personalisation is inappropriate within an office setting, has no place in a rational organisation, and serves no important function. Personalisation "is the deliberate adornment, decoration, modification or rearrangement of an environment by its occupants to reflect their individual identities" (Sundstrom, 1986, p. 218). That definition relates directly to the beliefs of the work aesthetic, chaos theory, and the trivial that we have discussed above. The belief that orderliness is indicative of efficiency, apparent in the views expressed by facilities managers in Donald's (1994b) study, seems to have been around for more than a century (Sundstrom, 1986). Certainly, disquiet at employees adapting their work areas was evident in the 1960s and 1970s too (Schumann, 1974).

In the environmental psychology literature on office environments, personalisation receives relatively little attention, especially in comparison to, for instance, lighting, ambient conditions, and spatial layout, raising the question of whether or not it plays an important role in employee experience at work. Evidence suggests that personalisation is important with between 70% and 90% of US office workers saying that they personalise their workspace (BOSTI, 1981; Sundstrom, 1986; Wells, Thelen, & Ruark, 2007). Regardless of the policy pursued by many organisations that ban or severely restrict forms of personalisation, many office workers continue to do it (Becker, 1990; Donald, 2001). Further, a major, highly influential study in the 1970s identified that for an office to reflect the personality of its occupant was the fourth most desirable quality in an office setting (Harris & Associates, 1978). In some ways, perhaps, people wanting to express their individual and social nature versus the corporate desire for uniformity and control is symbolic of the old division between classical theory and humanist theories. In relation to the idea of work aesthetic that is 'clean and efficient' and devoid of personalisation as an indication of productivity, Sundstrom (1986) concludes, "*Despite its long history and apparently widespread acceptance, the assumed link between superficial orderliness and efficiency seems to have no basis in empirical evidence*" (p. 221).

Theory and research indicate that the ability to personalise the office environment is potentially important for employees and has benefits for organisations. Empirical research focusing on personalisation in the workspace (Laurence, Yitzhak & Slowik, 2013; Wells, 2000; Wells & Thelen, 2002), along with reviews (Ashkenasy et al., 2014; Sundstrom, 1986), suggests that far from being trivial or detrimental to an organisation, personalisation can fulfil several essential purposes in the development of an effective work environment that is beneficial for both individual employees and their employer.

Drawing on the existing reviews (e.g., Ashkenasy et al., 2014; Donald, 1994a, 2001; Sundstrom, 1986; Wells, 2000; Wells & Thelen, 2002), we can see that personalisation can increase job satisfaction, improve well-being, reduce stress, regulate social interaction, express workers' personality, indicate status, demonstrate affiliations, express emotions, enhance mood, demonstrate commitment to the organisation, and facilitate place attachment to the work environment. It can also make for a more pleasant and enjoyable workplace. For the organisation, the advantages can be generally improved morale, more effective support for work practice with improved productivity, and reduced turnover of staff, which can result in a significant cost saving. At a group level, personalisation can help establish group coherence, identity, and provide demarcation from other groups. There is also evidence that teams that personalise tend to be more creative, though it is unclear if creative teams are more likely to personalise, or personalisation leads to more creative teams. Personalisation can also help new employees adapt and fit in.

Interestingly, Ashkenasy and colleagues (2014), as well as others (Gill, 1984; Hess, 1993; Wells, 2000), argue that personalisation is particularly important during times of change, such as during mergers, or when there are significant environmental changes including moves from cellular to open plan offices. Laurence et al. (2013) have shown that perceived lack of privacy is related to architectural privacy – having four walls and a door. In open plan offices, where architectural privacy is low, people experience less privacy, which is also associated with increased levels of emotional exhaustion. The researchers found that personalisation, including personal artefacts, mediated between the experience of privacy and the level of emotional exhaustion people felt. Consequently, personalisation is particularly important for employee well-being in low privacy environments such as open plan offices. The relationship of personalisation to privacy and privacy outcomes links back to the discussion of spatial behaviour in Chapter 3. It seems likely that personalisation operates as a territorial marker allowing greater control, or perceived greater control over interactions. It is also possible that the same territorial mechanism at a group level helps with the formation and identity of teams within organisations. What is apparent from the research is that personalisation is far from trivial and can have beneficial outcomes for workers and their organizations.

FINALLY

The experience of the 2020 pandemic has led to speculation about whether there will be a significant increase in homeworking in the future, with some asking if this is the death of the office (e.g., Economist, 29 April 2020). Data suggest that homeworking employees feel more productive and experience a better work-life balance, despite doing more unpaid hours (Office for National Statistics, 2021). Nevertheless, it seems likely that we will return to pre Covid-19 work patterns, although there might be some changes. It is therefore important that office environments provide a satisfying, healthy setting in which to work. Although it is clear that open plan offices have many drawbacks for their inhabitants compared to smaller or private offices, they are almost certainly going to continue to be the dominant design for some time. It is therefore important that we understand the way such offices affect their occupants.

At the beginning of the chapter we considered classical theory and the efforts to find simple and direct links between the environment and work output. From our consideration of some of the factors that shape working life in the office, it should be clear that the relationship between employees and the environment is much more complex than that. How an employee experiences their environment also involves their interaction history with that setting and with the management and organisational processes that brought it about and maintain it. In the same way that place is a bringing together of other experiences with the physical environment to create something more, so does experience of the office environment. To ensure productive offices and satisfied workers, the complexity of the relationship needs to be understood and form the basis of both design and environmental management.

REFERENCES

Ashkanasy, N. M., Ayoko, O. B., & Jehn, K.A. (2014). Understanding the physical environment of work and employee behavior: An affective events perspective. *Journal of Organizational Behaviour*, 35, 1169–1184.

Ayoko, O. B. & Ashkanasy, N. M. (2020). Introduction: Organizational Behaviour and the physical environment. In O. B. Ayoko & N. M. Ashkanasy (eds.), *Organizational Behaviour and the Physical Environment* (pp. 3–12). London: Routledge.

Ayoko, O. B. & Härtel, C. E. J. (2003). The role of space as both a conflict trigger and a conflict control mechanism in culturally heterogeneous workgroups. *Applied Psychology: An International Review*, 52, 383–412.

Becker, F. (1981). *Workspace: Creating Environments in Organizations*. New York: Praeger.

Becker, F. (1990). *The Total Workplace: Facilities Management and the Elastic Organization*. New York, NY: Van Nostrand Reinhold.

Becker, F. & Steele, F. (1994). *Workplace by Design*. San Francisco, CA: Jossey-Bass.

Bergström, J., Miller, M., & Horneij, E. (2015). Work environment perceptions following relocation to open-plan offices: A twelve-month longitudinal study. *Work*, 50, 221–228.

Bernstein, E. S. & Turban, S. (2018). The impact of the 'open' workspace on human collaboration. *Philosophical Transactions of the Royal Society B*, 373. http://dx.doi.org/10.1098/rstb.2017.0239

BOSTI (1981). *The Impact of Office Environment on Productivity and Quality of Life: Comprehensive Findings.* Buffalo: Buffalo Organization for Social and Technological Innovation.

Brand, J. L. & Smith, T. J. (2005). Effects of reducing enclosure on perceptions of occupancy quality, job satisfaction, and job performance in open-plan offices. *Proceedings of the Human Factors and Ergonomics Society Annual Meeting*, 49, 818–820.

Braverman, H. (1974). *Labor and Monopoly capital: The Degradation of Work in the Twentieth Century*. New York: Monthly Review Press.

Brennan, A., Clugh, J. S., & Kline, T. (2002). Traditional versus open office design: A longitudinal field study. *Environment and Behavior*, 34, 279–299.

Chigot, P. (2003). Controlled transparency in workplace design: Balancing visual and acoustic interaction in office environments. *Journal of Facilities Management*, 2, 121–130.

De Croon, E., Sluiter, J., Kuijer, P., & Frings-Dresen, M. (2005). The effects of open office concepts on worker health and performance: A systematic review of the literature. *Ergonomics*, 48(2), 119–134.

Ding, S. (2008). User's privacy preferences in open-plan offices. *Facilities*, 26, 401–417.

Donald, I. (1991). Managing the organic office. *Building Services: The CIBSE Journal*, 13(8), 28–30.

Donald, I. (1994a). The structure of office workers' experience of organizational environments. *Journal of Occupational and Organizational Psychology*, 67, 241–258.

Donald, I. (1994b). Management and change in office environments. *Journal of Environmental Psychology*, 14, 21-20.

Donald, I. (2001). Emotion and offices at work. In R. L. Payne & C. L. Cooper (eds.), *Emotions at Work. Theory, Research and Applications for Management (pp. 281–303). Chichester: Wiley.*

Donald, I. & Canter, D. (1987). Psychology in the United Kingdom. In A. R. Gilgen & C. K. Gilgen (eds.), *International Handbook of Psychology* (pp. 502–533). Westport, CT: Greenwood Press.

Duffy, F. (1979). Bürolandschaft '58–78. *The Architectural Review,* CLXV, January, 54–58.

Duffy, F. (1980). Office buildings and organizational change. In A. D. King (ed.), *Buildings and Society* (pp. 255–280). London: Routledge & Keegan Paul.

Ellis, P. (1986). Functional, aesthetic, and symbolic aspects of office lighting. In J. D. Wineman (ed.), *Behavioural Issues in Office Design* (pp. 225–249). New York: Van Nostrand Reinhold.

Fineman, S. (1993). Organizations as emotional arenas. In S. Fineman (ed.), *Emotion in Organizations* (pp. 7–35). London: Sage.

Gilbreth, F. B. (1912). *Primer of Scientific Management.* New York: Van Nostrand Company.

Gill, A. (1984). *Environmental Personalization in Institutional Settings.* Cardiff: University of Wales.

Haapakangas, A., Helenius, R., Keskinen, E., & Hongisto, V. (2008). Perceived acoustic environment, work performance and well-being–survey results from Finnish offices. *Proceedings of the 9th International Congress on Noise as a Public Health Problem* 21–25 July 2008. (ICBEN). Foxwoods, CT.

Harris, L., & Associates, Inc. (1978). *The Steelcase National Study of Office Environments: Do They Work?* Grand Rapids, MI: Steelcase.

Hedge, A. (1982). The open plan office: A systematic investigation of employees reactions to their environment. *Environment and Behaviour,* 14, 519–542.

Hedge, A. (1986). Open versus closed workspaces: The impact of design on employee reactions to their offices. In J. D. Wineman (ed.), *Behavioural Issues in Office Design* (pp. 139–176). New York: Van Nostrand Reinhold.

Hess, J. A. (1993). Assimilating newcomers into an organization: A cultural perspective. *Journal of Applied Communication,* 21, 189–210.

Irving, G. (2016). *Collaboration in Open-Plan Offices.* PhD Thesis, UQ Business School, The University of Queensland. https://doi.org/10.14264/uql.2016.668

Irving, G. L., Ayoko, O. B., & Ashkanasy, N. M. (2020). Collaboration, physical proximity and serendipitous encounters: Avoiding collaboration in a collaborative building. *Organizational Studies*, 41, 1123–1146.

Izawa, M. R., French, M. D., & Hedge, A. (2011). Shining new light on the Hawthorne illumination experiments. *Human Factors: The Journal of the Human Factors and Ergonomic Society*, 53, 528–547.

James, O., Delfabbro, P., & King, D. L. (2021). A comparison of psychological and work outcomes in open-plan and cellular office designs: A systematic review. *SAGE Open*, 11(1), 1–13. https://doi.org/10.1177%2F2158244020988869

Kabo, F. W. (2016). A model of potential encounters in the workplace: The relationships of homophily, spatial distance, organizational structure, and perceived networks. *Environment and Behavior*, 46, 638–662.

Kegel, P. (2017) The impact of the physical work environment on organizational outcomes: A structured review of the literature. *Journal of Facility Management Education and Research*, 1(1), 19–29.

Kim, J., Candido, C., Thomas, L., & De Dear, R. (2016). Desk ownership in the workplace: The effect of non-territorial working on employee workplace satisfaction, perceived productivity and health. *Building and Environment*, 103, 203–214.

Kim, J. & De Dear, R. (2013). Workspace satisfaction: The privacy-communication trade-off in open-plan offices. *Journal of Environmental Psychology*, 36, 18–26.

Kupritz, V. (2003). Accommodating privacy to facilitate new ways of working. *Journal of Architectural and Planning Research*, 20, 122–135.

Laurence, G. A., Fried, Y., & Slowik, L. H. (2013). "My space": A moderated mediation model of the effect of architectural and experienced privacy and workspace personalization on emotional exhaustion at work. *Journal of Environmental Psychology*, 36, 122–152.

Liebl, A., Jödicke, B., Baumgartner, H., Schlittmeier, S., & Hellbrück, J. (2012). Combined effects of acoustic and visual distraction on cognitive performance and well-being. *Applied Ergonomics*, 43, 424–434.

Mayo, E. (1933). *The Human Problems of an Industrial Civilization*. New York: Macmillan.

McCoy, J. M. (2005). Linking the physical work environment to creative context. *The Journal of Creative Behavior*, 39, 169–191.

Morrison, R. L. & Smollan, R. K. (2020). Open plan office space? If you're going to do it, do it right: A fourteen-month longitudinal case study. *Applied Ergonomics*, 82. https://doi.org/10.1016/j.apergo.2019.102933.

Mylonas, G. & Carstairs, J. (2007). Open plan office environments: The rhetoric and the reality. In A. I. Glendon, B. M. Thompson, & B. Myors (eds.), *Advances in Organisational Psychology* (pp. 443–458). Brisbane: Australian Academic Press.

Office for National Statistics (2021). *Homeworking Hours, Rewards and Opportunities in the UK: 2011 to 2020.* London: ONS.

Oommen, V. G., Knowles, M., & Zaho, I. (2008). Should health service managers embrace open plan work environments? A review. *Asian Pacific Journal of Health Management*, 3(2), 37–43.

Reagans, R. (2011). Close encounters: Analyzing how social similarity and propinquity contribute to strong network connections. *Organization Science*, 22, 835–849.

Regoeczi, W. C. (2003). When context matters: A multilevel analysis of household and neighbourhood crowding on aggression and withdrawal. *Journal of Environmental Psychology*, 23, 457–470.

Richardson, A., Potter, J., Paterson, M., Harding, T., Tyler-Merrick, G., Kirk, R., Reid, K., & McCesney, J. (2017). Office design and health: A systematic Review. *The New Zealand Medical Journal*, 130(1457), 29–49.

Roethlisberger, F. J. & Dickson, W. J. (1949). *Management and the Worker.* Cambridge, MA: Harvard University Press.

Schumann, A. (1974). Keeping blight from the open office. *Administrative Management*, 25(10), 26–28.

Smith-Jackson, T., & Klein, K. (2009). Open-plan offices: Task performance and mental work load. *Journal of Environmental Psychology*, 29, 279–289.

Sundstrom, E. (1986). *Work Places: The Psychology of the Physical Environment in Offices and Factories.* Cambridge: Cambridge University Press.

Taylor, F. W. (1911). *The Principles of Scientific Management.* New York: Harper and Row.

Värlander, S. (2012). Individual flexibility in the workplace: A spatial perspective. *Journal of Applied Behavioral Science*, 48, 33–61.

Vernon, H. M. (1919). *The Influence of Hours of Work and of Ventilation and of Output in Tinplate Manufacture.* Industrial Fatigue Research Board, Report No. 1. London: HMSO.

Vischer, J. (1989). *Environmental Quality in Offices.* New York: Van Nostrand Reinhold.

Weber, M. (1947). *The Theory of Social and Economic Organization.* Translated by A. M. Henderson & T. Parsons. New York: The Free Press.

Wells, M. (2000). Office clutter or meaningful personal displays: The role of office personalization in employee and organizational well-being. *Journal of Environmental Psychology*, 20, 239–255.

Wells, M. & Thelen, L. (2002). What does your work space say about you? The influence of personality, status, and workspace on personalization. *Environment and Behavior*, 34, 300–321.

Wells, M., Thelen, L., & Ruark, J. (2007). Workspace personalization and organizational culture: Does your workspace reflect you or your company? *Environment and Behavior*, 39, 616–634.

SUGGESTED READING

Ayoko, O. B. & Ashkanasy, N. M. (Eds.) *Organizational Behaviour and the Physical Environment.* London: Routledge.

8

ENVIRONMENTAL SUSTAINABILITY AND PRO-ENVIRONMENTAL BEHAVIOUR

INTRODUCTION

Environmental sustainability and pro-environmental behaviour are, surprisingly, relatively new areas of significant interest in environmental psychology. Although they have always been part of the discipline's discussion, it was not until towards the end of the twentieth century and the beginning of the twenty-first century that they became prominent. Sustainability and pro-environmental behaviour have now become one of the major research fields within the discipline, forming dominant areas of publications such as the *Journal of Environmental Psychology*, and texts in environmental psychology (e.g., Steg & de Groot, 2019). Comprehensive reviews of environmental psychology that appear from time to time demonstrate the shift in interest too. The first review of environmental psychology published in the *Annual Review of Psychology* (Craik, 1973) included no reference to pro-environmental behaviour or sustainability. The most recent review is almost entirely devoted to it (Gifford, 2014). There have also been books dedicated to conservation psychology, which examine a broad range of issues centred on creating a sustainable relationship between people and nature (Clayton & Myers, 2015).

Amongst the public, interest seems mixed. In the last year or so there does, anecdotally, seem to have been an increase in climate change-related events, or at least media coverage of them. A survey of four European countries conducted in 2016 asked people what

DOI: 10.4324/9780429274541-8

they thought the most important societal issue would be within the next 20 years (Steentjes et al., 2017). The results suggest that, at that time, climate change was not uppermost in people's concerns. In 2016 climate change was mentioned by 2% of the respondents in the UK, 3% in Germany, and 6% in France. In Norway, climate change was a more prominent concern and was the fourth most mentioned issue, with pollution the second. People's main concerns in France, Germany, and the UK were unemployment, the refugee crisis, and immigration. Interestingly, those concerns are all things that are affected by climate change. Asked what the phrase 'climate change' meant to them, the most frequent responses concerned global warming and weather change. The least frequently mentioned concerns were crop failure, food shortages, and hunger. Two percent of the sample said that they did not believe in climate change.

A more recent survey, carried out in 2019, found that just over half of people in the UK were *very concerned* about climate change, and 85% were concerned. That compares with 60% who were concerned in 2013 (Ipsos Mori, 2020), although the level concern fluctuates over time, probably in response to media interest and other activities in the public domain. To some extent that is indicated by Sisco et al. (2021), who examined people's interest in climate change in 46 countries, comparing internet search data between 2015 and 2019. Their results support the general impression that there is growing concern or at least interest in the subject amongst the public, with the data showing a 'marked increase' in searches relating to climate change in 2019. Interestingly, while governments in many countries put effort into informing the public about the problems and causes of climate change, the study found that it was after global climate marches that public interest, reflected in internet searches, appeared to increase. Although we need to remain cautious about using search terms to infer support rather than, for instance, annoyance, if demonstration and public activism do increase awareness, then governments should support rather than suppress climate protest.

In this chapter we will focus on some of the broad conceptual issues, such as the primary theoretical models that underpin the research and explain people's behaviour, as well as how to prioritise behaviour change interventions. Along the way we will refer to research findings in relation to substantive topics, such as transport use and domestic energy conservation. While much of the focus will be on drivers of climate change and the behaviours that underpin them, the research will be relevant to many other unsustainable and damaging actions that threaten our world. Many of these have been examined by environmental psychologists. For example, the sinking of the *Prestige* off the coast of Spain in 2002 was a major ecological disaster, leaving three hundred thousand tons of tar on the on the shores of Galicia. The disaster has been subject to important social science and in particular environmental psychology research. Studies have provided significant insight into the disaster, its causes and the impact it had on people's relationships to their environment (Garcia-Mira, 2013).

Although the scale of research on sustainability and pro-environmental behaviour is beyond the coverage possible within this chapter, it should provide the foundation for thinking about sustainability and pro-environmental behaviour, and provide a gateway for further exploration.

PSYCHOLOGY AND SUSTAINABILITY

A good place to start is by addressing the question of what psychology has to offer to such urgent, large-scale challenges as environmental sustainability and climate change. Paul Stern (2011) addressed this question directly when he wrote that "*Psychology can make a significant contribution to limiting the magnitude of climate change by improving understanding of human behaviors that drive climate change and human reactions to climate-related technologies and policies by turning that understanding into effective interventions*" (p. 303). The first point he is making is that psychology is important, or even central, because many of the drivers that are damaging to the environment have their origins in human behaviour. Consequently, if we can alter these behaviours, we can reduce some of the pressures on climate change. Stern also makes the point that reactions to technology and policy are important.

While there is no question that technological advances are, and will continue to make a major contribution to addressing many of the environmental challenges we face, they are unlikely to achieve their full potential without accompanying behavioural change. An example of this is the *rebound effect*, in which improved technology not only fails to live up to its potential but results in increased, rather than decreased, consumption (Berkhout, Muskens, & Velthuijsen,

2000; Khazzoom, 1980; Sorrell, 2007). This is potentially a significant problem, with some commentators arguing that efficiency gains are apparently 'eaten up' by the effect (Otto, Kaiser, & Arnold, 2014). The same authors contend that a rebound effect is what would be expected if people act rationally. Further, there is evidence that reliance on technology can undermine pro-environmental behaviour (Murtagh, Gatersleben, & Uzzell, 2015).

Furthermore, behaviour change can be more cost-effective and more rapidly achieved than technological change, which tends to be relatively slow and expensive. Psychology can also help suggest ways to speed up the adoption of technology, overcoming the 'energy efficiency gap' (Jaffe & Stavins, 1994), which is the time between technology being available and that technology being taken up.

To be effective, policy that aims to change behaviour also needs to be based on an understanding of the processes that underlie that behaviour. If those processes are not understood, policy changes can have unintended consequences. For instance, as we will see later, the introduction for financial incentives or disincentives to curtail harmful behaviours can unintentionally increase rather than reduce those behaviours (Gneezy & Rustichini, 2000a). Psychology then has a critical role to play in the implementation of technology and the development of strategy and policy for reducing our environmental impact through behaviour change.

Now that we have emphasised the importance of examining and changing people's behaviour, we need to add a caveat. While the behaviour of individuals is important, we cannot entirely focus on that. As Uzzell has argued,

> Successive governments, as well as civil society, have tended to treat climate change as a problem caused by individuals through their excessive consumption. . . By framing the issue of climate change as a problem caused by individuals, we not only restrict our understanding of the potential causes of the challenges that face us, but also close down many of the options for taking action.
>
> (Uzzell, 2018, p. 3)

As psychologists, we might emphasise individual behaviour, but we should not lose sight of the fact that behaviour takes place within a much broader structural, socio-political context, which will also encourage, constrain, and influence that behaviour (Shove, 2010).

TOO MANY CONSUMING TOO MUCH IS A MAJOR PROBLEM

This chapter is focused primarily on climate change, but that does not exclude other damaging actions, such as pollution and the destruction of ecosystems and biodiversity that often go hand in hand. According to the World Wildlife Fund (WWF), "*Until 1970, humanity's Ecological Footprint was smaller than the Earth's rate of regeneration. To feed and fuel our 21st century lifestyles, we are overusing the Earth's biocapacity by at least 56%*" (WWF, 2020, p. 6). They estimate that there has also been "*an average 68% decrease in population sizes of mammals, birds, amphibians, reptiles and fish between 1970 and 2016. . . and per person, our global stock of natural capital has declined by nearly 40% since the early 1990*s" (WWF, 2020, pp. 6–7). The impact of individual consumption becomes more problematic as the population grows. It is predicted by the United Nations that the world population will increase by around two billion over the next 20 years or so, achieving 9.7 billion by 2050 (United Nations, 2019). Much of that increase will be in the developing world, which is also where per capita consumption is likely to see the greatest rise, though in absolute levels, that consumption is less than in the advanced economies.

The challenge we face is to achieve a balance between the amount of the earth's available resources and our consumption. We cannot maintain both. We therefore need to 'increase' the world's resources, by developing new and renewable energy sources for instance, or reduce our consumption, by either changing our lifestyles or finding ways to maintain our lifestyles while consuming less. It is, of course, not a choice between mutually exclusive approaches, both technology and behaviour have a role to play in this. The likelihood is that we will need to change our lifestyles, reduce consumption, and develop better renewable, more efficient resources, including in energy, materials, and food.

In addition to the central issue of the psychology of pro-environmental behaviour, there is a role for environmental psychology in understanding how changes in the environment will affect us. There is a large and growing literature on the psychological impact of climate change and environmental degradation. We touched on these issues in Chapter 2 when we looked at the concept of place and place attachment, and the role they play in responses to forced migration. In a recent review of the impacts of climate change on behaviour, Evans paints a sobering picture of some of the effects:

> Droughts, floods, and severe storms diminish quality of life, elevate stress, produce psychological distress, and may elevate interpersonal and intergroup conflict. Recreational opportunities are compromised by extreme weather, and children may suffer delayed cognitive development. Elevated pollutants concern citizens and may accentuate psychological distress. Out-door recreational activity is curtailed by ambient pollutants.
>
> (Evans, 2019, p. 449)

Based on Evans' description, we face a grim future if we do not considerably reduce the damage we do to the planet and if we fail to prepare for the consequences of the damage we have already done.

PRIORITISING INTERVENTIONS

The challenges facing us are many and complex, raising the question of what we should focus on to reduce the negative impact of our behaviour on the environment. Rather than concentrating on the biggest, most threatening problems, Stern (2011) and others argue that most effort should be put into those things that can have the most *impact*. To calculate that, we should consider areas, (a) where there are potentially *technological alternatives*, (b) where there are *behaviours* that are potentially open to change, and (c) where it is likely that a *significant number* of people can be persuaded to change their behaviours (Stern, 2011).

The first step in deciding what to do is to identify the sources of the problems. To help simplify this, in the next sections we will primarily discuss CO_2 emissions, which majorly contribute to climate change.

MAIN SOURCES OF EMISSIONS

Although here we will mainly consider carbon-based emissions, the same general points, nonetheless, could be made in relation to other emissions, such as methane, or threats, including the destruction of biodiversity, the increase in plastics and other pollution, overuse of water resources, or any of the other ways in which we are damaging the planet.

While emissions include many gases and pollutants, one of the largest contributions to greenhouse gases and climate change is CO_2. Historically, industry accounted for the greatest overall level of emissions and other pollution. That has steadily declined in most Western countries to a point where, since the 1980s, it is below the emissions generated by transport (40%) and domestic energy use (29%) (BEIS, 2017), with a significant proportion of the transport energy use being from domestically owned vehicles (Uzzell, 2018). Worldwide, it is estimtated that 72% of total greenhouse gas emissions are generated by households (Dubois et al., 2019; Hertwich & Peters, 2009). While much of the reduction in industrial emissions has been achieved by technological advances and shifts in the economic base of Western economies, some of the reduction of emissions in the West is from 'offshoring', whereby the goods we consume are manufactured in other countries such as China and India (Uzzell, 2018). Carmichael (2019) notes that the UK has reduced its emissions by 40% in the last 30 years, primarily from an increase in non-carbon electricity generation. However, he adds, "*Up to now, behaviour change and societal change around lifestyles and consumption have not played a significant role in progress towards meeting UK emissions reductions targets*" (Carmichael, 2019, p. 15). He identifies the most significant potential contributions to reducing carbon as coming from households making changes in car and plane mobility, and reductions in animal-based foods, and changes to household heating. Dubois et al. (2019) classify the major areas of household consumption as mobility (34%), food (30%), and housing (21%). This shows us that it is ordinary people going about their daily lives who are the biggest contributors to emissions and therefore to climate change.

Breaking down domestic energy consumption helps us to see potential targets for action. The use of appliances, such as kettles, microwaves, televisions, and computers, is a relatively small contributor to emissions. Heating or cooling our homes, however, is by far the largest consumer of energy. Cooking and water heating generate the second highest level of emissions. While there will undoubtedly be national variation on these figures, it is likely that they will be relatively similar across Western nations. In developing countries, the picture might be different, but is moving in the same direction.

Even though there is good reason to focus on domestic energy consumption, it is worth emphasising that we still need to tackle other areas of people's lives to ensure sustainability. For example, many Western economies have shifted from an industrial base to a service economy. It is therefore important to understand how energy is used in office environments, the role of office workers' behaviour impacts upon that consumption and how energy use can be reduced. This is important as research suggests that behaviours are not readily carried over from domestic settings to behaviour at work (Tudor, Barr & Gilig, 2008). Examining how organizations' policies can influence employee behaviour, Garcia-Mira and his colleagues concluded that policy should strengthen participation and autonomy of the workforce. Moreover, they found that several medium intensity initiatives are more likely to be effective than higher intensity single or unrelated policies (Garcia-Mira et al., 2017).

CLASSIFYING BEHAVIOUR: CURTAILMENT, EFFICIENCY, AND MAINTENANCE

Because much of domestic emissions is a result of transport, and heating and cooling, there is potential for significant reductions. However, there are hundreds of specific behaviours that could be targeted to help people become more sustainable. To make research, policy, and interventions manageable, and to structure our thinking, we need to reduce those behaviours to a few pragmatically useful categories and dimensions. Over the last 40 years or so, several researchers have attempted to do that. Amongst the suggestions, two primary sets of behaviour have frequently been proposed. Those are behaviours aimed at *curtailment*, and others concerned with *efficiency* (Gardner & Stern, 2008). Focusing on these, Karlin et al. (2014) reviewed 28 published research papers. They content analysed the ways in which different behaviours had been classified. While their qualitative examination of the studies revealed a wide variation in the terms used to describe behaviours, factor analysis of the energy conservation behaviours provided empirical support for the curtailment-efficiency dichotomy and allowed them to identify some of the main characteristics of each.

Curtailment tends to be the behaviour change that has the most immediate, direct impact on domestic emissions. It involves people stopping behaviours that are not sustainable, and increasing those that are. The changes tend to be quite simple, not costly, and involve actions that are frequent, such as switching off lights or not leaving appliances on standby. While many of these actions have a minimal impact on people's daily lives, some, such as curtailing the use of private cars in favour of public transport, can be disruptive. Two areas of curtailment that could make a significant difference to a household's greenhouse gas emissions are reducing aviation use and changes to diet. As Carmichael (2019) points out, the emissions associated with a return flight between London and New York *per passenger* are around the same as heating a typical house for an entire year, and livestock for food generates 14.5% of worldwide greenhouse gasses.

Efficiency usually involves finding and purchasing less wasteful ways of having the same lifestyle and behaviour, but with less resource consumption and pollution. For instance, rather than curtailing private car use in favour of more sustainable public transport, people might purchase more efficient cars. Within the home, it might include buying more efficient heating boilers or ground-source heat pumps, changing to LED light bulbs, insulating the home, or installing double or triple glazing.

Efficiency and curtailment each have several defining real or perceived characteristics. For instance, curtailment is sometimes seen as reducing people's enjoyment, whereas efficiency is often considered costly. In their analysis, Karlin et al. (2014) identified *cost* and *frequency* as the primary two dimensions that both behaviours could be classified on. Curtailment happens often, but is usually inexpensive and can save money. Efficiency, however, tends to be expensive, but is usually infrequent.

Representing frequency and cost on the *X*- and *Y-axes* of the graph in Figure 8.1 gives us four quadrants, two of which are occupied by efficiency and curtailment. A third behaviour, which is low frequency and low cost, could be maintenance (Karlin et al., 2014; Van Raaij & Verhallen, 1983). Maintaining a vehicle and a well-maintained domestic heating system are examples of actions that could reduce emissions. The fourth quadrant suggests high-frequency high-cost behaviours. While there might be a variety of these, it is unlikely that at an individual level they are something that people would be prepared to engage in and so probably are not worth promoting.

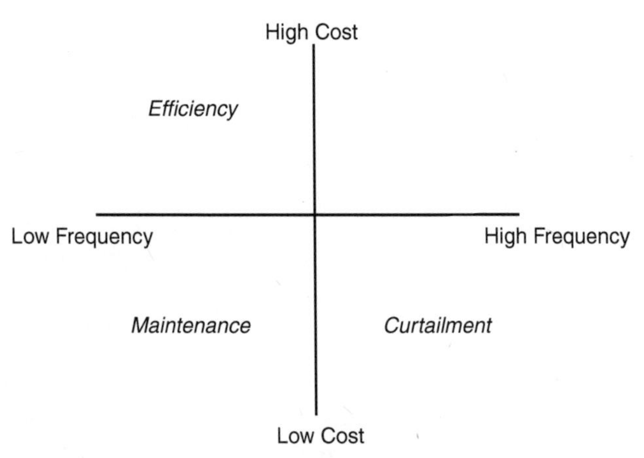

Figure 8.1 Dimensions of curtailment and efficiency.

There is a degree of overlap between the characteristics of curtailment, efficiency, and maintenance, as well as some interaction between them (Karlin et al., 2014). Occasionally, action in one area can undermine behaviour in another. For instance, a new more efficient heating boiler (efficiency) which may be cheaper to run, might be left on for longer as a result (inhibiting curtailment), which would be an example of a rebound effect. Those issues aside, emission reductions from efficiency are likely to be greater than from curtailment (Stern, 2011). Despite this, curtailment behaviours are more strongly represented within the sustainability and pro-environmental behaviour literature (Hafner, Elmes, Read, & White, 2019).

People tend to be more positive about efficiency policy measures than those that are aimed at curtailment (Poortinga et al., 2003). Schuitema and Bergstad (2013) note that even though efficiency measures can be expensive, curtailment can be perceived to affect people's freedom, which reduces the acceptability of the policies (Jakobsson, Fujiim, & Gärling, 2000). The response to curtailment is, however, likely to depend on the behaviour being targeted.

Although many researchers use a classification of efficiency and curtailment, there is evidence that it is not the way lay people think about or perceive pro-environmental behaviour (Truelove & Gillis, 2018). In their study, using factor analysis, Truelove and Gillis identify four dimensions that people use when perceiving pro-environmental behaviours: financial and behavioural cost, external pressures, environmental impact and financial savings, and health and safety impact. The results of their analysis are detailed and quite complex. Of direct relevance to the discussion of curtailment and efficiency Truelove and Gillis found that efficiency (buying more efficient products) is perceived to be time consuming and inconvenient. As efficiency is usually related to single infrequent actions it is perhaps surprising that the public perceive them in that way. However, the researchers speculate that they are perceived as time consuming because of the effort put into researching products and then sourcing vendors. Further, Truelove and Gillis suggest laypeople do not make the distinction between the same characteristics as experts do. As the authors note, it is important that focusing on the widely used dimensions of efficiency and curtailment, researchers do not create a 'blind spot' to other ways in which people think about pro-environmental behaviour.

THEORIES OF PRO-ENVIRONMENTAL BEHAVIOUR

When we address the range of factors that underlie people's behaviour, it helps to have robust psychological framework or theory. This allows us to group and organise the different influences on behaviour and see how they singularly or mutually interact to influence that behaviour. By providing a model for understanding the probable antecedents of behaviour, and a possible explanation of the behaviour, research can more readily be fed through into interventions, which in turn should be more effective because they are based on sound psychological principles.

Gifford (2014) identified some of the most useful theories which are amenable to translation into research and action. Of those, we will examine the three that are, arguably, the most influential: the *Value-Belief-Norm (VBN) theory* (Stern, 2000), *goal-framing theory* (GFT) (Lindenberg & Steg, 2007), and the *theory of planned behaviour* (TPB) (Ajzen, 1991). Although each of these theories is different, there is overlap in what they include and the perspectives they take. In one form or another they include people's actions (behaviour), feelings (emotions), and understanding (cognition). They also situate each of these within a normative framework, considering important social and contextual influences on behaviour. Further, the theories all include values, attitudes, or general orientations, which might or might not be pro-environment.

As behavioural norms play an important role in each of the theories, and the *New Environmental Paradigm* (NEP) is implicit in them, we should first consider different forms of norms and the NEP before moving onto the theories themselves.

THE NEW ENVIRONMENTAL PARADIGM

The term *New Environmental Paradigm* was coined in an article by Dunlap and Van Liere (1978). In proposing the concept, they were bringing together emerging views that were in opposition to the *Dominant Social Paradigm* (DSP) (Pirages & Ehrlich, 1974) of the time, which we will refer to as the anthropocentric paradigm, as it is no longer so dominant. In that paradigm, the world was viewed as anthropocentric (human-centric), with an emphasis on economic growth and ever-expanding economies, personal wealth, private ownership, and the unchecked exploitation of natural resources. Despite the DSP, there was also a growing but still fringe view at the time that saw the anthropometric perspective as unsustainable and the cause of the degradation of the environment. Of course, that view is no longer quite so fringe as it was.

Although Dunlap and Van Liere (1978; Dunlap, 2008) did not rigorously define the NEP, it is relatively easy to characterise from their writings and the measures they developed. Dunlap described the first three facets of the paradigm as a belief in the "*existence of ecological limits to growth, importance of maintaining the balance of nature, and rejection of the anthropocentric notion that nature exists primarily for human use*" (Dunlap, 2008, p. 6). As greater environmental awareness became widespread, Dunlap and others elaborated the concept to encompass such additional facets as exceptionalism and in particular the conviction that "*modern industrial society is exempt from ecological constraints*" and a belief in the likelihood of eco-crises (Dunlap, 2008, p. 9). Dunlap also renamed the NEP as the *New Ecological Paradigm*, though that has not caught on as well as the original term, the use of which continues to dominate in the literature. The ecological paradigm, however it is termed, is important in Stern's (1992) model described shortly.

BEHAVIOURAL NORMS

Social norms feature in most theories of pro-environmental behaviour in one form or another. They have also been found to be influential in helping to increase people's sustainable actions in many areas. It is therefore worth briefly describing the different types of norm. Social norms are rules that are understood by a group and that guide their behaviour, they are a set of beliefs a person has about what others do and what others would wish them to do (Hafner et al., 2019). Norms have been found to significantly influence pro-environmental behaviour in several different contexts (e.g., Cialdini, Reno & Kallgren, 1990; Goldstein, Cialdini & Griskevicius, 2008; Hafner et al., 2019).

Personal Norms and Moral Norms

In general, personal and moral norms can be taken as being the same concept. Although some authors might have slight differences in the way that they conceptualise them, others use them interchangeably (e.g., Raymond, Brown, & Robinson, 2011). Within environmental psychology, several researchers use Schwartz's (1977) concept of personal norms. Schwartz originally defined personal norms in this way: "*The term* personal norms *will be used to signify the self-expectations for specific action in particular situations that are constructed by the individual. Activated personal norms are experienced as feelings of moral obligation, not as intentions*" (Schwartz, 1977, p. 227). He goes on, "*There is often overlap between personal norms held by individuals and prevailing social norms. But while social norms are perceived to be shared by members of a group, personal norms typically vary from one individual to another*" (p. 231). Importantly, personal norms are feelings of *moral* obligation, which act as motivators. They are individually held and are not necessarily the same as the norms of others. Stern draws directly on Schwartz's ideas, placing personal norms centrally in his VBN theory (Stern, 2000, 2011; Gardener & Stern, 2008).

Descriptive Norms

Descriptive norms are the *perception* of what *most* other people do. By most we could mean members of a specific reference group or an entire population of a country. The important point is that it is a norm based on the observation or *perception* of what others do. The perceptions might be right or wrong, shared or not, the important thing is that people perceive them to be. An important characteristic of descriptive norms is that transgression of the norm does not necessarily involve any form of social sanctions.

Injunctive Norms and Subjective Norms

Injunctive norms are the perception of what you *ought* to do (Cialdini, Reno, & Kallren, 1990). They are norms about behaviour that will be approved or disapproved of by *others.* They are different from personal norms, which are about self-approval. Although personal norms might attract disapproval, that is not part of the consideration in personal norms. In injunctive norms, a failure to comply will result in some form of social sanction. If the norm is adhered to, it might be rewarded.

People do not always do what the majority think they should. If that was not the case, there would never be minority behaviour, some of which has shaped the world (Lapinski & Rimal, 2005). The TPB recognises those circumstances by including the concept of *subjective norms.* A subjective norm is in essence an injunctive norm in that it is concerned with the perception of what others think you *ought* to do. However, it also includes whether you care about what others think. This is called *motivation to comply*.

VALUE-BELIEF-NORM THEORY

Value-Belief-Norm theory (Stern, 1992, 2000) integrates several conceptual approaches to positive environmental behaviour. It is a development of the more general Norm Activation Model (NAM) proposed by Schwartz (1977) to explain social altruism. The NAM was adapted by Stern to do the same for pro-environmental behaviour, which can be conceptualised as a form of altruistic behaviour. The basic VBN model is quite straightforward. To begin with we can assume that people have pre-existing values. The model then comprises a chain of events starting with someone becoming aware of an issue, then either dismissing the matter, or moving through a series of steps ending with one or more pro-environmental

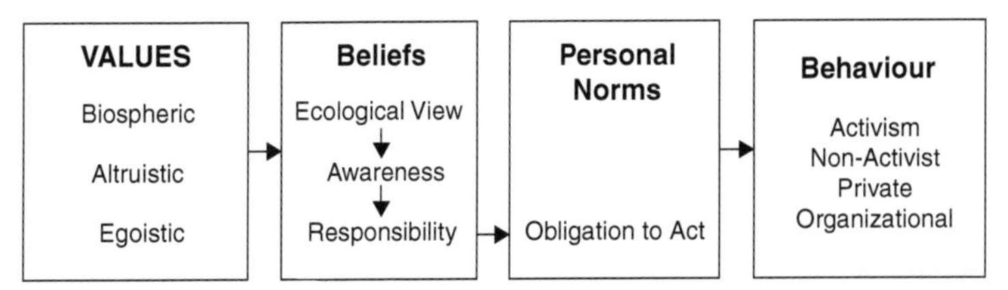

Figure 8.2 Representation ofValue-Belief-Norm theory (Adapted from Stern, 2000).

behaviours.These steps are shown in Figure 8.2 and comprise vales, beliefs, norms, and behaviours.

A key part of the process in Stern's model is the *values* that a person already holds. *Values are the principles that people have about a subject* including the environment. Stern suggests there are three main sets of values relevant to pro-environmental behaviour, which are *altruistic* (acting positively towards another person or living creature for their benefit rather than for personal gain), *biospheric* (values that recognise the importance of the planet's living organisms and the systems that support them), and *egoistic* (giving precedence to self-interest over other people, society, and the environment). One of those three values will be dominant, but which one will change over time and from circumstance to circumstance.The most dominant value will determine a person's response. If someone has altruistic and biospheric values they are likely to ultimately lead to pro-environmental action.When egoistic values are activated, they are unlikely to lead to pro-environmental behaviour, and may well lead to further damaging behaviour.

The next stage comprises a sequence of three sets of beliefs.The first is a belief in an *ecological worldview* (or belief in the *NEP*), second, a belief that a threat exists (*awareness of consequences*), and third, a belief that they have some responsibility for doing something about it (*ascription of responsibility*).The next stage in the process is dependent on their personal or moral norms and is whether they feel an obligation to do something. If they do feel they should act, the model moves to the final, action stage, which comprises four different behaviours: *private behaviour*, which has a direct impact, such as curtailment and efficiency; *activism* includes joining pro-environmental groups such Extinction Rebellion, protesting, or boycotting companies with poor environmental records; *non-activist* behaviour, which stops short of activism but supports positive environmental policy; and *organisational behaviours*, through which people can make an organisation more environmentally positive – for instance, employees might successfully campaign for office recycling, or the board of an investment bank might decide only to invest in shares of environmental positive companies. A failure at any stage along the values, beliefs, and norms process will result in non-action.

There has been some validation of VBN model, particularly of the relationships between the components. Steg, Dreijerink, and Abrahamse (2005) carried out a test of the full VBN model, which supported the causal stages of the theory, suggesting the process leading to pro-environmental is valid. Several researchers have found a relationship between biospheric values and pro-environmental behaviour (De Groot & Steg, 2008; Steg & De Groot, 2012; Rhead, Elliot, & Upham, 2015), while the role of anthropocentric values has not been supported (Rhead et al., 2015). Nevertheless, Rhead et al. did identify a 'denial' factor, which the authors linked to egoistic values, and was negatively related to behavioural intention to support the environment. Interestingly, research suggests that people with egoistic values also feel they have less control than do those with altruistic values. For instance, people high on egoism believe it is too difficult or pointless to try to do something about environmental challenges, which might explain the finding that they are less willing to make financial scarifies to support the environment (Kenz, 2016).

In addition, other research examining personal norms alone has shown them to have some predictive value in four different domains of pro-environmental behaviour (Harland, Staats, & Wilke, 1999). Overall, however, Ghazali et al. (2019) have concluded that the predictive power of the VBN model is unclear and questionable, especially when compared to approaches such as the TPB. Steg and others have also provided a mixed opinion of the model. Gifford, Steg, and Reser (2011) observe that the theory can predict low-cost behaviours and positive expressions of support for pro-environmental behaviour. It is not very good, however, at explaining high-cost behaviours such as buying a more efficient car. It is also weak in accounting for behaviour when other factors, such as structural constrains, are in play. The inability for the model to deal with external limitations on behaviour is likely to be why the TPB usually has more explanatory power than the VBN model (Gifford et al., 2011).

One interesting and productive development on Stern's original model is the addition of identity. Environmental self-identity has been described as reflecting, "*the extent to which an individual sees himself or herself as a type of person who acts pro-environmentally and prescribes a course of action that is compatible with this sense of how the individual sees himself or herself*" (Ruepert et al., 2016, p. 60). The concepts of social, personal, and environmental identity have been used in various areas of environmental psychology, some of which we have seen in other chapters. It is not surprising that identity has also been found to be useful in explaining and predicting pro-environment behaviour. Ruepert et al.'s (2016) Value Identity Personal Norm (VIP) model of behaviour has proved useful in predicting pro-environmental behaviour in a number of different contexts, including domestic and workplace settings (e.g., Ruepert et al., 2016; Van der Werff & Steg, 2016). In assessing the development of the model, van der Werff and Steg conclude that the "*value-identity-personal norm model is a... particularly promising model in promoting a range of environmental behaviours*" (p. 107). Finally, it is worth noting that researchers have also examined identity outside of the VIP framework. For instance, Murtagh and colleagues, using the framework provided by Breakwell (1986), found identify useful in explaining pro-environmental behaviour in relation to transport use (e.g., Murtagh, Gatersleben, & Uzzell, 2012a, 2012b).

GOAL-FRAMING THEORY

Throughout this book we have emphasised the importance of goals and purposes in understanding person-environment-behaviour relations. They are also central to the GFT of pro-environmental behaviour. Much of the writing on this approach comes from Steg and her colleagues at the University of Groningen in the Netherlands. Lindenberg and Steg (2007) provide a very useful article that sets out the theory in detail and is well worth consulting.

The basic idea of goal framing is that at any point in time, we have a primary goal relative to our environment or wider context. That primary goal gives us a perspective or *frame*work within which to view the world. The goal-related frame shapes our perceptions, thoughts, and actions, what knowledge and attitudes are accessible and how they are evaluated, and which outcomes are considered (Lindenberg and Steg, 2007). As our primary goal changes, so do our frames, perceptions and motivations. Most of the time, we have several goals which we hold simultaneously, and all of which colour our thinking and behaviour, although only one frame is dominant at a time. Recognising multiple goals acknowledges that there can be several different motivations underlying behaviour, and behavioural outcomes can satisfy more than one goal.

Lindenberg (2001) proposes that for behaviour there are three relevant, broad frames: *hedonic*, *normative*, and *gain* goal frames. Hedonic goals are directed at immediate gratification or feelings of pleasure. Normative goals are the desire to align behaviour with the norms of external bodies or groups. The norms can be either injunctive (what other's think you ought to do), descriptive (what you think most people do), or both. Gain goals focus on gaining or keeping possessions, income, and other resources.

As we have noted, only one of these frames will be dominant but other frames will continue to be influential. For example, while a gain goal frame (keeping or increasing resources) might be dominant, the hedonic goal (immediate gratification or pleasure) may be in the background. The hedonic goal would consequently modify the behaviour being driven by the gain frame (Steg & Vlek, 2009). For instance, if someone has a dominant gain goal frame they might turn down their heating at home to save money. However, that might conflict with the hedonic goal of being warm and comfortable, which will therefore weaken the influence of the gain goal. Over time the dominant frame can change, but when two or more goals are achieved by the same action, it is likely to strengthen the probability of that behaviour happening. When goals conflict, they may weaken the likelihood of the behaviour. Changing people's behaviour in a pro-environment direction can be thought of as a process of tapping into or manipulating people's goal frames. Because there are different combinations of goal frames there is no one simple way to bring about pro-environmental behaviour.

Normative goal frames are the frames most associated with positive environmental behaviour. For them to be dominant you first need to be aware that a particular behaviour is damaging. However, just giving people information about the damaging effects is not necessarily going to change their behaviour (McKenzie-Mohr, 2000; Owens & Driffill, 2008), people also need to know what they should do. Without that knowledge, other goal frames are likely to become dominant (Lindenberg & Steg, 2007). In any intervention to help people to become more pro-environmental in their behaviour, it is important that information is given about environmental threats, *and* what can be done to mitigate those threats.

Both hedonic and gain frames can work against people engaging in pro-environmental behaviour by often emphasising self-interest over wider societal benefit. Further, Lindenberg and Steg (2007) argue that people holding a hedonic goal frame can be fickle, acting in accordance with their mood, carrying out actions only if they 'feel like it' and it is not a hassle (De Groot & Steg, 2009). Since moods can be unstable and change easily, hedonic goal frames are also unreliable.

Tapping into the more selfish motivations can still prove useful. It may be possible to strengthen pro-environmental norms by using hedonic and gain frames to work *with* norms in a complimentary way (Lindenberg & Steg, 2007). In essence, this requires making positive environmental behaviour more enjoyable or rewarding (Steg et al., 2014). In some cases that is quite easy. For instance, many pro-environmental measures that reduce energy consumption also reduce the cost of utility bills (gain frame). Other activities are more difficult to encourage. For example, it may be difficult to convince people to use public transport if their hedonic goal frame is dominant, unless the positive benefits of public transport are emphasised. For instance, telling people that on a train journey they can get coffee and something to eat, read a book, and relax might appeal to their hedonistic goals. That can be reinforced by comparing that experience with being stuck in a traffic jam in a hot car that takes longer to get to their destination. In fact, that is exactly the image some train companies have used in their advertising, with slogans like 'let the train take the strain'. Potentially then, we could encourage environmentally positive train use by linking to all goal frames, emphasising the benefit to the environment, along with personal comfort and convenience (Steg et al., 2014).

When introducing interventions to encourage pro-environmental behaviours, it is important to understand the possible long-term consequences and to consider any unexpected outcomes. For instance, if financial incentives are introduced when normative goal frames are not strong, and the opportunity is not taken to strengthen them, once the incentives are removed, people may resort to their previous actions (Steg et al., 2014). Worse still, the use of incentives and disincentives has the potential to increase rather than reduce negative behaviour. Some interesting experiments carried out by behavioural economist Gneezy and his colleagues help illustrate this point.

In one study, a nursery had a problem with parents arriving late to collect their children (Gneezy & Rustichini, 2000a). As a result, the school told parents that if they were any more than ten minutes late, they would have to pay a fine. Following the introduction of the incentives to be on time, the late arrival of parents increased. Two things had happened which led to the unexpected change in behaviour. First, the new sanctions implied that being ten minutes late was acceptable, because fines were only applied after that time. Second, it changed the parent-nursery time keeping relationship. Until the introduction of fines, collecting a child on time was a *moral* obligation; it was the right thing to do. Introducing the fines shifted the relationship to a business or financial transaction in which there was no longer a moral imperative to be on time. Parents perceived the payment as buying extra time from the nursery rather than a fine for poor behaviour. As Fehr and Falk (2002) describe it, the introduction of fines "transformed the act of being late from a rule violation to a market transaction" (p. 709). The parents had purchased the right for their child to stay longer. Even when the fine was removed, the level of late collections remained higher than before the fines being introduced. There are lessons here for the use of fines to encourage pro-environmental behaviour. For instance, the use of fines such as congestion charges in cities might give drivers the feeling that they can buy the right to drive there. Less congestion can also, incidentally, appeal to a hedonistic goal, encouraging new drivers who go on to form the habit of driving in the city.

In another interesting study, Gneezy and Rustichini (2000b) examined the impact of incentives on another existing moral behaviour. In this study they looked at a group of school age children who collected money for charities. The collectors were not paid and were motivated by moral, normative incentives only. Once the researchers introduced payments for the children's achievement, the amount they collected fell. The results again suggest a shift from a moral goal frame to a gain goal frame. To begin with, the children's moral motivation was stronger than their financial one. When their moral motivation was replaced with a less motivating financial reward, the children's effort fell. Kopelman, Weber, and Messick's (2002) argument that sanctioning systems (disincentives) can undermine intrinsic motivation, such as social approval or the moral satisfaction of doing the right thing, supports Gneezy and Rustichini's conclusions.

These brief examples demonstrate that introducing initiatives is not as straightforward a matter as some policy makers would wish. It is important not to remove the underlying normative motivations for behaviour by making payments and moving people towards gain and hedonic goal frames. As Gneezy et al. (2011) summarise, "*using incentives. . . could backfire, because extrinsic incentives may in some way crowd out intrinsic motivations that are important to producing the desired behavior*" (p. 191).

Despite the warnings derived from Gneezy and colleagues' work, other researchers have demonstrated some successful campaigns based on financial incentives. Meta-analysis has indicated that there can be a small to medium change in behaviour achieved with incentives and that the change tends to be maintained at a similar level after the incentive is removed (Maki et al., 2016). It is possible in such cases that while the incentives are in place, people develop 'habits' (which we discuss in detail later) that are then maintained. Further, Maki et al. (2016) did find that the success of cash incentives varied between different types of pro-environmental behaviour; they were effective for encouraging recycling, but less effective than non-cash incentives for changing people's transport choices.

THE THEORY OF PLANNED BEHAVIOUR

The theory of planned behaviour (Ajzen, 1991) is one of the most widely used models in social psychology, and perhaps the most widely used when looking at sustainability and pro-environmental behaviour. The model comprises several core components, with numerous research studies adding other constructs to make it more comprehensive or applicable. The model is based on the idea that people systematically consider, process, and use the information available to them to make a behavioural decision. The TPB stops short of predicting behaviour; instead, it usually aims to predict *intention to act*. It is assumed that if someone intends to behave in a particular way, they will, if there is nothing stopping them from doing so. The extent to which that assumption is justified varies. However, when appropriately specified measures are used, there is a strong relationship between intention and behaviour (Sheeran, 2002).

The three main stages in the psychological process that leads to behaviour are shown in Figure 8.3. We can see that indirect influences (referred to as indirect measures) lead to *direct influences* (direct measures), which in turn result in the formation of *behavioural intention*, which should result in behaviour. The key components of the TPB model that tend to be reported in research and used in developing initiatives are the direct influences, shown in the second column of Figure 8.3. These are *attitudes*, *subjective norm*, and *perceived behavioural control*.

Attitude is a result of *behavioural beliefs* and *outcome evaluations*. Essentially, people hold beliefs about the likely outcome of a particular action and an evaluation of whether those outcomes are desirable. For instance, a person might consider that taking fewer flights cuts down on emissions, and reduced emissions is desirable. In that case their attitude would be in favour of less flying. The attitude of someone who thinks that climate change is not a result of human action

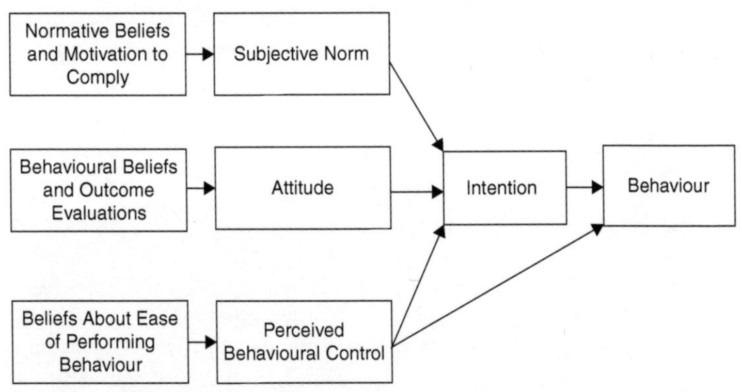

Figure 8.3 Representation of the theory of planned behaviour.

or emissions will have different beliefs and evaluations, probably not seeing cutting down on flights as a good thing to do.

Subjective norm allows the incorporation of social influences into the model. As described in the previous sections, subjective norm is a result of what a person believes others think (normative beliefs), and their motivation to comply with those beliefs. For example, a person might think that their friend believes that they should use their car less. As they value their friend's opinion, they would wish to comply with it, resulting in a strong subjective norm in favour of using their car less. In another case, someone feels that the government thinks they should travel to work by public transport, but if they do not care what the government thinks, then they are not motivated to comply with those beliefs. Consequently, the subjective norm will not support using public transport. There is overlap with GFT's normative frame and TPB subjective norm. However, it does not overlap with the VBN model because subjective norms are injunctive and the norms in the VBN model are moral. However, as we will see, studies have added other normative components to extend the TPB, creating an overlap between all three approaches (e.g., Donald et al., 2014; Wall, Divine-Wright & Mill, 2007).

Perceived behavioural control (PBC) usually increases the predictive power of the model especially when compared with the VBN. The construct allows the inclusion of contextual constraints that might prevent a behaviour that would otherwise result from the attitudes and subjective norms. Researchers often link behavioural control directly to behaviour as well as to behaviour via intention. Perceived behavioural control is similar to Bandura's concept of *self-efficacy* (Bandura, 1982). It is the extent to which a person believes that they can, in practice, carry out a particular action in a way that is acceptable. For example, a person might believe that public transport would reduce carbon emissions, which they believe is a good thing. They might also believe that their family think that they should use public transport, and as the person cares what their family thinks, they are motivated to comply. Without PBC you would therefore predict they would at least intend to use public transport. Unfortunately, their nearest bus stop, or train station, is a four-mile walk from their home. So, although they think it is a good idea to use public transport, they might conclude that it is too difficult for them to do so in practice.

It is possible to link TPB to GFT. For instance, if the hedonic goal frame is dominant, walking to a transport stop might be perceived as too tiring, over-ruling the normative motivation to use public transport. However, a dominant gain frame might result in the saving made by using public transport justifying the walk. It might also increase fitness and reduce the need for a costly gym subscription.

The TPB has been widely and successfully used in many domains in general psychology as well as environmental psychology. Within sustainability and positive environmental action, the model has been used to examine a diverse range of behaviours including energy saving (Liobikienė, Dagiliūtė, & Juknys, 2021), activism (Fielding, McDonald, & Louis, 2008), transport mode choices (Bamber & Schmidt, 2003; Donald, et al. 2014; Gardner & Abraham, 2010; Harland et al., 1999; Heath & Gifford, 2002), air travel decisions (Morten, Gatersleben, & Jessop, 2018), recycling (Chan & Bishop, 2013; Chen & Tung, 2010; Mannetti, Pierro, & Livi, 2004; Taylor & Todd, 1995), and meat consumption (Wolstenholme et al., 2021).

EXPANDING THE THEORY OF PLANNED BEHAVIOUR

Each of the models has some weaknesses. For instance, Gifford et al. (2011) draw attention to the difficulty the VBN model has explaining behaviour when there are external constraints on people's actions. The TPB includes evaluation of the restrictions to carrying out a target action, and so it is likely to be more complete than VBN. However, the TPB lacks consideration of a wider set of norms, and especially moral norms, which are found in GFT. Adding additional normative constructs to the basic model of the TPB is particularly useful as subjective norm tends to be weakest predictor of intention (e.g., Armitage & Conner, 2001). Several authors have responded to this by adding to or combining features of the major theories of pro-environmental behaviour. The results tend to suggest some form of hybrid theory is perhaps the most fruitful (Bamberg & Schmidt, 1992; Wall, Divine-Wright & Mill, 2007).

Moral, Personal, and Descriptive Norms

Although not necessarily a result of making direct comparisons between models, it is not uncommon for researchers to extend the

TPB by including other variables, which is in effect integrating components of other theories. Most common seems to be extending the range of normative influence considered. For instance, moral or personal norms have been added in several studies (e.g., Donald et al., 2014; Gardner & Abraham, 2010; Heath & Gifford, 2002). Harland, Staats, and Wilke (1999) found that inclusion of moral norms improved the predictive ability of the TPB model in relation to four pro-environmental behaviours, with evidence that after taking attitude, subjective norm, and PBC into account, moral norms can help provide a fuller explanation and prediction of pro-environmental behaviour (Harland, Staats, & Wilke, 1999). Those results have been echoed in relation to specific actions including transport use (e.g., Donald et al., 2014) and recycling (e.g., Chan & Bishop, 2013; Chen & Tung, 2010).

Although personal and moral norms are influential in predicting pro-environmental intentions and behaviour, this does not necessarily mean that behaviours are determined primarily by personal rather than social factors. The finding may be attributed to inadequate measurement of social pressure (Donald & Cooper, 2001; Terry & Hogg, 1996). Research that has included descriptive norms, which have a social element, supports this by also giving a fuller account of the social pressures that impact on intentions (Donald & Cooper, 2001; Rivis & Sheeran, 2003).

In general, studies have shown that people's perceptions that others perform a behaviour are associated with stronger intentions to act themselves, though this is not universal. It might be expected that people will tend to follow the crowd and do what they think most other people do. However, as we have already seen, people's responses are not always as expected. For instance, one study examining car use found that descriptive norm had an inverse relationship with intentions. People were less motivated to drive when they thought other people would be driving (Gardner & Abraham, 2010). We can explain this in several ways, including GFT. It makes sense that someone with a biospheric set of beliefs, or a pro-environmental goal frame, would take an opposite stance to the norm if they perceive a lot of damage is already resulting from others driving. From a more selfish hedonic goal frame, it could be felt that more people driving would create congestion making car use more uncomfortable.

Environmental Concern

The study of driving by Gardner and Abraham (2010) suggests the importance of environmental concern in people's intentions. Donald et al. (2014) explicitly included that construct, along with others, in an examination of commuter's transport mode choices. They found that environmental concern did not directly influence intention to use either a private vehicle or public transport. However, it did show an indirect negative effect on behaviour through its influence on habit, meaning that an increase in environmental concern does reduce driving by reducing habitual driving behaviour. Or to put that another way, people who are concerned about the environment are more likely to think before they drive. The results of that research confirm other studies in which habits have been found to be important in determining behaviour.

HABIT

One of the criticisms of the three main theories we have looked at is that they focus on rational cognitive processes in which people form an intention or decide to act after consciously considering all the relevant issues involved. However, several authors have pointed to the potentially significant part played by habits as much environmentally relevant behaviour is thought to be habitual (e.g., Donald et al., 2014; Klöckner & Verplanken, 2013; Verplanken & Whitmarsh, 2021). While most behaviour begins as considered and intentional, there are certain circumstances that can lead them to become habitual, including occurring frequently, being stable over time, and successfully achieving the appropriate goal. Once established through regular repetition, behaviour often takes place without conscious thought. If this were not the case, the number of conscious decisions we would need to make during a day would be overwhelming.

Habit can usefully be thought of as being like the script-based behaviour discussed in Chapter 4 (Donald et al., 2014; Fujii & Gärling, 2003; Klöckner & Mattheis, 2012). Like habit, scripted behaviour is frequent, stable, and successful. The habits that are relevant to environmental sustainability have parallels with the scripts that influence behaviour in emergencies (Donald & Canter, 1992). Both habits and scripts are usually maintained until events challenge them, forcing people to engage in conscious thought about what they are doing.

One activity that provides insight into how habits can be changed is transport use. At a domestic level, the use of private vehicles rather than more sustainable public transport negatively impacts our lives in many ways. Collins and Chambers (2005), for instance, note that "*personal car use contributes to environmental pollution, decreased air quality, greenhouse gas emissions, and fossil fuel consumption*" (p. 640). One solution would be switching to electric vehicles supported by national charging infrastructure, but that will take a long time, so finding ways to get people to move to public transport could be a partial solution that can be achieved more rapidly.

Habit has been identified in several studies as an underlying factor in people using private vehicles (e.g., Bamber & Schmidt, 2003; Donald et al., 2014; Fujii & Gärling, 2003; Gao et al., 2020; Jing et al., 2018; Klöckner & Mattheis 2012; Ramos, Bergstad, & Nässén, 2020; Verplanken et al., 1998, 2008). The consistency of the research findings points to the important role habit plays in transport choice. To encourage change it may therefore be necessary to break transport habits as part of behaviour change initiatives. One key strategy for changing habitual behaviour that has been shown to have an effect is creating or exploiting naturally occurring *discontinuities*. A discontinuity is when an event interrupts the normal routine of everyday life, creating the need for conscious reflection, assessment, and evaluation of behaviour choices. Discontinuity therefore provides an opportunity for behaviour change.

Discontinuities can disrupt habitual behaviour in any area of a person's life. Changing job, moving house, going to university, and even incidental road closures are all examples of naturally occurring interruptions. Policy makers and politicians can also purposefully introduce disruptions. Reducing the number of parking spaces, increasing parking costs, imposing congestion changes, or designating bus lanes could all create a discontinuity that results in people reflecting on their transport choices.

A small number of studies have focused on naturally occurring discontinuities and travel mode choice. Verplanken et al. (2008) conducted a study of staff in a UK university and found that moving residence increased the likelihood of reducing car use. Fujii, Gärling, and Kitamura's (2001) research in Japan demonstrated that interrupting habitual car use and, importantly, showing commuters that they have opportunities to adopt other transport modes increased the use of public transport. Bamberg's (2008) German study showed that an intervention following residential relocation had a greater effect than an intervention on a non-relocation sample in persuading participants to adopt public transport.

The Covid-19 pandemic of 2020–2021 is probably the largest discontinuity that most people have experienced. With a very large fall in travel for leisure and for commuting, for example, it has given people the opportunity to consider alternative modes of transport. Unfortunately, there is little evidence that this unique opportunity has been grasped. It is unlikely that changes towards greater public transport use will be the results. One reason is that the lockdowns experienced in many countries removed the need for travel altogether rather than creating a need to travel in a different or novel way. In fact, it is probable that where conscious decisions were made, they are likely to have been towards reducing public transport use because mixing with others was perceived as more risky than private vehicle use. Early indications from official government statistics seem to support this with public transport use remaining lower than pre-Covid-19 levels.

Even if the pandemic did not create a discontinuity in travel mode choice, other than greater car use, there was a discontinuity in working habits. In pre-pandemic times, Wall et al. commented "*Although some journeys might be avoidable for some people, commuting is perhaps one type of travel that is nonnegotiable*" (Wall et al., 2007, p. 732). The lockdowns demonstrated that commuting is negotiable. It was evident that large numbers of the workforce did not need to travel into a central workplace. Perhaps the critical question should not be which mode of transport commuters should use, but whether they need to commute at all. Following the lockdowns, many large multinational companies have expressed enthusiasm for at least part-homeworking. However, the UK government is pushing for a return to the workplace and so indirectly also pushing for return to unsustainable behaviour.

Habits are sometimes seen as a barrier to pro-environmental behaviour. However, that is not necessarily the case, as some positive behaviours are habitual, such as turning off lights when leaving a room. Because habit can be disrupted by change, there are opportunities that can be exploited to establish new, sustainable behaviours, which are then automatically maintained. In this sense, habits can be beneficial to sustainable behaviour, but sustainable habits must be encouraged, not inhibited.

INFORMATION AND FEEDBACK

Environmental campaigns and initiatives are often based on the idea that, as rational beings, if people know the threats of unsustainable behaviour and lifestyles, they will act in a more pro-environmental way. This 'information deficit model' (Burgess, Harrison & Filius, 1998; Owens & Driffill, 2008) does not receive much empirical support. There are many factors that shape people's behaviour, only one of which is information. We have seen this in each of the three models of environmental behaviour that we have considered in the chapter. For example, in VBN theory, for personal norms to be activated, there needs to be relevant information. But information on its own is insufficient. Research generally shows that although information increases knowledge, it only has a small effect on pro-environmental behaviour (McKenzie-Mohr, 2000; Owens & Driffill, 2008). It is useful, in making the point, to quote an anonymous participant in one of Verplanken's studies, "*Whilst I do acknowledge that the issue of climate change is probably the most important problem humanity has faced, I surprise myself in my ability to ignore this*" (Verplanken, 2014).

One form of information that is receiving attention is feedback. For more than a century psychologists have been aware that feedback can be useful in changing and maintaining behaviour and improving performance. Feedback has been used as a way of improving pro-environmental behaviour in several areas, including recycling (Abrahamse & Steg, 2013; Varotto & Spagnolli, 2017), despite it being rather impractical for that activity (Katzev & Mishima, 1992), and energy-efficient driving (Birrell & Young, 2011). Domestic energy consumption, however, has probably received most attention from researchers interested in the role of feedback. That is partly because it is a significant contributor to emissions, but also because it is something that is open to behavioural influence, with studies showing consumption can vary by up to 260% in identical accommodation (Karlin, Zinger & Ford, 2015). Finally, and importantly, domestic energy consumption is also an area in which giving detailed and useful feedback is possible.

It is quite difficult to effectively reduce energy consumption without feedback. For many years that is what has been expected of people trying to achieve more sustainable consumption. Traditionally, every three months or so a bill arrived saying how much was owed, but not providing easily understandable information about the energy used. More recently, many countries are rolling out the installation of smart meters and other technologies that provide detailed information about how energy is consumed. Innovations like smart meters are costly, so it is helpful if their design, installation, and use are informed by empirical research.

The use of feedback in reducing energy consumption raises several questions about how to present the information. For instance, we need to consider whether to just provide information on the amount of energy used, or whether we should make some comment on it. If some comment is provided, should it be simply about the amount used, or would it be helpful to draw on normative processes and compare a person's energy use with other people or groups? If a comparison is made, which social or normative group should it be made with? There are a number of possibilities including previous household use, neighbours' use, or average use. We need to consider whether the information on usage should be given in watts, cubic metres for gas, or in terms of the financial cost. Finally, we need to know how often the information should be presented, in what form and using which medium. Research has tried to answer these and other questions.

Usually, the provision of feedback on energy use is part of a wider initiative, and this makes it difficult to compare research results without disentangling the impact of feedback from other aspects of an intervention. For instance, researchers might introduce feedback along with goal setting, leaving the question of which is having an impact on behaviour. Karlin et al. (2015) have summarised the situation, saying that we know that feedback works, but we do not really know what works most effectively.

To move closer to answering the question of how most effectively to use feedback, Karlin et al. (2015) carried out a meta-analysis of studies of the impact of feedback on energy consumption. They looked at 42 research studies examining variables including, for instance, frequency, the medium it is given in, the metric used, the level of detail, and the duration of time over which feedback is given. As making comparisons between studies is difficult, the results of the meta-analysis, though interesting, need to be taken as indicative, rather than definitive.

Overall, the meta-analysis shows that feedback does reduce residential energy use of between 8% and 12%. However, individual studies showed a lot of variability in the results. This fits with other reviews of feedback and energy consumption. For instance, Vine, Buys, and Morris (2013) in their review found reductions in energy use of between 5% and 20%, again demonstrating some quite wide variation. Karlin et al. (2015) found that 5% of the studies reviewed demonstrated no effect, 12% showed a negative effect, and the majority, 83%, revealed a positive relationship.

As usual, when comparing the findings of different research studies, we have to be aware that different results could be an artefact of the way the various studies were conducted. It is likely that feedback has a different effect in different circumstances, which highlights the fact that to have the most impact, feedback needs to be tailored to its specific context. Nevertheless, there appear to be several characteristics of feedback that do not result in significant differences in people's behaviour. These include the frequency with which feedback is given, the units in which energy use is measured and the granularity of the measures, and whether consumption was compared to historic data on people's own consumption or to other's energy use (Karlin et al., 2015). However, when a person has set a goal and can see how they are doing against that goal, feedback can lead to savings. The medium by which feedback is given does have an effect but only when the information was provided using computers, which might be because they are interactive. The smallest effect is when a utility bill provides the information. Giving feedback in combination with other interventions, such as goal setting, showed a significant improvement in energy saving, as did the duration over which the feedback was given (Karlin at al., 2015).

The results of the meta-analysis by Karlin et al. are interesting and indicate several areas where feedback is useful. As the authors themselves note, some of the conclusions that can be drawn from their analysis do not agree with some existing studies. For instance, normative comparisons have been found to be effective in studies and reviews of energy conservation (e.g., Bergquist & Nilsson, 2016; Nolan et al. 2008; Schultz, 2014). Further, Nolan et al. (2008) found that descriptive norms (perception of what most other people do) are predictive of energy conservation. Moreover, they also demonstrated that social norms were more influential in bringing about behaviour change than being given information about other reasons to reduce energy use. Karlin et al.'s review also contradicts Darby's review, in which she concludes that providing historic feedback of past energy use does effect current energy consumption more than goal-related feedback (Darby, 2006). What these differences tell us is not that there are problems with the reviews, but that there are difficulties in comparing studies that can vary widely in their methods and analysis. That is one of the challenges of conducting applied research.

FINALLY

There are two observations that stand out in this chapter on sustainability and pro-environmental behaviour. The first is the significant increase in research that has taken place to the point that it now dominates the discipline of environmental psychology. The second is the observation by Carmichael (2019) that, so far, there has been very little impact on reducing greenhouse gas emissions by changing people's behaviour. Ernst and Wenzel (2014) have said that the impact of behavioural change has not been as visible or as successful as we would wish. If these observations are correct, it raises questions about the efficacy of research and its implementation. It is unlikely that the research itself is of poor quality, or that the behaviour change initiatives that have been based on it are completely wrong. That leaves us with the question of whether carrying out more and more of the same research, conceived of in the same way, will somehow begin to produce results and interventions that will significantly impact climate change. Is it that we have not done enough research and behaviour change work, or is it perhaps that we are thinking about the problems in fundamentally the wrong way?

Perhaps environment-behaviour researchers need to rethink the problem and our approach to it. Rather than focusing on the causes of what are perceived to be our individual wrong choices and why we make them, maybe we should be looking our relationships to our wider environment, including our social, political, economic, cultural, and physical rootedness. As environmental psychologists, we should be able to examine how we mutually interact and coexist with the environment and suggest effective ways to make that coexistence sustainable.

REFERENCES

Abrahamse, W., & Steg, L. (2013). Social influence approaches to encourage resource conservation: A meta-analysis. *Global Environmental Change*, 23, 1773–1785.

Ajzen, I. (1991). The theory of planned behaviour. *Organizational Behavior and Human Decision Processes*, 50, 179–211.

Armitage, C. J. & Conner, M. (2001). Efficacy of the theory of planned behaviour: A meta analytic review. *British Journal of Social Psychology*, 40, 471–500.

Bamberg, S. (2008). Is a residential relocation a good opportunity to change people's travel behavior? Results from a theory-driven intervention study. *Environment and Behavior*, 38, 820–840.

Bamberg, S. & Schmidt, P. (2003). Incentives, morality, or habit? Predicting students' car use for university routes with the models of Ajzen, Schwartz, and Triandis. *Environment and Behavior*, 35, 264–283.

Bandura, A. (1982). Self-efficacy mechanism in human agency. *American Psychologist*, 37, 122–147.

BEIS. (2017). *Energy Consumption in the UK*. London: Department of Business, Energy and Industrial Strategy. July 2017.

Bergquist, M., & Nilsson, A. (2016). I saw the sign: Promoting energy conservation via normative prompts. *Journal of Environmental Psychology*, 46, 23–31.

Berkhout, P. H. G., Muskens, J. C., & Velthuijsen, J. W. (2000). Defining the rebound effect. *Energy Policy*, 28, 425–432.

Birrell, S. A. & Young, M. S. (2011). The impact of smart driving aids on driving performance and driver distraction. *Transportation Research Part F*, 14, 484–493.

Breakwell, G. M. (1986). *Coping with Threatened Identities*. London: Methuen.

Burgess, J., Harrison, C., & Filius, P. (1998). Environmental communication and the cultural politics of environmental citizenship. *Environment and Planning A, Economy and Space*, 30, 1445–1460.

Carmichael, R. (2019). *Behaviour Change, Public Engagement and Net Zero*. A report for the Committee on Climate Change. Retrieved from https://www.theccc.org.uk/publications/ and http://www.imperial.ac.uk/icept/publications/

Chan, L. & Bishop, B. (2013). A moral basis for recycling: Extending the theory of planned behaviour. *Journal of Environmental Psychology*, 36, 96–102.

Chen, M.-F. & Tung, P.-J. (2010). The moderating effect of perceived lack of facilities on consumers' recycling intentions. *Environment and Behavior*, 42, 824–844.

Cialdini, R., Reno, R., & Kallgren, (1990). A focus theory of normative conduct: Recycling the concept of norms to reduce littering in public places. *Journal of Personality and Social Psychology*, 58, 1015–1026.

Clayton, S., & Myers, G. (2015). *Conservation Psychology: Understanding and Promoting Human Care for Nature, Second Edition*. Oxford: Wiley-Blackwell.

Collins, C. & Chambers, S. (2005). Psychological and situational influences on commuter transport-mode choice. *Environment and Behavior*, 37, 640–661.

Craik, K. H. (1973). Environmental psychology. *Annual Review of Psychology*, 24, 403–422.

Darby, S. (2006). *The Effectiveness of Feedback on Energy Consumption: A Review for DEFRA of the Literature on Metering, Billing and Direct Displays*. Environmental Change Institute, University of Oxford, Oxford. https://www.eci.ox.ac.uk/research/energy/downloads/smart-metering-report.pdf

De Groot, J. M. I., & Steg, L. (2008). Value orientations to explain beliefs related to environmental significant behaviour: How to measure egoistic, altruistic, and biospheric value orientations. *Environment and Behavior*, 40, 330–354.

De Groot, J. M. I., & Steg, L. (2009a). Value orientations to explain beliefs related to environmental significant behaviour: How to measure egoistic, altruistic and biospheric value orientations. *Environment and Behavior*, 40, 330–355.

De Groot, J. M. I., & Steg, L. (2009b). Morality and prosocial behaviour: The role of awareness, responsibility and norms in the norm activation model. *Journal of Social Psychology*, 149, 425–449.

Donald, I. & Canter, D. (1992). Intentionality and fatality during the King's Cross underground fire. *European Journal of Social Psychology*, 22, 203–218.

Donald, I. & Cooper, S. R. (2001). A facet approach to extending the normative component of the theory of reasoned action. *British Journal of Social Psychology*, 40, 599–621.

Donald, I., Cooper, S. R., & Conchie, S. (2014). An extended theory of planned behaviour model of psychological factors affecting commuters' transport mode use. *Journal of Environmental Psychology*, 40, 39–48.

Dubois, G., Sovacool, D., Aall, C., Nilsson, M., Barbier, C., Herrmann, A., Bruyère, S., Andersson, C., Skold, B., Nadaud, F., Dorner, F., Richardsen, K., J. P. C. Moberg, Fischer, H., Amelung, D., Baltruszewicz, M., Fischer, J., Benevise, F., Louis, V. R., & Sauerborn, R. (2019). It starts at home? Climate policies targeting household consumption and behavioral decisions are key to low-carbon futures. *Energy Research & Social Science*, 52, 144–158.

Dunlap, R. E. (2008). The new environmental paradigm scale: From marginality to worldwide use. *The Journal of Environmental Education*, 40, 3–18.

Dunlap, R. E. & Van Liere, K. D. (1978). The "New Environmental Paradigm": A proposed measuring instrument and preliminary results. *The Journal of Environmental Education*, 9(4), 10–19.

Ernst, A. & Wenzel, U. (2014). Bringing environmental psychology into action: Four steps from science to policy. *European Psychologist*, 19, 118–126.

Evans, G. W. (2019). Behavioral Impacts of Climate Change. *Annual Review of Psychology*, 70, 449–474.

Fehr, E., & Falk, A. (2002). Psychological foundations of incentives. *European Economic Review*, 46, 687–724.

Fielding, K. S., McDonald, R., & Louis, W. R. (2008). Theory of planned behaviour, identity and intentions to engage in environmental activism. *Journal of Environmental Psychology*, 28, 318–326.

Fujii, S. & Gärling, T. (2003). Development of script-based travel mode choice after forced change. *Transport Research Part F*, 6, 117–124.

Fujii, S., Gärling, T., & Kitamura, R. (2001). Changes in drivers' perceptions and use of public transport during a freeway closure. *Environment and Behavior*, 36, 796–808.

Gao, K., Yang, Y., Sun, L., & Qu, X. (2020). Revealing psychological inertia in mode shift behaviour and its quantitative influences on commuting trips. *Transportation Research Part F: Traffic Psychology and Behaviour*, 71, 272–287.

Garcia-Mira, R. (ed.) (2013). *Readings on the Prestige Disaster: Contributions from the Social Sciences.* A Coruña, Spain: Institute for Psychosocial Studies and Research '*Xoan Vicente Viqueira*'.

Garcia-Mira, R., Dumitru, A., & Alonso-Betanzos, A., Sánchez-Maroño, N., Fontenla-Romero, Ó., Craig, T., & Polhill, J. G. (2017). Testing scenarios to achieve workplace sustainability goals using backcasting and agent-based modelling. *Environment and Behavior*, 49, 1007–1037.

Gardner, B. & Abraham, C. (2010). Going Green? Modelling the impact of environmental concerns and perceptions of transportation alternatives on decisions to drive. *Journal of Applied Social Psychology*, 40, 831–849.

Gardner, G. T. & Stern, P. C. (2008). The short list: The most effective actions US households can take to curb climate change. *Environment: Science and Policy for Sustainable Development*, 50(5), 12–25.

Ghazali, E. M., Bang, N., Dilip, S. M., & Su-Fei, Y. (2019). Pro-environmental behaviours and Value-Belief-Norm Theory: Assessing unobserved heterogeneity of two ethnic groups. *Sustainability*, 11(12), 3237. https://doi.org/10.3390/su11123237 Downloaded from https://www.mdpi.com/2071-1050/11/12/3237

Gifford, R. (2014). Environmental psychology matters. *Annual Review of Psychology*, 65, 541–579.

Gifford, R., Steg, L., & Reser, J. P. (2011). Environmental psychology. In P. R. Martin, F. M. Cheung, M. C. Knowles, M. Kyrios, L. Littlefield, J. B. Overmier, & J. M. Prieto (eds.), *IAAP Handbook of Applied Psychology*, (pp. 440–470). Oxford: Blackwell.

Gneezy, U., Meier, S., & Rey-Biel, P. (2011). When and why incentives (don't) work to modify behavior. *Journal of Economic Perspectives*, 25(4), 191–210.

Gneezy, U. & Rustichini, A. (2000a). A fine is a price. *Journal of Legal Studies*, 29, 1–18.

Gneezy, U. & Rustichini, A. (2000b). Pay enough or don't pay at all. *Quarterly Journal of Economics*, 115, 791–810.

Goldstein, N. J., Cialdini, R. B., & Griskevicius, V. (2008). A room with a viewpoint: Using social norms to motivate environmental conservation in hotels. *Journal of Consumer Research*, 35, 472–482.

Hafner, R., Elmes, D., Read, D., & White, M. P. (2019). Exploring the role of normative, financial and environmental information in promoting uptake of energy efficient technologies. *Journal of Environmental Psychology*, 63, 26–35.

Harland, P., Staats, H., & Wilke, H. A. M. (1999). Explaining pro-environmental intentions and behavior by personal norms and the theory of planned behavior. *Journal of Applied Social Psychology*, 29, 2505–2528.

Heath, Y. & Gifford, R. (2002). Extending the theory of planned behaviour: Predicting the use of public transportation. *Journal of Applied Social Psychology*, 32(10), 2154–2185.

Hertwich, E. & Peters, G. (2009). Carbon footprint of nations: A global, trade-linked analysis. *Environmental Science and Technology*, 43, 6414–6420.

Ipsos Mori (2020). https://www.ipsos.com/ipsos-mori/en-uk/concern-about-climate-change-reaches-record-levels-half-now-very-concerned Accessed 16 October 2021.

Jaffe, A. B. & Stavins, R. N. (1994). The energy paradox and the diffusion of conservation technology. *Resource and Energy Economics*, 16(2), 91–122.

Jakobsson, C., Fujii, S., & Gärling, T. (2000). Determinants of private car users' acceptance of road pricing. *Transport Policy*, 7, 153–158.

Jing, P., Wang, J., Chen, L., & Zha, Q. F. (2018). Incorporating the extended theory of planned behavior in a school travel mode choice model: A case study of Shaoxing, China. *Transportation Planning and Technology*, 41, 119–137.

Karlin, B., Davis, N., Sanguinetti, A., Gamble, K., Kirkby, D., & Stokols, D. (2014). Dimensions of conservation: Exploring differences among energy behaviors. *Environment and Behavior*, 46, 423–452.

Karlin, B., Zinger, J. F., & Ford, R. (2015). The effects of feedback on energy conservation: A meta-analysis. *Psychological Bulletin*, 141, 1205–1227.

Katzev, R. & Mishima, H. R. (1992). The use of posted feedback to promote recycling. *Psychological Reports*, 71, 259–264.

Kenz, I. (2016). Is climate change a moral issue? Effects of egoism and altruism on pro-environmental behaviour. *Current Urban Studies*, 4(2), 157–174.

Khazzoom, J. D. (1980). Economic implications of mandated efficiency in standards for household appliances. *Energy Journal*, 1(4), 21–40.

Klöckner, C. A. & Matthies, E. (2012). Two pieces of the same puzzle? Script-based car choice habits between the influence of socialization and past behavior. *Journal of Applied Social Psychology*, 42, 793–821.

Klöckner, C. A., & Verplanken, B. (2013). Yesterday's habits preventing change for tomorrow? The influence of automaticity on environmental behaviour. In L. Steg, A. van der Berg, & J. I. M. de Groot (eds.), *Environmental Psychology: An Introduction* (pp. 198–209). Oxford: BPS-Blackwell.

Kopelman, S., Weber, J. M., & Messick, D. M. (2002). Factors influencing cooperation in commons dilemmas: A review of experimental psychological research. In E. Ostrom, T. Dietz, N. Dolsak, P. C. Stern, S. Stonich, & E. U. Weber (eds.), *The Drama of the Commons* (pp. 113–156). Washington, DC: National Academy Press.

Lapinski, M. K., & Rimal, R. N. (2005). An explication of social norms. *Communication Theory*, 15(2), 127–147.

Lindenberg, S. (2001). Social rationality versus rational egoism. In J. Turner (ed.), *Handbook of Sociological Theory* (pp. 635–668). New York: Kluwer Academic/Plenum.

Lindenberg, S. & Steg, L. (2007). Normative, gain and hedonic goal frames guiding environmental behaviour. *Journal of Social Issues*, 65, 117–137.

Liobikienė, G., Dagiliūtė, R., & Juknys, R. (2021). The determinants of renewable energy usage intentions using theory of planned behaviour approach. *Renewable Energy*, 170, 587–594.

Maki, A., Burns, R. J., Ha, L., & Rothman, A. J. (2016). Paying people to protect the environment: A meta-analysis of financial incentive interventions to promote proenvironmental behaviors. *Journal of Environmental Psychology*, 47, 242–255.

Mannetti, L., Pierro, A., & Livi, S. (2004). Recycling: Planned and self-expressive behaviour. *Journal of Environmental Psychology*, 24, 227–236.

McKenzie-Mohr, D. (2000). Promoting sustainable behavior: an introduction to community-based social marketing. *Journal of Social Issues*, 56, 543–554.

Morten, A., Gatersleben, B., & Jessop, D. C. (2018). Staying grounded? Applying the theory of planned behaviour to explore motivations to reduce air travel. *Transportation Research Part F: Traffic Psychology and Behaviour,* 55, 297–305.

Murtagh, N., Gatersleben, B., & Uzzell, D. (2012a). Multiple identities and travel mode choice for regular journeys. *Transportation Research Part F,* 15, 514–524.

Murtagh, N., Gatersleben, B., & Uzzell, D. (2012b). Self-identity threat and resistance to change: Evidence from regular travel behaviour. *Journal of Environmental Psychology*, 32, 318–326.

Murtagh, N., Gatersleben, B., & Uzzell, D. (2015). Does perception of automation undermine pro-environmental behaviour? Findings from three everyday settings. *Journal of Environmental Psychology*, 42, 139–148.

Nolan, J. M., Wesley Schultz, P., Cialdini, R. B., Goldstein, N. J., & Griskevicius, V. (2008). Normative social influence in underrated. *Personality and Social Psychology Bulletin*, 34, 913–923.

Otto, S., Kaiser, F. G., & Arnold, O. (2014). The critical challenge of climate change for psychology: Preventing rebound and promoting more individual irrationality. *European Psychologist*, 19, 96–106.

Owens, S., & Driffill, L. (2008). How to change attitudes and behaviours in the context of energy. *Energy Policy*, 36, 4412–4418.

Pirages, D. C. & Ehrlich, P. R. (1974). *Ark II: Social Responses to Environmental Imperatives.* San Francisco, CA: W. H. Freeman.

Poortinga, J. O., Steg, L., Vlek, C., & Wiersma, G. (2003). Household preference for energy-saving measures: A conjoint analysis. *Journal of Economic Psychology*, 24, 49–64.

Ramos, É. M. S., Bergstad, J., & Nässén, J. (2020). Understanding daily car use: Driving habits, motives, attitudes, and norms across trip purposes. *Transportation Research Part F: Traffic Psychology and Behaviour*, 68, 306–315.

Raymond, C. M., Brown, G., & Robinson, G. M. (2011). The influence of place attachment, and moral and normative concerns on the conservation of native vegetation: A test of two behavioural models. *Journal of Environmental Psychology*, 31, 323–335.

Rhead, R., Elliot, M., & Upham, P. (2015). Assessing the structure of UK environmental concern and its association with pro-environmental behaviour. *Journal of Environmental Psychology*, 43, 175–183.

Richetin, J., Perugini, M., Conner, M., Adjali, I., Hurling, R., Sengupta, A., & Greetham, D. (2012). To reduce and not to reduce resource consumption? That is two questions. *Journal of Environmental Psychology*, 32, 112–122.

Rivis, A. & Sheeran, P. (2003). Descriptive norms as an additional predictor in the theory of planned behaviour: A meta-analysis. *Current Psychology: Developmental, Learning, Personality, Social*, 22, 218–233.

Ruepert, A., Keizer, K., Steg, L., Maricchiolo, F., Carrus, G., Dumitru, A., Mira, R. G., Stancu, A., & Moza, D. (2016). Environmental considerations in the organizational context: A pathway to pro-environmental behaviour at work. *Energy Research & Social Science*, 17, 59–70,

Schuitema, G. & Kakobsson-Bergstad, C. (2013). Acceptability of environmental policies. In L. Steg, A. van der Berg, & J. I. M. de Groot (eds.), *Environmental Psychology: An Introduction* (pp. 255–266). Oxford: BPS-Blackwell.

Schultz, P. W. (2014). Strategies for promoting pro-environmental behavior. *European Psychologist*, 19, 107–117.

Schwartz, S. H. (1977). Normative influence on altruism. In L. Berkowitz (Ed.), *Advances in Experimental Social Psychology*, Vol. 10, (pp. 221–279). New York: Academic Press.

Sheeran, P. (2002). Intention-behaviour relations: A conceptual and empirical review. In M. Hewstone & W. Stroebe (eds.), *European Review of Social Psychology, Volume 12* (pp. 1–36). Chichester: Wiley.

Shove, E. (2010). Beyond the ABC: Climate change policy and theories of social change. *Environment and Planning A*, 42, 1273–1285.

Sisco, M. R., Pianta, S., Weber, E. U., & Bosetti, V. (2021). Global climate marches sharply raise attention to climate change: Analysis of climate search behavior in 46 countries. *Journal of Environmental Psychology*, 75, https://doi.org/10.1016/j.jenvp.2021.101596. Available online 2 April 2021.

Sorrell, S. (2007). *The Rebound Effect: An Assessment of the Evidence for Economy-Wide Energy Savings from Improved Energy Efficiency.* A report produced by the Sussex Energy Group for the Technology and Policy Assessment function of the UK Energy Research Centre, October 2007, ISBN 1-903144-0-35.

Steentjes, K., Pidgeon, N., Poortinga, W., Corner, A., Arnold, A., Böhm, G., Mays, C., Poumadère, M., Ruddat, M., Scheer, D., Sonnberger, M., & Tvinnereim, E. (2017). *European Perceptions of Climate Change: Topline Findings of a Survey Conducted in Four European Countries in 2016.* Cardiff: Cardiff University.

Steg, L., Bolderdijk, J. W., Keizer, K., & Perlaviciute, G. (2014). An integrated framework for encouraging pro-environmental behaviour: The role of values, situational factors and goals. *Journal of Environmental Psychology*, 38, 104–115.

Steg, L. & De Groot, J. I. M. (2012). Environmental Values. In S. Clayton (ed.), *The Oxford Handbook of Environmental and Conservation Psychology* (pp. 81–92). Oxford: Oxford University Press.

Steg, L. & de Groot, J. I. M. (eds.) (2019). *Environmental Psychology: An Introduction, Second Edition.* Oxford: BPS Blackwell.

Steg, L., Dreijerink, L., & Abrahamse, W. (2005). Factors influencing the acceptability of energy policies: A test of VBN theory. *Journal of Environmental Psychology*, 25, 415–425.

Steg, L., Lieke, D., & Wokje, A. (2005). Factors influencing the acceptability of energy policies: A test ofVBN theory. *Journal of Environmental Psychology*, 25, 415–425.

Steg, L. & Nordlund, A. (2013). Models to explain environmental behaviour. In L. Steg, A. E. van den Berg, & J. I. M. de Groot (eds.), *Environmental Psychology: An Introduction* (pp. 186–195). Oxford: BPS Blackwell.

Steg, L. & Vlek, C. (2009). Encouraging pro-environmental behaviour: An integrative review and research agenda. *Journal of Environmental Psychology*, 29, 309–317.

Stern, P. (2011). Contributions of psychology to limiting climate change. *American Psychologist*, 66(4), 303–314.

Stern, P. C. (2000). Toward a coherent theory of environmentally significant behaviour. *Journal of Social Issues*, 56, 407–424.

Taylor, S. & Todd, P. (1995). An integrated model of waste management behavior: A test of household recycling and composting intentions. *Environment and Behavior*, 27, 603–630.

Terry, D. J. & Hogg, M. A. (1996). Group norms and the attitude-behavior relationship: A role for group identification. *Personality and Social Psychology Bulletin*, 22, 776–793.

Triandis, H. (1977). *Interpersonal Behaviour.* Monterey, CA: Brooks/Cole.

Truelove, H. B. & Gillis, A. J. (2018). Perception of pro-environmental behavior. *Global Environmental Change*, 49, 23–31.

Tudor, T. L., Barr, S. W., & Gilg, A. W. (2008). A novel conceptual framework for examining environmental behaviour in large organizations – A case study of the Cornwall National Health Service (NHS) in the United Kingdom. *Environment and Behavior,* 40, 426-450.

United Nations. (2019). *World Population Prospects 2019: Highlights.* United Nations Department of Economic and Social Affairs, Population Division, (ST/ESA/SER.A/423).

Uzzell, D. (2018). Changing Behaviour: Energy Consumption. Briefing Paper. British Psychological Society.

Van der Werff, E. & Steg, L. (2016). The psychology of participation and interest in smart energy systems: Comparing the value-belief-norm theory and the value-identity-personal norm model. *Energy Research & Social Science*, 22, 107–114.

Van Raaij, W. F. & Verhallen, T. M. M. (1983). A behavioral model of residential energy use. *Journal of Economic Psychology*, 3, 39–63.

Varotto, A. & Spagnolli, A. (2017). Psychological strategies to promote household recycling. A systematic review with meta-analysis of validated field interventions. *Journal of Environmental Psychology*, 51, 168–188.

Verplanken, B. (2014). If you don't understand habits, how can you hope to change them? Challenges and opportunities to encourage sustainable living. https://www.behaviourworksaustralia.org/wp-content/uploads/2014/12/BasVerplankenhabits.pdf Accessed June 2016.

Verplanken, B., Aarts, H., van Knippenberg, A., & Moonen, A. (1998). Habit versus planned behaviour: A field experiment. *British Journal of Social Psychology*, 37, 111–128.

Verplanken, B., Walker, I., Davis, A., & Jurasek, M. (2008). Context change and travel mode choice: Combining the habit discontinuity and self-activation hypotheses. *Journal of Environmental Psychology*, 28, 121–127.

Verplanken, B. & Whitmarsh, L. (2021). Habit and climate change. *Current Opinion in Behavioral Sciences*, 42, 42–46.

Vine, D., Buys, L., & Morris, P. (2013). The effectiveness of energy feedback for conservation and peak demand: A literature review. *Open Journal of Energy Efficiency*, 2, 7–15.

Wall, R., Divine-Wright, P., & Mill, G. A. (2007). Comparing and combining theories to explain proenvironmental intention: The case of commuting-mode choice. *Environment and Behavior*, 39, 731–753.

Wolstenholme, E., Carfora, V., Catellani, P., Poortinga, W., & Whitmarsh, L. (2021). Explaining intention to reduce red and processed meat in the UK and Italy using the theory of planned behaviour, meat-eater identity, and the Transtheoretical model. *Appetite*, 166, https://doi.org/10.1016/j.appet.2021.105467

WWF. (2020). *Living Planet Report 2020- Bending the curve of biodiversity loss.* R. E. A. Almond, M. Grooten & T. Petersen (eds). WWF, Gland, Switzerland.

SUGGESTED READING

Abrahamse, W. (2019) *Encouraging Pro-Environmental Behaviour: What Works, What Doesn't, and Why*. London: Academic Press.

Clayton, S., & Myers, G. (2015). *Conservation Psychology: Understanding and Promoting Human Care for Nature, Second Edition*. Oxford: Wiley-Blackwell.

Gifford, R. (2014). Environmental psychology matters. *Annual Review of Psychology*, 65, 541–579.

Steg, L. & de Groot, J. I. M. (eds.) (2019). *Environmental Psychology: An Introduction, Second Edition*. Oxford: BPS Blackwell.

INDEX

affiliative behaviour in emergencies 89–90; *see also* behaviour during fires and emergencies
agency 12, 17
aggression: driving 70; emergencies, during 83; psychiatric hospitals 140–142, 151; in sport 70; temperature and 111; territory 67, 69, 75
altruism values 210–212
American Psychological Association (APA) 7
animal studies, relevance of 59, 71; *see also* territory
anthropocentric paradigm 208; values 212
anti-essentialism 41; *see also* essentialism
architects 6, 7, 12, 15, 16, 172, 177
architectural psychology *see* environmental psychology
architecture 6–7, 16–18
arousal 73, 111, 154
arson 124
assault 114–115, 122, 124, 128, 135
assistive technology 144–145
attention restoration theory (ART) 149–151, 152, 154–155
attitudes and place 41, 47–48; sustainability 208, 214, 218–219, 221; theory of planned behaviour 218
autism: neuro-typical approach 146–147; prevalence 146; school design 138, 146, 160; sensory-centric approach 146–147
autochthony and refugees 42

behaviour change and sustainability 198, 200, 203–204, 223, 228; *see also* pro environmental behaviour; sustainability
behavioural geography 5–6, 14; *see also* geography
behavioural intention 212, 218, 220, 222; *see also* theory of planned behaviour
behavioural scripts *see* scripts
behavioural sinks 58–59; *see also* sink estates
behaviour during fires and emergencies: affiliative 89; cues 94–95, 97, 101; domestic settings 94–95; general model of 97; hospitals 96; interpreting cues 85–86, 88, 92–93, 97, 99,

101, 105; multiple occupancies 95–96; normative 90–91; rules and roles 91; social identity and self-categorisation 90; *see also* decision-making; disaster myths; exit choice; gender roles; King's Cross Underground; panic; scripts
being away 150, 155
biodiversity 201–202
biospheric: beliefs 221; values 211–212
British Psychological Society (BPS) 17
Building Performance Research Unit (BPRU) 16
burglary: location 121–123; spatial pattern 124, 128; territorial markers (and defensible space) 118–120; weather 113–115
bürolandschaft 176–179

Canter, David 14–18, 123
childsex abuse and environment 136
Churchill, Winston 21
City University New York (CUNY) 8
classical organisational theory *see* organisational theory
climate change: adaption to 44; crime 110; effects 43, 45–46; migration 40; psychology 199–202, 228; public concern 197–198; *see also* emissions; sustainability
clinical psychology and environment 135–136
cognitive maps 6, 122–123
commuter model of crime 123–125, 127–128
commuting and travel mode choice 222, 224
consumption of resources 199–201, 203–205, 215, 220, 223, 225–228
control and social interaction 62–63, 66, 69; in hospitals 141; in offices 172, 179–180, 182, 183, 190
cost benefit model of crime 114, 119
Covid-19 40, 46, 61, 72, 110, 168, 190, 224
Craik, Ken 9
crime: crowding 58; defensible space 117–119; design 115–117; during disasters 82–83; environment 109, 126; temperature 110–113, 115
Crime Prevention through Environmental Design (CPTED) 119–120
crime and weather 109–115; methodological problems with 112, 115
criminal range 123; *see also* home range
crowding: definition 60, 76; stress 60–61, 141; *see also* density
culture and personal space 74–75
curtailment behaviour 204–207, 211

decision-making: emergencies 88, 95, 99, 101; environment 2–3, 5, 21, 150, 152
defensible space 117; burglars' judgement 118–119; characteristics 117–119; criticism 118, 120, 129; spatial zones 117
dementia: design 143–145, 148; prevalence 142; symptoms 143–144
density 58–61, 73, 180; social density 60, 141–142; spatial density 60, 186
design 16–17, 19; autism 146–147; clinical settings 136; crime 115–119; dementia 142–145; emergencies 81, 85–87, 96;

hospitals 140–141; organizational theory 169–173, 176–179, 186; place 32; prisons 138–139; social interaction 63–66; therapeutic goals 137, 147–148, 160
determinism 12, 19–21, 23–24, 34, 65, 115, 128, 173–174, 183
diet and sustainability 67, 201, 203, 205
directed attention fatigue (DAF) 150
disaster management 85, 87, 90, 92
disaster myths 82, 85
disasters *see* behaviour during fires and emergencies; King's Cross Underground Fire
disaster shock 82
disaster syndrome 82
dominant social paradigm (DSP) 208

ecological worldview 211
EDRA (Environmental Design Research Association) 17
efficiency behaviour and sustainability 200, 204–206, 211
egoistic values 211–212
emergencies *see* behaviour in fires and emergencies
emissions: reduction of 205, 218–219, 223, 228; sources 202–205, 223, 225
energy conservation 204, 228
energy efficiency gap 200
Environment and Behavior 18
environmental determinism *see* determinism
environmental interaction *see* interactionism
environmental psychologist, becoming 7–8
environmental psychology: characteristics 3–4, 10–13; definition 8–9; history and origins 13–18
environmental range 123
environmental role 33
environmental sociology 5
environmental sustainability *see* sustainability
environmental transaction *see* transactionism
environmental trigger: in mental health 135; of panic 84, 85
ergonomics 4–5, 8
essentialism 34, 41
evolution 73–74, 152–153, 156
exit choice in emergencies 90–91, 101
experimental psychology 1–2, 4, 11
extent: restoration 150–151, 155
extrinsic change in offices 187; *see also* intrinsic change

facilities management 182, 186–188
factories 170–171
fascination 149–151, 155–156
feedback and sustainability 225–228
fire alarms 23, 84–86, 89, 95, 97
fires *see* behaviour during fires and emergencies
flexible space in offices 76, 78
flood risk 44–45, 202
Ford, Henry 171
framing *see* goal framing

Gaudi, Antonio 64
gender roles *see* roles
genius loci *see* place
geographical profiling 109, 121, 123, 126–128; home and home range 122–126; use in investigation 127–128; *see also* arson; murder; offender profiling; property crime; rape
geography: place 29–31
general affect model (GAM) 111

global warming *see* climate change
goal-directed environmental behaviour 17
goal framing theory (GFT) 207, 213–217, 220
goal setting with feedback 227
greenhouse gasses 203, 205, 223, 228
green medicine 138, 149, 158–160
green space, positive impact of 136, 139, 158–160
groupsat work 169, 174, 176, 178, 180, 182, 184, 187, 189

habit: characteristics of 222; private transport use 216, 222–225
Hawthorne studies 20, 173–175
hazards: hazardous technology 48; response to natural hazards 44–45; *see also* risk
health supportive environments 135–136
hedonic goal frames 214–217, 220–221
high security hospitals 139–140
Hillsborough disaster and the media 82
home range 123
homeworking 168, 190, 224
hospitals: design 140–141, 147; early research 75; fires in 96; windows 154–155; *see also* ergonomics; human factors
humanistic organisational theory *see* organisational theory
Hurricane Katrina 44

identity process model 36–37
immigrants 43
injunctive norm 210
intentionality and place 33
interactionism 19, 21
International Association for People-Environment Studies (IAPS) 17
interpersonal distance *see* personal space
intimate distance 72–73
intrinsic motivation and behaviour 217
intrinsic satisfaction: crime 115; work 170
involvement at work *see* participation
isolation 61, 63, 76; offices 179–180; prisons 138

job satisfaction 170, 174, 189
Journal of Environmental Psychology 18, 197

King's Cross underground station fire 98–104
Kingston Polytechnic 6, 17

landscape offices *see* bürolandschaft; open plan offices
landscape preference 153, 156
Larkin building 123
Lee, Terrance 6–7, 14–16
Lewin's equation 21
Lipman, Alan 6
long hot summer 110
Lynch, Kevin 6

mainstream psychology 5, 10
maintenance and sustainability 204–206
Man-Environment Research Association (MERA) 18
Manning, Peter 6, 16–17
marauder model of criminal behaviour 124–125, 127
Markus, Tomas 6, 16
meat and sustainability *see* diet
mental fatigue 151–152
mental health and environment 135, 137–138–142, 149, 151,

154, 158–160; and aggression (*see* aggression)
micro-restorative settings 155; *see also* restoration; restorative environments
migrants 43; *see also* immigrants
migration 39–41, 202
mortality rate and density 58–59
murder 112, 123, 126
museums and galleries as restorative environments 155–156

natural environment *see* restorative environments
negative effect escape model (NAE) 111
new ecological paradigm 211
new environmental paradigm (NEP) 208, 211
NIMBYism (not in my backyard) 47
noise: annoyance 19–20; autism 147; in offices 168–169, 178–179; in prison 138; in psychiatric hospital 141
normal activation model (NAM) 210
normative goal frames 215–217
normative goals 214
norms, types: behavioural norms 209; descriptive norms 209–210; injunctive and subjective norms 210; moral and personal norms 209; *see also* theory of planned behaviour; Value Norm-Belief theory
nuclear power, attitudes towards 48

obesity and environment 135–136, 159
obsessive compulsive behaviour (OCD) 135
offender: cognitive map 123; decision making 112, 114, 122, 125–127; environmental familiarity 122–123, 126, 128; motivated 114; spatial pattern of offences 123, 125–128; travel distance 122
offender profiling 121; *see also* geographical profiling
office landscape 177
office lighting and emotion 183, 184
office personalisation 167–168, 182, 187–190
offices *see* open plan offices
open plan office 177; communication 179; economic benefits 182; negative effects 179; 182, 190; privacy 179–180; 190; sustainability 204
organisational theory: classical 170–172, 176, 185, 189; humanistic 170, 175–177, 189; *see also* Hawthorne studies; productivity in offices

panic 82–90, 93; causes 84–85; characteristics 83; emergency preparedness 87–89; media portrayal 85–87, 104
Parc, Guell 64
participation: lack of in design 145; in offices 176, 184–185, 188, 204
People and Physical Environment Research (PAPER) 18
people environment transactions *see* transactionalism
perceived behavioural control (PBC) 218–219, 221
performance *see* productivity in offices
personal norms 209–212, 221, 225
personal space 57, 63, 71–76; biological basis 74; culture 75; definition 71; proxemics 71–72; and territory 75–76; theories 73–74; zones 73; *see also* privacy

Pilkington Research Unit (PRU) 16
place: definition 29–30, 32; facets of 30, 33, 39; in geography 29–30, 32; *genius* loci 32–33; intrinsic meaning 31–32, 34, 41; phenomenological approach 30–31; positivist approach 30–31; sense of 31; social construction of meaning 31, 33–34, 41; *see also* anti-essentialism; essentialism; place attachment; place identity
place attachment 30, 34; applications 39–40; climate change 40; components 38–39; definition 37–38; functions 42–43; homesickness 40; opposition to migrants 41–42; refugees 42; response to threat 44–46; sustainability and pro-environmental behaviour 47, 49; *see also* risk
place disruption 40–41
place identification 35
place identity 35–36; functions 36–37; migrants 40–41; social identity 36; sustainability 46, 48; *see also* anti-essentialism; essentialism
placelessness 31–33
place schema 92
planning: discipline 6; town planning 15
police: investigations 109, 127–128; involvement in disasters 82, 87, 99–101
pollution 136, 198, 201, 203, 205, 223
population: control 57; density 59–60; growth 57–58, 201; other species 201
post-traumatic stress disorder (PSTD) 135
Prestige: sinking 199
prisons 137–139; aims 138–139; gardens 138–139; privacy 138; well-being 138–139
privacy 57, 61–64; definitions 61; functions 62–63; personalisation in offices 189–190; regulation 64, 66, 71, 76; therapeutic settings 137–138; types of 63; *see also* plan offices
productivity in offices 171, 177, 180–183, 187, 189; employee regulated 175; Hawthorne Studies 173–174
pro-environmental behaviour 197, 203–207; consumption 201; environmental concern 198; financial incentives 216–217; growth of research 197; habit 222–225; interventions 200, 202; psychology, role of 199–200; and technology 199–200; theoretical approaches 207, 221; *see also* curtailment; efficiency; emissions; feedback; maintenance; sustainability
property crime *see* burglary
Proshansky, Harold 14
prospect 153, 156
prospect-refuge theory 153
proxemics 71–73; distance zones 73
psychophysics 4–5
public territory *see* territory

rape 113, 115, 122, 124, 126
rational choice theory (RAT) 114, 119, 121
rebound effect 199–200, 206
recycling: encouraging 212, 217, 220–221; and feedback 225
refuge 153, 156

restorative environments 149–151, 154–160; benefits 149, 151, 156–158, 160; nature benefit assumption 154; qualities 150–151; urban environments 154–155, 158–159; *see also* attention restoration theory; directed attention fatigue; micro-restorative settings; museums; stress recovery theory
riots 58, 109–110, 115
risk: perception 44; and place attachment 43–44; planning and adaption 45–46; *see also* hazards
road rage 69–70
roles: gender 95; place related 33–34; purposes 33; rules during fires (disasters and emergencies) 90–92, 95–96, 104; work 175–176; *see also* environmental role
routine activity theory (RAT) 114, 121
Royal Institute of British Architects (RIBA) 16–17

Schwartz's value theory 209–210
Scientific Management 170–173, 175; *see also* organizational theory
scripts 12, 23, 88, 92–93, 96, 222
secondary territory 68
self-categorisation theory 89–90
self-efficacy 36–37
self-identity: environmental 213; place 37, 40, 42; and privacy 62; *see also* place identity
sense of place 30–34, 42, 48; *see also* place
serial offenders 123–126
sink estates 59
social breakdown 58
social construction of place *see* place
social density *see* density
social identity 36, 89
social norms: pro-environmental behaviour 209, 228; rats 58; *see also* norms
social roles *see* roles
sociofugal space 64–66
sociopetal space 64–66
Sommer, Robert 71
spatial density *see* density
status in offices 169, 179, 189
stress recovery theory (SRT) 149, 151–155; preferenda 152; psycho-evolutionary explanation 152; *see also* restorative environments; windows
Stringer, Peter 15
subjective norms 210, 218–221
Surrey University 15–16
sustainability 197–199; consumption 201–204; growth in research 197; place and location of infrastructure 46–49; psychology 199–200; *see also* place attachment; pro-environmental behaviour

target hardening 116–117, 120
task performance *see* performance
Taylor, Fredrick 170–171
temperature and crime *see* crime
territoriality *see* territory
territory: aggression 69–70; animal *vs* human 58, 67, 70; crime 117, 120; defensible space 117, 120; definition 66; functions of 66; home advantage 70–71; markers 68–69, 117; offices 182; personalisation 189–190; and personal space 73, 75–76; primary territory 67–70; privacy regulation 66; public territory 68–69; secondly territory 68

terrorist attacks 81, 83, 88, 97, 116
theory of planned behaviour (TPB) 207, 210, 212–213, 217, 218–221
therapeutic environments, approaches: custodial 137–139, 148, 160; enhancement 137, 139, 147–148; growth 137, 148; medical 137, 139–140, 142, 147; normalisation 137, 139, 142, 144, 147–148; prosthetic 137, 144, 147–148, 160
transactionism 8–9, 19, 21–22, 34, 36, 151
transport mode choice 205, 213, 215, 217, 219, 220, 222–224

United Nations (UN) 201
University of California, Irvine 8
University of Liverpool 6, 16
University of Strathclyde 6, 16–17

Value-Belief-Norm Theory (VBN) 207, 209–213, 219–220, 225
Value Identity Personal Norm (VIP) 213
view *see* window
volcanoes 29, 45

wandering: dementia 143, 150
wayfinding: dementia 143
weather *see* aggression; crime; riots
Weber, Max 170–171
Wells, Brian 16
wilderness 3
wildfires 43; place attachment 45
windows: health benefits 155; status in offices 171, 178; view 153–157
work environment *see* open plan offices
working from home *see* homeworking
World Wildlife Fund for Nature (WWF) 201

zero responders 88